CASE STUDIES IN
CULTURAL ANTHROPOLOGY

SERIES EDITORS

George and Louise Spindler

STANFORD UNIVERSITY

ETHNIC IDENTITY IN CHINA
The Making of a Muslim Minority Nationality

ETHNIC IDENTITY IN CHINA
The Making of a Muslim Minority Nationality

DRU C. GLADNEY

University of Hawai'i
East-West Center

HARCOURT BRACE COLLEGE PUBLISHERS

Fort Worth   Philadelphia   San Diego   New York   Orlando   Austin   San Antonio
Toronto   Montreal   London   Sydney   Tokyo

Publisher	Earl McPeek
Acquisitions Editor	Brenda Weeks
Product Manager	Julie McBurney
Project Editor	Louise Slominsky
Production Manager	Andrea Johnson
Art Director	Don Fujimoto
Electronic Publishing Coordinator	Ellie Moore/Michael Bryant

Cover photo by Dru C. Gladney

ISBN: 0-15-501970-8

Library of Congress Catalog Card Number: 97-72355

Address for orders:
Harcourt Brace & Company
6277 Sea Harbor Drive
Orlando, FL 32887-6777
1-800-782-4479

Address for editorial correspondence:
Harcourt Brace College Publishers
301 Commerce Street, Suite 3700
Fort Worth, TX 76102

Web site address:
http://www.hbcollege.com

Printed in the United States of America

7 8 9 0 1 2 3 4 5 6   039   9 8 7 6 5 4 3 2 1

Foreword

ABOUT THE SERIES

These case studies in cultural anthropology are designed for students in beginning and intermediate courses in the social sciences, to bring them insights into the richness and complexity of human life as it is lived in different ways, in different places. The authors are men and women who have lived in the societies they write about and who are professionally trained as observers and interpreters of human behavior. Also, the authors are teachers; in their writing, the needs of the student reader remain foremost. It is our belief that when an understanding of ways of life very different from one's own is gained, abstractions and generalizations about the human condition become meaningful.

The scope and character of the series has changed constantly since we published the first case studies in 1960, in keeping with our intention to represent anthropology as it is. We are concerned with the ways in which human groups and communities are coping with the massive changes wrought in their physical and sociopolitical environments in recent decades. We are also concerned with the ways in which established cultures have solved life's problems. And we want to include representation of the various modes of communication and emphasis that are being formed and reformed as anthropology itself changes.

We think of this series as an instructional series, intended for use in the classroom. We, the editors, have always used case studies in our teaching, whether for beginning students or advanced graduate students. We start with case studies, whether from our own series or from elsewhere, and weave our way into theory, and then turn again to cases. For us, they are the grounding of our discipline.

ABOUT THE AUTHOR

Dru C. Gladney is Professor of Asian Studies and Anthropology at the University of Hawai'i at Manoa. He is also a Senior Research Fellow at the East-West Center in Honolulu. He received his M.A. and Ph.D. degrees in Social Anthropology from the University of Washington, Seattle. He also holds two M.A. degrees from Fuller Theological Seminary in Theology and Cross-Cultural Studies.

At the age of 17, Gladney traveled to Hong Kong in order to teach English to mainland Chinese refugees living in the resettlement districts. While studying Mandarin, living with a Swatow-speaking family, and walking the streets of the predominantly Cantonese city, he was struck by the complexity and variety of Chinese society. This interest in Chinese ethnic diversity led him to study the anthropology of China at the University of Washington, and the Mandarin language at Beijing University in 1981. From 1983 through 1985 he was a Fulbright and National Academy of Sciences scholar in China, where he carried out his dissertation field research. He has traveled to China every year since that time for a total of over 6 years of fieldwork in the People's Republic. In 1992 and 1993, Dr. Gladney was a

Fulbright Research Scholar at Bosphorus University in Istanbul, Turkey, where he conducted research on Turkic Central Asians from China and Inner Asia. He has also served as Assistant Professor of Anthropology at the University of Southern California, as a lecturer in Anthropology at Harvard University, and as a visiting scholar in Aarhus University, Denmark; King's College, Cambridge, England; Xiamen University and Central Nationalities University, China. He has held post-doctoral fellowships from the Institute for Advanced Study, Princeton, and Harvard University, Center for International Affairs.

In addition to China and Turkey, Gladney has carried out more recent research projects in Kazakhstan, Kyrgyzia, Uzbekistan, and Egypt. Currently, Associate Editor for China and Inner Asia for the journal, *Central Asian Survey,* he has also served as a consultant to UNESCO, the Smithsonian Institution, and the National Academy of Sciences. Recently, he was asked by the National Committee on U.S–China Relations to travel to Tibet as part of a team of social scientists studying "cultural survival among Tibetans in Sichuan and Tibet."

Professor Gladney is the author and editor of several books, including *Muslim Chinese: Ethnic Nationalism in the People's Republic* (Harvard University Press); *Dislocating China: Muslims, Minorities, and Other Subaltern Subjects* (C. Hurst, London, in press); *Making Majorities: Constituting the Nation in Japan, China, Korea, Malaysia, Fiji, Turkey, and the United States* (Stanford University Press); *Islam in China: International Perspectives* (C. Hurst, London and IMMA Press, Saudi Arabia); as well as numerous book chapters and articles in *Public Culture, The Journal of Asian Studies, History and Anthropology, Current History, Central Asian Survey, and Cultural Survival Quarterly.* Gladney has received grants and fellowships from the National Academy of Sciences, Fulbright, UNESCO, the American Academy of Arts and Sciences, IREX, the Social Science Research Council, the Wenner-Gren Foundation for Anthropological Research, the Woodrow Wilson Foundation, the Harvard Academy for International and Area Studies, and the National Endowment for Humanities.

Professor Gladney continues his research on ethnic problems in China, Central Asia, and Turkey. When not on the road, Gladney lives in an old Chinese house on the beach in Honolulu, teaching his dog Liko how to surf tandem.

ABOUT THIS CASE STUDY

The common outlook on China is that it is a monolithic nation-state with billions of people very much like each other. In fact, China is seen as potentially threatening because it is so huge and so homogeneous. Nothing could be further from the truth. After the revolution and Chiang Kai-shek's forces had retreated to Taiwan, over 400 separate "ethnic" groups applied for state recognition. Only 55 were officially recognized. Of those 55, the Hui, the object of Professor Gladney's case study, are the largest Muslim nationality, and third largest minority group. The Han majority, however, is by no means homogeneous. There are eight mutually unintelligible linguistic groupings, with associated cultural differences, among the Han. Contrary to popular notions, China is a multiculturally and ethnically diverse nation and potential ethnic separatism has become a concern for the People's Republic of China.

Having selected one of the many minority groups in China for study, one would think that Dru Gladney could go about his research in customary ways—locating commonalities and describing a culture, divergent from a majority standard, but interdependent with it and sharing many characteristics with it, but always with a touch, at least, of difference. It is difficult today to proceed with the stock assumptions of anthropology in the study of any presumed group of human beings, whether "tribal," village, class, and most of all, nation. But it is impossible when studying and "writing up" a people like the Hui. The more Gladney traveled about China over a period of years, meeting and talking to Hui in more than 400 households and in every territory of the People's Republic from north to south and east to west, the less he knew about what ties these people into one ethnic group. For the Hui there is no "we." The Hui consist of widely divergent communities living within varying ecological contexts and experience their ethnicity in radically different ways.

Even religion, which is widely thought to unify the Hui ("because they are Muslim"), does not work to define them as an ethnic group. In some areas, to be Hui is to be Muslim, and in others Islam is almost totally irrelevant and Hui identity is based largely on genealogical descent from foreign Arab ancestors.

Hui inhabit every major metropolitan area of China and are considered China's major urban ethnic group, but they have received scant attention in the growing anthropological literature on China's cities, perhaps because they are so internally diverse and their presumed ethnicity so ambiguous.

The Hui exist, however. The state recognized them as a minority group (thus leading to a further invention of ethnicity) and they recognize themselves. The problem is to define this identity in meaningful ways. They are strongly endogamous, so they recognize their own identity. It is important to them that a *"qing zhen" (halal* or *kosher)* lifestyle be preserved, so there must be one that the Hui themselves recognize and celebrate. This is the author's problem: to discover how the Hui view themselves, how they recognize who is Hui, how they define and defend a *qing zhen* lifestyle under widely varying circumstances. How he does this we leave to the reader to discover. This case study makes most interesting reading and raises questions about the nature of ethnic groups everywhere, not just in China. It is relevant to a wide audience, extending well beyond the students of affairs Chinese. This work will be especially useful to those interested in the anthropology of religion, particularly the comparative study of Muslim societies outside of the Middle East and in Asia, where Muslims now have their largest populations. Also, it can tell us much about minority groups in America, that are also internally diverse and have "floating," indeterminate, unifying characteristics but are treated as homogeneous by the majority group and in much official policy.

George and Louise Spindler
Series Editors
Ethnographics
Box 38
Calistoga, CA 94515

Acknowledgments

This book represents a rewriting and condensation of an earlier book (*Muslim Chinese: Ethnic Nationalism in the People's Republic,* Harvard University Press) so that it might become more widely available to an undergraduate audience. I am therefore most grateful to the Council on East Asian Studies in the John King Fairbank Center for East Asian Research at Harvard University and Harvard University Press for allowing much of the earlier book to be reworked and reproduced here in order to make it more accessible to a larger readership. I would also like to acknowledge those who helped make the earlier volume such a success and who supported much of my earlier research and study in China.

Updating and rewriting of the earlier volume has been conducted largely while teaching at the University of Hawai'i at Manoa and conducting research through the East-West Center. I would especially like to express my appreciation to my colleagues at both institutions for their support and encouragement in this project, in particular (and in alphabetical order): Roger T. Ames, Elizabeth Buck, Daniel Cole, Edward L. Davis, John DeFrancis, James P. Dorian, Carol Eastmen, P. Bion Griffin, Eric Harwit, Daniel Y. W. Kwok, Reginald Kwok, Judy Ledgerwood, Cynthia Ning, Larry Smith, Ricardo D. Trimillos, Geoffrey White, and Mingbao Yue.

In the midst of revisions, I codirected a National Endowment for Humanities summer seminar on "Ethnic Diversity in China," in which my codirector, Prasenjit Duara, provided invaluable insights into the revisions, as well as the members of the seminar who are all undergraduate teachers. The Harcourt Brace editorial staff, especially Louise Slominsky, have provided painstaking assistance. Mary Hammond has continued to provide support and insight.

Finally, just after the book went to press I had the opportunity to travel to their mountain home in Calistoga and meet for the first time George and Louise Spindler. It was such an inspiring meeting that I would like to dedicate this volume to the memory of Louise Spindler.

Contents

Introduction

"We have made Italy, now we have to make Italians."
> —Massimo d'Azeglio at the first meeting of the parliament of
> the newly united Italian Kingdom (Hobsbawm, 1991, p. 44)

How are Muslims "made" in China? This book suggests that while they are born at home (or in hospitals) they may well be *made* in the process of interaction between self-identity and state policy. While there are at least 10 official Muslim nationalities in China, with extremely divergent histories and diverse identities, this book suggests that through centralized, state-sponsored policies directed at Muslims and other minorities, ethnic and cultural identity in China has taken a certain form of expression. This form tells us much about cultural politics and identity in contemporary Chinese society, and perhaps in many other places as well.[1]

THE RESEARCH: A PERSONAL SEARCH FOR THE HUI

I went to China as a graduate student in search of a Muslim people known as the "Hui" minority nationality. Although I encountered them everywhere in China, I had great difficulty deciding *who* they were. My reflections on the question of ethnic identity in China were guided by a similar feeling of ambiguity that Michael Moerman experienced when he was confronted with the question: "Whom did you study in the field?" (Moerman, 1965, p. 1215). After almost 3 years of fieldwork in China, the longer I searched for the Hui the less I understood what made them Hui. One Hui I encountered was particularly puzzling: Old Mr. Ma was a party communist official who was a staunch atheist, went to mosque every Friday, and resolutely refused to eat pork! I arrived in Beijing in the summer of 1982 to initiate a study of the Hui, one of the 55 officially identified minority nationalities who are portrayed clearly in the government nationality publications as having a long and uninterrupted history in China. Unlike many of the other minority nationalities of China, the Hui are distinguished negatively: They generally do not have their own language, peculiar dress, literature, music, or the other cultural inventories by which more "colorful" minorities are portrayed. As one Hui ethnologist stated to me, "We Hui don't sing, we don't

As a symbol of China's "Unified Nationalities," this ethnic dance troupe was filming a modern rock video on the steps of the Great Hall of the People to the tune of a song based on a poem by President Jiang Zemin stressing "nationality unity." September 9, 1995.

dance, but we're still ethnic!" How was I to find, let alone describe in classical ethnographic fashion, this people who supposedly lacked any special cultural characteristics?

When I arrived in Beijing I began to carry out my rather narrowly defined original proposal: an in-depth social study of an urban Muslim community concentrated mainly in one neighborhood, with a citywide population of more than 200,000 Hui. Through the auspices of the Central Nationalities University, I was assigned to a supervisory committee where two Hui professors would oversee my research in Beijing and my study at the Institute. It was not long, however, before my advisors and other Hui classmates at the Institute said that if I wanted to *really* understand the Hui I would have to travel to where they are "typical," such as, I was told, the Northwest. During my year of fieldwork on the Hui workers in Beijing City, I went on two trips through the Northwest and the Southeast. On a 1-month research trip to Northwest China, I followed the historic 1936 northwestern route of the Chinese ethnographer Fan Changjiang (1936), recorded in his book *China's Northwest Corner* (*Zhongguode Xibeijiao*), and visited Hui communities in Inner Mongolia (Huhehot); Ningxia (Yinchuan, Wuzhong); Gansu (Lanzhou) and Shaanxi (Xi'an). In the spring, I made a 6-week escorted trip to dispersed Hui communities in Southern and Southeastern China, including Shanghai, Hangzhou, Suzhou, Nanjing, Zhenjiang, Yangzhou, Jiaxing, Fuzhou, Quanzhou, Xiamen, and Guangzhou. The problem was that in all of these trips, as I traveled further, I found less and less that tied all of these diverse peoples together into one ethnic group.

I applied to renew another year, and through delicate and protracted bureaucratic negotiations, I managed to move to Ningxia, the Hui Autonomous Region in the rural Northwest. After 10 months in Ningxia, I returned to the United States to begin the process affectionately known as "writing up." As this endeavor raised more questions than it answered, in the summer of 1986, I went back to China to do some follow-up and carry out further research on the Southeast Coast. I have visited China every year since then, where I have had the opportunity to meet with Hui colleagues and to meet again with some key informants. In each community visited, I conducted household interviews with an informal interview schedule focusing on three major areas: migration and family ethnohistories; basic household economic and occupational data; and ethnoreligious knowledge of the Islamic world, Hui history, minority polity, and Hui cultural and religious differentiation. Whenever possible, I attempted to be sensitive to longitudinal and gender distinctions. Talking with Hui rural women in the northwest was much more difficult, as they tend to be even more conservative than Han women. Much that I learned of the identity of Hui rural woman was obtained informally in Hui homes, among those Hui families who knew me well.

On the few formal research forays when I was accompanied by government officials and academics, local authorities, though generally nervous, were for the most part helpful in allowing me to interview both well-known "model" households, as well as worker and farming households of average income. In addition to the Hui scholar who accompanied me on arranged visits to mosques and households, I was often accompanied by one cadre, and once by as many as five cadres, from the local Commission for Nationality Affairs (CNA) (*Minzu Shiwu Weiyuanhui*), the United Front Bureau (*Tongzhanbu*), or the Chinese Islamic Society (*Zhongguo Yisilanjiao Xiehui*). While these cadres were sometimes a hindrance to more casual, unrestricted conversation, they often proved to be extremely knowledgeable and forthcoming about local conditions and policies, as well as helpful in providing the official stamp of approval on my research. I often revisited households alone on later occasions, sometimes several times.

Finally, and most importantly, in addition to these more formal, arranged interviews and research trips, I engaged wherever possible in informal "participant observation" in which I talked with local Hui regarding their ethnic background on an individual basis, without accompaniment by any local officials or scholars.

As I lived in China for nearly 3 years as a "foreign student," it was not difficult to spend almost all of my time with Hui. Travel in China is generally tedious, troublesome, and time-consuming. The innumerable hours I spent on trains and buses— or waiting to buy tickets for them—provided ample opportunity to discuss Hui identity with fellow Han and Hui travelers. For this reason, and personal preference, I always traveled in a hard berth or seat (third and fourth class) and ate exclusively in Hui *qing zhen* restaurants. This last requirement became most difficult when traveling in southern China where Hui restaurants are less numerous, but it gave me an insider's view of the hardships imposed on a *qing zhen* lifestyle.

In Ningxia, I negotiated a research contract that guaranteed unrestricted and unescorted informal access to Hui households in Yinchuan City and two nearby Hui villages (Luojiazhuang and Najiahu). This was cleared with city and village officials. At one point, while riding through the countryside on my bicycle, I even heard an official open-air radio broadcast on the local loudspeaker system explaining my research project and purpose to workers busy with the fall harvest. Even though the broadcaster accurately described what I looked like and who I was, there were so few foreigners in the region that once, while I was cruising through a small Muslim village along a dirt path on my Phoenix bicycle, several children ran out, pointing at me and shouting: "A Japanese, a Japanese!" (*riben ren, riben ren!*). Our presence as the first and only Americans to live long-term in Ningxia since 1949 was a source of interest and concern to residents and officials throughout the region. Due to restrictions on foreign researchers in China, I never lived independently in a peasant home, though I stayed at length in the village retirement unit in Na Homestead (see chapter 3). In Ningxia, residence in the Chinese faculty building of Ningxia Educational College (*Ningxia Jiaoyu Xueyuan*) provided normal social-living conditions and frequent, unrestricted access to Chinese society. Fortunately, the college itself was located on the land of the Luo Family Village (*Luojiazhuang*). I only had to walk outside the front gate to be in the village and could look out my back window to see Hui villagers in their fields.

Language was a problem. In the north, I was able to rely on the "standard language" (*putong hua*) of Mandarin, based on the Beijing dialect. In the Northwest, I had to cope with Ningxia, Gansu, and Shaanxi dialects, and by the end of my stay I was able to understand general conversation without too much repetition. Familiarity with these dialects became useful when visiting with Soviet Central-Asian Dungans in Almaty, who maintained their Gansu dialect. In this case, my limited Turkish was helpful, but in Xinjiang I relied primarily on Mandarin. Only in Quanzhou did it become necessary to work through a research assistant, who was a Hui from the area and spoke Southern Min (Hokkien). In Tibet, Yunnan, Guangdong, Hainan, and Sichuan, most of the younger Hui spoke Mandarin or interpreted their elder's speech into something understandable to me.

An example of Muslim language diversity, this restaurant sign indicating halal *(ritually purified food) according to Islamic requirements (Chinese,* Qing Zhen, *literally, "Pure and True") is written in Chinese, Arabic, Uygur, Russian, and English. Kashgar, Xinjiang Uygur Autonomous Region. September 15, 1996.*

"Being There" in the Chinese Nation-State

Given the well-known restrictions placed on foreign social-science researchers in China, by now the reader must be asking how I was seemingly able to so easily "waddle in" (Geertz, 1988, p. 143n). More importantly, once there, why did I keep moving? This is a fundamental issue for my research on the Hui in the Chinese nation-state. It certainly departs from the traditional Malinowski-style ethnography where an anthropologist attempts to "squat" in one community for an extended period of time. Not only was I urged to visit as many Hui communities as possible by my Hui colleagues, but it also became immediately apparent that a book on the Hui that was based solely on one community would mislead rather than inform readers about their identity. Unlike Raymond Firth's (1936) classic ethnography, *We, the Tikopia*, there was no single voice that spoke for the Hui. For the Hui, there is no "we." There is no community, nor individual, that even begins to represent all the Hui of China.

Certainly, the voice of the state in its numerous nationality publications could not be taken for granted, nor the view of the Imam, the worker, the villager, or the entrepreneur. Instead we find a polyphony of voices—from urban to rural, religious to secular, elite to commoner, modernist to "traditionalist"—each contradicting the other, sharing different visions of Hui-ness, and subscribing to separate imagined communities (Anderson, 1991). Of course, I could have remained in Beijing and spent all of my 27 months among the Oxen Street Hui community. An urban ethnography of the Hui in Beijing would reveal much about Hui identity in the city—and this very much needs to be done—but it would reveal very little about the vast majority of agriculturist Hui. How would one begin to understand the devoutly religious northwestern Hui communities from the reference point of the secularized workers who predominate in the city?

At an even more fundamental level, the basic nature of nationality identity in the nation-state is diffused—it depends on the local juxtapositions of power, constantly in flux, interacting with the significant others in socially specific contexts, as well as the local state apparati. Central nationality policy, as this study will show, often bears little relation to what happens at the local level. Particularized, long-term ethnographies are indeed needed to gain a greater understanding of unique Hui identities, and it is hoped that these may take place. The problem that this study seeks to address, however, is one of national identity: what it means to be Hui in the Chinese nation-state. To address this question, I realized that an overall perspective must be attempted. My research trips exposed me to widely divergent communities of Hui living under varying ecological and socioeconomic contexts and expressing their identity in radically different ways. This diversity convinced me that I should not concentrate my study of the Hui on one isolated community, but should use the time and opportunities provided to travel and observe as much of Hui life as possible, in order to build a more comprehensive understanding of Hui identity and nationalism in the Chinese state. These travels convinced me of the wide variety of Hui identity and adaptation, an aspect of Hui identity not expressed in earlier accounts of the Hui in China (see Andrew, 1921; Broomhall, 1910; Israeli, 1978).

There were, of course, practical considerations. When I was in China, field research was still formally limited to a 2-week stay in any one village. I was able to get around some limitations by returning often to certain villages and by living long-term as a foreign graduate student in Chinese institutional housing with other Chinese, including Hui. Bus and bicycle carried me to most outlying households and communities, such as Na Homestead, Chang Ying, and Niujie. However, there were frustrating times when I was restricted and denied access to Hui communities for various reasons. Once, after traveling in southern Ningxia for 4 days by Beijing jeep on dirt roads, across a large area of the Gobi desert, and over the Liu Pan mountains, I finally arrived late one evening in Xiji, a Hui Sufi Naqshbandiyya center and one of the poorest towns in China, only to be told by the local county chairman that it would be inconvenient (*bu fangbian*) for me to stay beyond the next morning. Out of respect for China's national sovereignty and laws, I never transgressed these boundaries by entering off-limit areas (*fei kaifang diqu*) without permission, or tried to pass as a local—which would have been easy to do in the Northwest where I was often mistaken for another minority.[2] I doubt, too, that I would have been given the same kind of access if I were a visiting foreign scholar. Foreigners are generally watched much more closely in China.

While I was not in any one village during my entire stay, I did manage to invest substantial time and energy in at least four communities, and visited several other communities. Under the constraints of fieldwork in China, I was fortunate to have picked the Hui, as they are to be found everywhere, in every city, small town, and village. On rare occasions when I could not be among Hui, it was often just as en-lightening to discuss ethnic problems with Han colleagues and informants. The state could keep me from going to the Hui, but it could not always keep them from com-ing to me. On my first trip to Quanzhou, on the southeast coast, several Hui from a village that I was not allowed to visit heard of my interest, rented a bus, and met with me an entire day in the local mosque. I was able to eventually travel to the vil-lage in 1986 and carry out further study (see chapter 7).

In many ways, this kind of research seeks to avoid the gross generalization of one community or individual as exemplary of the whole. It also does not lend itself to what Marcus (1986, p. 165) described as "salvage" or "redemptive" modes of ethnography, where the community is thought to be either on the verge of modern-ization or still struggling to preserve remnants of its tradition "after the deluge" of modernity has set in. Each community and individual must speak for itself, himself, or herself. By not assuming a certain identity for each community or individual, or regarding it as representative of some abstract whole, this approach seeks more par-ticularized understanding, attempting to avoid the "Orientalism" on which so many travelogues, and even some ethnographies, are based (Said, 1978).

There are, of course, important costs involved. My research suffered from the lack of long-term daily observation that only comes with classic-style ethnography in one locality. The study was thesis- and problem-oriented, rather than village- or locale-oriented. Thus, it represents a substantial departure from traditional field-work. I do not attempt to describe the complete community, but examine a problem of identity across several communities. The project was intensive, rather than exten-sive, not in the Margaret Mead style of studying one culture for 6 months and then moving to a totally new one—I did spend almost 3 years in China studying primar-ily one nationality, all of whom could communicate in the national language—but in the sense that I did not devote my entire study to one specific community in time and place.

I have no single, central paradigmatic community or individual around whom my ideas of Hui-ness are formed. I can point to no standard ideal type by which to judge all other varieties (though, I would argue, this is not necessarily a flaw). I missed the opportunity to see the year-round daily agricultural cycle in one commu-nity, although I was able to observe many of the major ecological transitions in Luo Village across from my home. I might have formed deeper relationships with the lo-cals if I had stayed in one village the entire time. I also discovered, however, that some people were often more willing to tell me about themselves (and their neigh-bors) if they thought I was not too tightly woven into the web of their immediate so-cial relations. In a politically permeated society such as China, a foreigner staying in one place for a long time tends to focus and intensify attention on that place and those individuals, whereas this approach may have diffused some of that exposure.

In addition, I am not able to point to any one community as "my village," as other "lone stranger" anthropologists have traditionally claimed with exclusivity and pride (Salzman, 1989, p. 44). I not only have difficulty in briefly answering the question, "Whom did you study?" but also, "Where did you study them?" The claim of exclusivity may become more difficult to make as fieldwork continues to become more public and publicized in complex societies, occurring, as Elizabeth Pratt (1986) has noted, in less exotic "common places." This is particularly true when the actions of the fieldworker become interesting, or even perhaps threatening, to the regimes where he or she works. As Marcus (1986, p. 166) argues, no longer can the world of larger systems be "seen as externally impinging on and bounding little worlds, but not as integral to them." Smaller ethnic communities are tied into the larger nationality to which they belong and may be assigned by the state, and these ethnic communities are influenced by international events and relations. I do hope to go back and "camp out" in one place for a longer term, and more importantly, I hope that my carefulness has increased the possibility for others to follow. It is my desire that they start with the communities I have most come to know, which certainly are not "mine."

Fieldwork and Anthropological Careers in the Post-Colonial World

There is another issue at stake here: Classical long-term fieldwork has traditionally been modeled on those situations where the ethnographer is able to exercise at least some control over lifestyle and environment. Geertz (1988, pp. 23–24) reminds us that "being there" for the anthropologist in the past involved:

> at the minimum hardly more than a travel booking and permission to land; a willingness
> to endure a certain amount of loneliness, invasions of privacy, and physical discomfort;
> a relaxed way with odd growths and unexplained fevers; a capacity to stand still for
> artistic insults, and the sort of patience that can support an endless search for invisible
> needles in infinite haystacks.

Having endured these "minimal" difficulties, the anthropologist was generally left to do what he or she wanted. The thought of government employees looking over one's shoulder, living in state-owned institutions or hotels, restricted access to one's informants, and having to obtain multiple bureaucratic applications and approvals is distasteful, if not completely unacceptable, to most anthropologists. As a result, modern ethnographers have tended to avoid those places where such restrictions apply, favoring fieldwork where they could, for the most part, pitch their tent with impunity. It is no surprise that many of these field sites are in countries closely tied to Western economic and political interests (see Gough, 1967, pp. 12–27; Wax, 1983).

Western field research in China basically ground to a halt at the end of the Second World War with the decline of the notion of Western "extra-territoriality"—a right to immunity from Chinese prosecution that foreigners generally possessed to one degree or another since the Unequal Treaties were signed in the mid-nineteenth century. It became illegal to conduct field research in China without specific permission from the People's Republic, and for the most part few Westerners were granted that permission. Those that were allowed to conduct fieldwork were so circumscribed and sympathetic to state policy that their works generally lacked the dispassionate stance thought necessary for ethnographic credibility (see Crook, 1959).

Since 1949, field research on Chinese communities has been carried out primarily in Taiwan, Hong Kong, and Southeast Asia. There, due to international economic and power alliances, fieldwork could be conducted with the degree of autonomy deemed necessary by Western anthropologists. When I first proposed to conduct fieldwork in the People's Republic of China (PRC) in 1981, I received the advice generally given at the time by Western anthropologists: Since it was assumed I would never be able to do "real" fieldwork in China, it would be better to go to Taiwan or Hong Kong where "I could do what I wanted." In China, I might waste my time and then never be able to get a job. After writing a "solid" dissertation in Taiwan and obtaining an academic position, I was advised that I could afford to risk some short stints in China. When I then devised the idea of working on minorities, several people warned that I would be putting my career in jeopardy. I was constantly reminded that since there were so few minorities in China (less than 9% of the population), it would not be of any long-term value to our understanding of Chinese society to do research on minorities. The head of a major Chinese-studies center once said to me, "Why study the minorities? We still don't know enough about the Han." One of my students recently mentioned that he was warned by a senior Chinese anthropologist in the spring of 1989 that he would never find a job if he studied minorities in China.

The issue of anthropological careers and the limitations placed on anthropological research by the academic industry is of paramount concern when we consider contemporary research in complex nations (Marcus, 1986, pp. 262–267). I discovered in China, however, what few Sinologists could have predicted: It was precisely the work on the Han that was most restricted, and minority research was possible, if not encouraged. Traditionally, it was Chinese anthropologists who, influenced by the British social–anthropological tradition, worked mainly on minorities. In a classic division of labor, sociologists devoted themselves to the Han. When Western anthropologists attempt to study the Han in China, it is not only bureaucratically difficult, I have also noticed a tangible resentment and conviction that only anthropologists should study "backward peoples." The Han, as the "vanguard of the proletariat," do not wish to be regarded or studied as such. Anthropology (*ren lei xue*) in China, until recently, has been almost exclusively limited to physical anthropology. Ethnography (*minzu xue*) was devoted to the study of minorities and it was generally carried out in the nationalities institutes and nationalities research centers, rather than in the universities. Ethnography and anthropology, though later criticized, in general were more protected than sociology as a tool of the state in dominating the minorities. In China, anthropology became the "people's anthropology" (Fei, 1981), because it concerned itself exclusively with the cultural study of the minority peoples, generally ignoring such issues as political economy, social structure, religious authority, and socioeconomic change.

As a result, when I introduced myself in China as an ethnographer studying minorities, I generally was better received than when I said I was an anthropologist. One Chinese anthropologist said, "It's good you're studying the minorities, the Han people don't like to be regarded as 'primitives' to be studied by 'advanced' foreigners." My application to study minorities appeared to follow the contours of power within the Chinese social-science tradition, and though still difficult, it met with less resistance.

But one is never detached from the power structures of Chinese, or any, society. "Waddling in," to use Geertz's phrase, always involves leaving a wake behind. To some degree I was, of course, perceived by locals as a representative of the Chinese state (since I had their approval to be there), as well as a representative of American interests. Most cadres simply assumed I was a spy and treated me as such. As a Han official challenged me in Yinchuan one day, "Why else would I be in the middle of nowhere studying such an uninteresting, insignificant people?" I am certain that they never believed my lengthy explanation about why I found the Hui so fascinating. More practically, the institutes and individuals who hosted me were very aware of the political risks, costs, and benefits involved. My presence as a foreign researcher, in addition to being a threat, added prestige and some compensation to their institutions. There was an exchange, but not one that can be measured in quantifiable terms.

The past several years have demonstrated that, for whatever reasons, anthropological research has indeed made progress among the minorities. While my situation was admittedly quite unique, due to the subject of study, others (generally graduate students) have been granted long-term admittance to villages and communities in diverse minority areas from Yunnan to Xinjiang. Since my earlier study, several long-term studies have been carried out in minority areas with considerable success (see Harrell, 1995). Not only will this research among minorities continue to offer more opportunity in China, but more significantly, it will reveal much about the power relations and social identities within China. Ethnicity studies have the potential to reveal a great deal about the Chinese state and society in general, including the Han. After all, the Han also are a *minzu*.

Notes

[1]A more detailed treatment of this research is presented in Dru C. Gladney *Muslim Chinese: Ethnic Nationalism in the People's Republic,* 1991. Cambridge: Harvard University Press, East Asia Monograph Series, 1996. This represents a more condensed, and in many places updated version of the larger study. The author is grateful to the East Asia Council for permission to publish much of the earlier material in this form.

[2]On issues related to disguised observation, see Denzin, 1968, pp. 502-504; Erikson, 1967.

1 / The Uniting of China

China is a multicultural and ethnically diverse nation-state with tremendous cultural, geographic, and linguistic diversity among its dispersed population. Yet, China usually is not thought of as a multiethnic country, but rather as one nation with one majority population, the Han, and a few inconsequential minorities on its border areas.[1] Discussions of China generally take cultural uniformity for granted and China is often portrayed as an "homogeneous" monoethnic state. This study takes exception to this conceptualization of China and its population; not only is there tremendous ethnic diversity among China's "official" minority nationalities, but there are equally important cultural differences among China's majority population, identified as the "Han" people. This cultural and ethnic diversity will be of increasing importance and vibrancy in the post-Cold War era, with a rising politics of difference that we must take seriously if we are to understand China in the 1990s. By looking at ethnic identity formation among one Muslim nationality in China, we can begin to understand the nature of ethnic identity in the People's Republic.

The People's Republic of China is comprised of 56 "official" nationalities. These include a total population of 91 million "official" minorities, living in every province, region, and county, speaking a wide variety of languages that belong to four of the world's largest language families, including Sino-Tibetan (Mandarin, Tibetan, Kam-Tai, Miao-Yao), Turkic-Altaic (Kazakh, Uygur, Mongolian, Manchu-Tungus, Korean), Austro-Asiatic (Hmong, Vietnamese), and Indo-European (Tadjik, Russian; see Table 1.1). These groups have always been important for China's domestic and international relations (Pye, 1975). The significance of these official nationalities has increased dramatically in the 1990s, now that China is confronted with several new nations that have significant similar populations on both sides of the border. Ethnic separatism is a major concern to leaders in Beijing.

In addition to the official minority nationalities, the state-recognized majority nationality, known as the Han, which in 1990 occupied 91% of the total population, is comprised of a wide variety of culturally and ethnically diverse populations, including eight mutually unintelligible linguistic groupings (Mandarin, Wu, Yue, Xiang, Hakka, Gan, Southern and Northern Min). There is also marked linguistic and cultural diversity among these Chinese language subgroups. Among the Yue language family, for example, the Cantonese- and Taishan-speakers are barely intelligible to each other, and among southern Min-speakers, Quanzhou, Changzhou, and Xiamen dialects are equally difficult to communicate across. The North China dialect, known as Mandarin, was imposed as the national language in the first part

TABLE 1.1
CHINA'S OFFICIALLY RECOGNIZED NATIONALITIES, 1982 AND 1990 CENSUS

Name(s) of Group	1990 Population	1982 Population	Percent Increase	Language Family	Location
Achang	27,708	20,441	36%	Tibeto-Burman	South: Yunnan
Bai	1,594,827	1,132,010	41%	Tibeto-Burman	South: Yunnan
Bao'an (Bonan)	12,212	9,027	35%	Mongolian	North: Gansu
Benglong	15,462	12,295	26%	Mon-Khmer	South: Yunnan
Bulang (Blang)	82,280	58,476	46%	Mon-Khmer	South: Yunnan
Buyi	2,545,059	2,122,389	20%	Kam-Tai	South: Guizhou
Dai (Thai)	1,025,128	840,590	22%	Tai	South: Yunnan
Daur	121,357	94,014	29%	Mongolian	Manchuria, Xinjiang
Dong (Kam)	2,514,014	1,426,335	76%	Kam-Tai	South: Guizhou
Dongxiang (Santa)	373,872	279,347	34%	Mongolian	North: Gansu
Dulong (Drung)	5,816	4,682	24%	Tibeto-Burman	South: Yunnan
Elunchun (Oroqen)	6,965	4,132	68%	Tungus	North: Manchuria
Evenki (Ewenk)	26,315	19,343	36%	Tungus	North: Manchuria
Gaoshan	2,909	1,549	87%	Austronesian	Taiwan, Fujian
Gelao	437,997	53,802	714%	Miao-Yao	South: Guizhou
Hani	1,253,952	1,059,404	18%	Tibeto-Burman	South: Yunnan
Hezhe	4,245	1,476	19%	Tungus	North: Manchuria
Hui	8,602,978	7,227,022	19%	Diverse	Nationwide
Jing (Vietnamese)	18,915	11,995	58%	Mon-Khmer	South: Guangxi
Jingbo	119,209	93,008	28%	Tibeto-Burman	South: Yunnan
Jinuo	18,021	11,974	51%	Tibeto-Burman	South: Yunnan
Kazakh	1,111,718	908,414	22%	Turkic	North: Xinjiang
Kyrgyz	141,549	113,999	24%	Turkic	North: Xinjiang
Korean (Chaoxian)	1,920,597	1,766,439	9%	Altaic	North: Manchuria
Lahu	411,476	304,174	35%	Tibeto-Burman	South: Yunnan
Li	1,110,900	818,355	36%	Tai	South: Hainan
Lisu	574,856	480,960	20%	Tibeto-Burman	South: Yunnan
Luoba (Lhopa)	2,312	2,065	12%	Tibeto-Burman	Tibet
Manchu (Man)	9,821,180	4,304,160	128%	Tungus-Manchu	North: Manchuria
Maonan	71,968	38,135	89%	Tai	South: Guangxi
Menba	7,475	6,248	20%	Tibeto-Burman	Tibet
Miao (Hmong)	7,398,035	5,036,377	89%	Miao-Yao	South
Mongolian (Meng)	4,806,849	3,416,881	41%	Mongolian	North
Mulao (Mulam)	159,328	90,426	76%	Tai	South: Guangxi
Naxi (Moso)	278,009	245,154	13%	Tibeto-Burman	South: Yunnan
Nu	27,123	23,166	17%	Tibeto-Burman	South: Yunnan
Pumi (Primi)	29,657	24,237	22%	Tibeto-Burman	South: Yunnan
Qiang	198,252	102,768	93%	Tibeto-Burman	South: Sichuan
Russian (Eluosi)	13,504	2,935	360%	Indo-European	Manchuria, Xinjiang
Salar	87,697	69,102	27%	Turkic	North: Gansu
She	630,378	368,832	71%	Miao-Yao	South: Fujian

(Continued)

TABLE 1.1 (CONTINUED)
CHINA'S OFFICIALLY RECOGNIZED NATIONALITIES, 1982 AND 1990 CENSUS

Name(s) of Group	1990 Population	1982 Population	Percent Increase	Language Family	Location
Shui (Sui)	345,993	286,487	20%	Tai	South: Guizhou
Tadjik	33,538	26,503	27%	Indo-European	North: Xinjiang
Tatar	4,873	4,127	18%	Turkic	North: Xinjiang
Tibetan (Zang)	4,593,330	3,874,035	19%	Tibeto-Burman	Tibet, Qinghai, Sichuan
Tu (Monguor)	191,624	159,426	20%	Mongolian	North: Qinghai
Tujia	5,704,223	2,834,732	101%	Miao-Yao	South: Hunan
Uygur (Weiwuer)	7,214,431	5,962,814	21%	Turkic	North: Xinjiang
Uzbek	14,502	12,453	16%	Turkic	North: Xinjiang
Wa	351,974	298,591	19%	Mon-Khmer	South: Yunnan
Xibo	172,847	83,629	107%	Tungus	Manchuria, Xinjiang
Yao (Mien)	2,134,013	1,403,664	52%	Miao-Yao	South
Yi (Lolo)	6,572,173	5,457,251	20%	Tibeto-Burman	South
Yugur	12,297	10,569	16%	Turkic	North: Gansu
Zhuang	15,489,630	13,388,118	16%	Kam-Tai	South: Guangxi
Other nationalities still unidentified	749,341	881,838			
Chinese citizens of foreign origin	3,421	4,842			
Total Minorities	91,200,314	67,295,217	35%		
Han Majority	1,042,482,187	940,880,121	10%		
Total Population	1,224,882,815	1,075,470,555	12%		

Note. Name(s) of group based on most commonly used and Chinese *pinyin* transliterations.

Sources. Renmin Ribao, "*Guanyu 1990 nian renkou pucha zhuyao de gongbao*" [Report regarding the 1990 population census primary statistics], 14 November 1991, p. 3; Judith Banister, *China's Changing Population* (Palo Alto: Stanford Press, 1987) p. 323.

of the twentieth century and it has become the *lingua franca* (medium of communcation between peoples of different languages) most often used by these peoples to communicate with each other, but it still must be learned in school. Yet, as any Mandarin-speaking Beijinger will tell you, buying vegetables or radios in Canton and Shanghai is becoming increasingly difficult due to the growing expressions of pride in the local languages of these areas, with nonnative speakers always paying a higher price. Despite strong restrictions and discouragement from the state government, the appearance and resurgence of local languages, such as Cantonese, in film, radio, and television is just one indication of this increasing interest in cultural difference.

Yet, despite growing awareness of the enormous cultural and ethnic diversity within China, most introductions to the study of China have devoted themselves primarily to the larger issues of state and society, especially economics, politics, religion, family, and the arts, with little attention to the impact of cultural diversity on any of these issues. When cultural differences have been noted, generally they have been explained as "regional" and not important for our understanding of national identity in China. When ethnic identity is addressed, usually it has been devoted to the study of the official minorities who are generally marginalized to the geographic and sociopolitical borderlands of Chinese society (Dreyer, 1976; Heberer, 1989; Ma, 1989; Mackerras, 1994a). Although the official minorities are certainly important in terms of their overall estimated population of 91 million, and groups such as the Tibetans, Mongols, and Uygurs have gained international attention, their occupying only 8% of China's total population makes them inconsequential to most studies of China's overall economy, politics, and society. Discussions of ethnicity in China have generally been restricted to these official minorities, and since they are such a small proportion of China's population, little attention has been paid to ethnicity outside the official groups. This book will introduce further aspects of ethnic identity in China and explores some of the reasons that we have neglected to focus only on official ethnicity in the past, as well as why this is no longer possible to do so in the 1990s. The study of minorities in China must not be divorced from our understanding of ethnic and national identity in general, nor should the study of minorities ignore the increasing importance of the politics of difference throughout China.

THE POLITICS OF ETHNIC IDENTIFICATION

Shortly after the founding of the People's Republic, state planners in Beijing sent teams of researchers, social scientists, and Communist Party cadres to the border regions of China to identify and recognize groups seeking to be registered as official nationalities (*minzu*), a generic term with a complex and relatively recent history in China that has been translated in English as "nation," "nationality," "ethnicity," or "people." Although more than 400 separate groups applied for nationality recognition, only 41 nationalities were initially listed in the first census in 1953. The 1964 census included 53 nationalities, and the 1982 and 1990 censuses identified 56 separate nationalities. What happened to the nearly 350 other groups who applied to be recognized? Some of them are still trying. There are at least 15 groups who are officially being considered for nationality recognition, including the Sherpas, Kucong, and Chinese Jews (see Table 1.2). Significantly, the 1990 census revealed that there are still 749,341 individuals still "unidentified" and awaiting recognition. This means that these people are regarded as ethnically different, but do not fit into any of the official nationality categories recognized by the state.

The majority of the groups that did not get recognized were either considered to belong to the Han majority or were grouped with other minorities with whom they shared some similarities. While there has not been much written about the exact nature of how some groups were recognized or others excluded, Fei Xiaotong, China's preeminent social anthropologist, revealed that the nationality categories employed by the Soviet Union in its identification programs were also influential in China. Known as the "four commons," outlined by Joseph Stalin, these categories included "a common language, a common territory, a common economic life, and a common psychological makeup," what Stalin (1953, p. 349) later generalized as a common "culture." It is clear from Figure 1.1 that language was a major factor in the identification of China's 56 nationalities.

TABLE 1.2
PEOPLES UNDER CONSIDERATION FOR RECOGNITION AS OFFICIAL NATIONALITIES

Name(s) of Group	Estimated Population	Language Family	Location
Sherpas	400	Nepalese	Tibet
Pingwu-Tibetans	3,000+	Tibetan	Tibet, Sichuan, Gansu
Deng	20,000	Tibetan	Tibet, Yunnan
Laji	1,500	—	Yunnan, Maguan District
Khmu (Khmer?)	2,100	Mon-Khmer	South: Yunnan
Mangren	500	—	South: Yunnan
Hu	2,000	Kam-Tai	Yunnan, Xishuanbana
Kucong (Yellow Lahu)	25,000	Tibeto-Burman	South: Yunnan
Jews (You tai ren)	2,000?	Sino-Tibetan	Nationwide

As an example of this process, Fei (1981, pp. 76–77) discusses the case of the "Chuanqing Blacks" in Guizhou, noting that although they had a close relationship with the Han in the region, they possessed unique features in language, locality, economic life, and psychological makeup that would warrant recognition according to Stalin's criteria. Upon more detailed study by government researchers, however, it was determined that, according to linguistic and historical analyses, the Chuan-qing were not a separate nationality after all, but actually descendants of Han garri-son troops who intermarried with the local population after they were sent to the south to conquer remnant forces of the preceding period during the Ming dynasty. Apparently, however, this conclusion was not accepted by the Chuanqing, and in the late 1970s they were among the more than 80 groups totaling 900,000 people who petitioned for recognition in Guizhou alone (see Heberer, 1989, pp. 37–38).

Other groups, however, have been more successful. The Jinuo, who live on the border of northern Burma and southern Yunnan, were the most recent group to be officially recognized. They were granted official minority nationality status in 1979.[2] In 1978, even though they no longer practiced Islam, approximately 30,000 Fujianese who were able to prove descent from foreign Muslims were recognized as members of the primarily Islamic Hui nationality. In this case, their genealogical proof of descent from foreign Muslim officials and traders who settled on the south coast between the ninth and fourteenth centuries was sufficient for recognition (see chapter 6). This led the way for many groups to begin to press for nationality recog-nition based on the historical records of foreign ancestry alone, even though they may lack any cultural markers of ethnicity, such as language, locality, economy, or religion (see Gladney, 1994e).

Why would anyone want to be recognized as an official minority nationality in China, and why would the government want to recognize them in the first place?

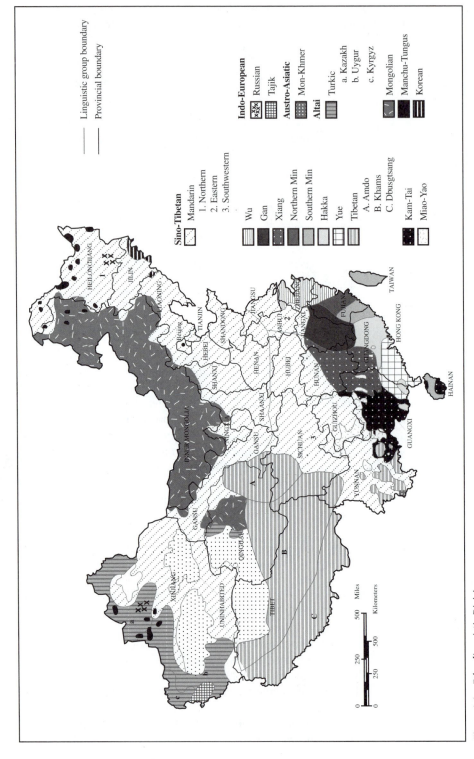

Figure 1.1   Ethnolinguistic Divisions

The answer may lie in the history of the Chinese Communist Party (CCP) and the influence of the "Long March" of 1934–1935, which was the Party's 6,000-mile escape from the threat of annihilation by Chiang Kai-shek's Kuomintang forces. During the Long March, the Chinese communist leaders became acutely aware of the vibrant ethnic identity of the many diverse peoples they encountered on their arduous trek from the southwest to the northwest. The march led them through the most concentrated minority areas of China, where they encountered peoples not always sympathetic to the communist cause. Edgar Snow graphically described the desperate plight of the Long Marchers, harried on one side by the Japanese and the Kuomintang, and on the other side by the "fierce" barbarian tribesmen (Snow, 1938). The Party was faced with the choice of extermination or making promises of special treatment to the minorities, specifically including the Miao, Yi (Lolo), Tibetan, Mongols, and Hui, should the CCP ever win national power. Once the Long Marchers reached the relatively safe haven of the mountain caves of Yenan, they had to devise a plan to appease the numerous Mongols in the north, Hui Muslims to the west, and their powerful warlord Ma Hongkui of Ningxia. One solution was to promise recognition of the Hui as a separate nationality and establish the first minority autonomous region in Tongxin, in southern Ningxia. These pledges of recognition and autonomy, in exchange for support for the Communists, were just a few of the many promises made to minorities prior to the establishment of the People's Republic in 1949.

From the beginning, the Chinese Communist Party followed the Soviet policy of offering the possibility of true secession for its minority republics, a policy that ultimately resulted in the dissolution of the USSR in 1991. China, however, did not maintain its commitment to a secessionist policy after the founding of the People's Republic. Before coming to power, Chairman Mao Zedong had followed and frequently referred to Article 14 of the 1931 CCP constitution, which clearly stated that the Party "recognizes the right of self-determination of the national minorities in China, their right to complete separation from China, and to the formation of an independent state for each minority" (in Brandt, 1952, p. 220). This policy was supported right up to the establishment of the PRC. In 1948, Liu Shaoqi stated that the CCP "advocates the voluntary association and voluntary separation of all nations" (Liu, 1948, pp. 127–128). Once the PRC was founded, however, all real possibilities of secession were revoked as no longer necessary.

Aside from the strategic enlistment of a "united ethnic front" in support of China's precarious new nation, there was another issue at stake in the formulation of the minority identification policy: the nature of the Chinese nation itself. Since early in the century, Chinese reformers, whether Kuomintang or Communist, were concerned that the Chinese people lacked a sense of nationhood, unlike the British, Germans, Japanese, and even the Tibetans and Manchu. In Dr. Sun Yat-sen's poignant words:

> The Chinese people have shown the greatest loyalty to family and clan with the result that in China there have been family-ism and clan-ism but no real nationalism. Foreign observers say that the Chinese are like a sheet of loose sand. . . . The unity of the Chinese people has stopped short at the clan and has not extended to the nation. (Sun, 1924, pp. 2, 5)

The identification of certain groups within China as "minorities" and the recognition of the Han as a unified "majority" played a fundamental role in forging a unified Chinese nation. For the Kuomintang, this reformulation of national identity as one people, with one history, helped to galvanize a sense of identity in relation not only to China's internal ethnic peoples, but also toward the foreign nations encroaching on China's soil.

This idea of Han unity became fundamentally useful to the Communists, who incorporated it into a Marxist ideology of progress, with the Han people in the forefront of development and civilization. In the Communists' portrayal, the Han were placed in the "vanguard" of the people's revolution. The minorities were induced to follow the Han example. The more backward, or primitive, the minorities were, the more advanced and civilized the so-called Han seemed and the greater the need for a unified national identity.

THE POLITICS OF HAN NATIONALISM

While research on the rise of Russian nationalism has been popular in Soviet studies since the 1970s, both by foreign and Russian scholars (Dunlop, 1983; Yanov, 1987), as yet no larger studies of the creation of Han nationalism have emerged—mainly because it is assumed, by scholars trained in the dominant tradition of sinology, that "Han" is generally equal to "Chinese"—a tradition maintained by the current regime in power. With the dismantling of the Soviet Union, and the rise of significant ethnic nationalisms in the new states on Russia's borders (and the emergent ones within), "Russification" paradigms have been discarded and attention has turned more seriously toward the politics of difference within and around the former Soviet Union. This has not been the case for China studies. In China, preoccupation with Sinification has paralleled the Russification assimilationist discourse, revealing an interest mainly in how much the so-called minorities and other foreigners in China's midst have been absorbed into the dominant Chinese civilization, a civilization dubbed as "Han" (Ch'en, 1966; Lal, 1970).

Recently, there has been an outpouring of scholarly interest in Chinese nationalism and China's "quest" for a national identity (Unger, 1996). However, most studies have continued to conflate the issue of the creation of the Han majority with larger questions of Chinese identity (Befu, 1993; Dittmer & Kim, 1993). Few have questioned how the Han became the 91% majority of China, merely accepting the Han as representative of the Chinese in general.

The notion of "*Han ren*" (Han person) has clearly existed for many centuries as those descendants of the Han dynasty (206 B.C.–220 A.D.) that had its beginnings in the Wei River valley. However, the notion of "*Han minzu*" (Han nationality) is an entirely modern phenomenon, which arose with the shift from Chinese empire to modern nation-state (see Duara, 1995). While the concept of a Han person certainly existed, it probably referred to those subjects of the Han empire, just as "Roman" referred to those subjects of the Roman empire (roughly concurrent with the Han). This tells us little about their "ethnicity," however, and we would be hard-pressed to determine who was Roman today. The Han are still thought to be around, however. The notion of a unified Han nationality, now said to occupy 91% of China's population, gained its greatest popularity under Sun Yat-sen. The leader of the republican movement that toppled the last empire of China in 1911, Sun was most certainly influenced by strong currents of Japanese nationalism during his long-term stay there. The Chinese term *minzu* is taken directly from the Japanese term *minzoku* and does not enter the Chinese language until the start of the twentieth century. Sun argued that the ruler–subject relation that had persisted throughout China's dynastic history would need to be fundamentally transformed if a true nationalist movement were to sweep China and engender support among all its peoples. More practically, Sun needed a way to mobilize all Chinese against the imperial rule of the Qing, a dynasty founded by a northeastern people who became known as the Manchu. By invoking the argument that a vast majority of the people in China were Han, Sun effectively found a symbolic national countermeasure against the Manchu and other foreigners to which the vast majority of the diverse peoples in China would surely rally.

Sun Yat-sen advocated the idea that there were "Five Peoples of China" (*wuzu gonghe*): the *Han*, *Man* (Manchu), *Meng* (Mongolian), *Zang* (Tibetan), and *Hui* (a term that included all Muslims in China, now divided into the Uygur, Kazakh, Hui, etc.). This recognition of the Five Peoples of China served as the main platform for his republican revolution that overthrew the Qing empire and established the first Republic. The notion of the peoples of China became key to the success of a people's revolution. The critical link between Sun's Five-Peoples policy and his desire to unify all of China is made clear from his discussion of nationalism, the first of his Three People's Principles (*Sanmin Zhuyi*), which he argued was a prerequisite for Chinese modernization.

It is also not at all surprising that Sun should turn to the use of the all-embracing idea of the Han as the national group, which included all the diverse peoples belonging to Sino-linguistic speech communities. Sun was Cantonese, raised as an overseas Chinese in Hawaii. As one who spoke heavily accented Mandarin, and with few connections in Northern China, he would have easily aroused traditional northern suspicions of southern radical movements extending back to the Song dynasty (960–1279 A.D.). The traditional antipathy between the Cantonese and northern peoples would have posed an enormous barrier to his promotion of a nationalist movement. Sun found a way to rise above deeply embedded north–south ethnocentrisms. The employment of the term *Han minzu* was a brilliant attempt to mobilize other non-Cantonese, especially northern Mandarin speakers and the powerful Zhejiang and Shanghainese merchants, into one overarching national group against the Manchu and other foreigners then threatening China. The Han were seen to stand in opposition to the "internal foreigners" within their borders—the Manchu, Tibetan, Mongol, and Hui—as well as the "external foreigners" on their frontiers, namely the Western imperialists. By identifying these "internal foreigners" in their midst, the Nationalists cultivated a new, broadly defined identity of the Han. In Benedict Anderson's (1991, p. 87) terms, Sun was engaged in helping to construct a new "imagined community" of the Chinese nation, by "stretching the short tight skin of the nation over the gigantic body of the empire."

The Communists stretched this skin even further, following the Soviet model, by identifying not 5, but 56 nationality groups, including the Han majority. Both for the Nationalists and the Communists it was not only the political necessity of enlisting the support of the ethnics on their borders that led them to recognize minority nationalities, but it was the desire to unify the nation against the outsiders, by de-emphasizing internal difference. Now that China no longer faces an external threat, internal differences must be considered if we are going to understand the full complexity of local politics and identity in contemporary China.

The best analogy today may be that of the new Europe and the ancient Roman empire. Lucian Pye has recently observed that "China today is what Europe would have been if the unity of the Roman Empire had lasted until now and there had not been the separate emergence of the separate entities of England, France, Germany and the like" (Pye, 1993, p. 130). Yet, one rarely thinks of the Cantonese and Shanghainese as being as different as the French and Spanish. Modern linguists might agree with this novel idea, however. Chinese ethnolinguists such as John DeFrancis and Jerry Norman have demonstrated that there is as much diversity "among the Chinese dialects as . . . among the Romance languages. . . . To take an extreme example, there is probably as much difference between the dialects of Peking and Chaozhou as there is between Italian and French; the Hainan Min dialects are as different from the Xian dialect as Spanish is from Rumanian" (Norman, 1988, p. 187). As Fred Blake (1981, p. 7) notes in his study of ethnic groups in southern China, "Cantonese, Hakka, and Hokkien (Fujianese) with their common root in ancient Chinese are as diverse from one another as are French, Italian, and Spanish with the Latin taproot." Much like Latin in the Middle Ages, these diverse language groups are all served with one standard writing system, Chinese ideographs (which do vary in some styles, such as Cantonese), although the speech communities are mutually exclusive (see Table 1.3). What has held these diverse communities together has been the power of the Chinese state, and the fear of foreign domination. Now that China is not threatened externally, and economic reforms have given increased autonomy to local regions, age-old internal divisions along official and unofficial ethnic lines may become one of Beijing's greatest concerns as it approaches the twenty-first century, especially with the return of Hong Kong on July 1, 1997.

THE POLITICS OF "UNOFFICIAL" ETHNICITY

There is a new feeling in China, a revalorization of ancestral and ethnic ties, especially in the south. Accompanying the dramatic economic explosion in southern China, southerners and others have begun to assert their cultural and political differences. Cantonese rock music, videos, movies, and television programs, all heavily influenced by Hong Kong, are now popular throughout China. Whereas comedians used to make fun of southern ways and accents, southerners now scorn northerners for their lack of sophistication and business acumen. Recent studies have demonstrated a new rising importance of the politics of ethnic and cultural difference *within* China proper (Friedman, 1993; Gladney, 1995b; Honig, 1991). Not only have the official minorities in China begun to strongly assert their identities, pressing the government for further recognition, autonomy, and special privileges, but different groups from within the so-called Han majority have begun to rediscover, reinvent, and reassert their ethnic differences.

TABLE 1.3
MAIN LANGUAGE FAMILIES OF CHINA

A. Sino-Tibetan

1. Mandarin
   1.1 Northern (Beijing)
   1.2 Eastern (Nanjing)
   1.3 Southwestern (Sichuanese)

2. Southern Languages
   2.1 Wu (Shanghai, Suzhou)
   2.2 Yue (Cantonese, Taishan)
   2.3 Xiang (Changsha, Shuangfeng)
   2.4 Hakka (Meishan, Wuhua)
   2.5 Southern Min (Xiamen, Taiwanese)
   2.6 Gan (Nanchang, Jiayu)
   2.7 Northern Min (Fuzhou, Shouning)

3. Tibetan
   3.1 Amdo
   3.2 Khams
   3.3 Dbusgtsang

4. Kam-Tai
   4.1 Tai (Dai)
   4.2 Zhuang
   4.3 Others

5. Miao-Yao

B. Mon-Khmer

1. Khmer
2. Vietnamese
3. Others

C. Altaic

1. Turkic
   1.1 Uygur, Uzbek, etc.
   1.2 Kazakh, Kirghiz
   1.3 Salar

2. Mongolian
   2.1 Mongolian
   2.2 Mongour (Tu)
   2.3 Bao'an
   2.4 Dongxiang
   2.5 Dong

3. Korean

4. Manchu-Tungus
   4.1 Manchu
   4.2 Oroqen (Elunchen)
   4.3 Ewenk (Evenki)
   4.4 Hezhe
   4.5 Xibo

D. Indo-European

1. Tadjik (Persian)
2. Russian (Slavic)

Note. Most language families listed are mutually unintelligible. Languages and speech communities listed are neither exhaustive nor exclusive, however, and though distinct, there may be some overlap and various degrees of mutual intelligibility.

Sources. John DeFrancis, *The Chinese Language: Fact and Fantasy* (Honolulu: University of Hawai'i Press, 1984); Jerry Norman, *Chinese* (Cambridge: Cambridge University Press, 1988); Robert S. Ramsay, *The Languages of China* (Princeton: Princeton University Press, 1989).

In the south especially, there has been a recent rewriting of history, illustrated by a newfound interest in the southern Chu kingdom as key to southern success. Museums dedicated to the glorious history of the southern Kingdom of Chu have been established throughout southern China. Many southerners now see the early Chu as essential to Chinese culture, to be distinguished from the less-important northern dynasties. In a significant departure from traditional Chinese historiography, southern scholars are beginning to argue that by the sixth century B.C., the bronze cultures of the Chu spread north and influenced the development of Chinese civilization, not the other way around as supposed by conventional wisdom. This

Hui Muslim farmers, Southern Pastures district, Tianshan Mountains, Xinjiang Uygur Autonomous Region. September 1988.

supports a reevaluation of the importance of the south to China's past, as well as its economic and geopolitical future.[3]

Rising consciousness of the southern Cantonese is paralleled by reassertions of identity among the Hakka (*Kejia*) people, the southern Fujianese Min (or *Hokkien*), the Swatow, as well as a host of other previously ignored peoples now empowered by economic success and embittered by age-old restraints placed on them from the north. Interestingly, most of these southern groups traditionally regarded themselves as Tang people, not Han people, descendants of the great Tang dynasty (618–907 A.D.) and its southern bases. Most Chinatowns in the west and southeast Asia are known as, and built around, the "Tang Person Streets" (*Tang ren jie*) as they are peopled by the descendants of Chinese émigrés from the mainly "Tang" areas of southern China. The 1990s may well witness the resurgence of Tang nationalisms in southern China in opposition to the northern Hans.

The resurgence of ethnic identities in southern China may well be influenced by similar movements in Taiwan. Increased traffic across the Formosan Straits has afforded access to information about recent widespread debates concerning minority and ethnic rights in Taiwan. Lao Ping-hui (1993) and Hsieh (1986), both Taiwanese scholars, report a dramatic reassertion of the "aboriginal" (*gaoshan*) peoples to their indigenous rights and claims on Taiwan, particularly through the public media. Age-old Taiwanese–Mainlander ethnic cleavages have given way to a predominance of Taiwanese language and political figures in everyday life, as well as a host of other groups maneuvering along traditional cultural and linguistic grounds for political power.

There has been an enormous outpouring of interest in Hakka origins, language, and culture in Taiwan as well, which also may be spreading to the mainland. The Hakka are thought to have moved southward in successive migrations from northern China as early as the Eastern Jin (317–420 A.D.) according to one Hakka historiographer, or as late as the Song dynasty (960–1279 A.D.) according to many Hakka, who claim to be "Song" people (Lo, 1965; Constance, 1995). They have also identified themselves as southerners and as "Tang people." The Hakka, however, have been registered as members of the Han nationality, perhaps because of a desire to overcome their long-term stigmatization by Cantonese and other southerners as uncivilized barbarians. This may stem from the unique Hakka language (unintelligible to other southerners), to the isolated and walled Hakka living compounds, or to the refusal of Hakka women to bind their feet. Either due to increasing pride in Hakkaness, or resurgent stigmatizations, the popular press in China is beginning to note the Hakka origins of important political figures, and it is not unusual to hear reports he has therefore acted in a certain way (leading figures considered to be Hakka or part-Hakka include Deng Xiaoping, Hu Yaobang, and Ye Jianning, father of Guangdong's last governor). It is now widely known that all of China's CCP-led southern bases of the 1920s and 1930s were Hakka, as were their leaders (Peng Pai, Fang Zhimin, Wang Zuo, and Deng Zihui). People now often praise Zhou Enlai, by stressing his southern Jiangnan linkages and even Chiang Kai-shek is lauded as a southerner who knew how to get money out of the United States.

These assertions of the politics of difference within the majority Han society argue against traditional assumptions about the "homogeneous" Chinese and the monoculturalism of China. Local differences are now becoming recognized as "ethnic," whereas they were previously dismissed as merely "regional" and therefore less important to understanding China. This semantic shift, from regional to ethnic, reflects a new salience placed on the politics of difference in the People's Republic.

Traditional China studies emphasized China as one civilization, one country, and one culture. Rarely was there serious attention paid to cultural and political difference in China studies, unless it concerned the "exotic" minority border peoples, almost always regarded as marginal to power and politics in the People's China. This goes against an historical perspective that notes China's long divisiveness over cultural, linguistic, and other fault lines, which led to ethnic feuds. As one historian of race in China noted, these feuds "strove to 'clear the boundaries' by ejecting exogenous groups from their respective territories. Such ethnic clashes could be extremely violent: A major conflict between the Hakka and Punti [locals] in 1856–67 took a toll of 100,000 victims" (Dikötter, 1992, pp.70–71). Such cultural and ethnic fault lines continue to influence social life in China today.

Notes

[1]Eric Hobsbawm repeats this widely accepted idea of Chinese monoethnicity in his classic work, *Nations and Nationalism Since 1780* (Cambridge: Cambridge University Press, 1992), p. 66, "...China, Korea, and Japan, which are indeed among the extremely rare examples of historic states composed of

a population that is ethnically almost or entirely homogeneous." Hobsbawm continues, "Thus of the (non-Arab) Asian states today Japan and the two Koreas are 99% homogeneous, and 94% of the People's Republic of China are Han" (p. 66, nt. 37).

[2]Ma Yin's discussion of the Jinuo does not indicate how they were recognized in 1979, but he does reveal why it was perhaps useful to recognize them, since they fit nicely into the Marxist evolutionary scheme of "primitive" minorities. Ma (1989, p. 334) writes, "The Jino matriarchal society gave way to a patriarchal one some 300 years ago. But the Jinos were still in the transitional stage from primitivity to a class society at the time the People's Republic was founded in 1949."

[3]In an important ethno-historical study, David Faure (1989, pp. 4–36) has noted that the Cantonese people are descended from the southern "Yue" people, who were regarded as subjects of the Song empire primarily because they paid taxes. Yue people who lived in the mountains often refused to pay taxes to the Song and they became known as the "Yao" people, now classified as a minority nationality of China, whereas the tax-paying Yue are now regarded as Cantonese Han. It is clear that politics was critical to ethnic identity even in the premodern period.

2 / Creating Ethnic Identity in China: The Making of the Hui Nationality

Before we begin to describe the wide variety of Muslim peoples in China, and ethnic identity formation among those people known as the Hui, we must first begin to understand a key concern to almost all Muslims in China. Central to Muslim identity is the Chinese translation and interpretation of Islam, as revealed in a nineteenth-century Muslim tract appended at the end of Marshal Broomhall's *Islam in China,* written in 1910, the first and only book on Muslims in China based on extensive field and survey work. If we are to understand Hui Muslim identity in China, we must begin here.

The Muslim tract stated:

> But our Pure and True Faith [*Qing Zhen Jiao*], the Correct Religion, arose and gradually reached this land from the Sui and T'ang dynasties onward. The statement of the recognition of the Lord (derived) from Adam was not yet lost. Moreover they obtained the most Holy Mohammed's very detailed account of the plain commands of the True Lord. Therefore our Religion is very Pure and very True, and only holds what is correct, not vainly taking the name, while lacking the ability to prove its truth. . . . Why (have we written) like this? Only in the hope that those who look at (the words) will clarify their heart and breast, and enlarge their horizon beyond the common and the visible, and sweeping away heresy will consider the traces of origin and exit, (and) will investigate the essential matter of reversion to the Source. Thus you will almost get hold of the correct Doctrine of Purity and Truth (in Broomhall, 1910, pp. 304–305).

The "Pure and True" mentioned in this Muslim tract refers to the two Chinese characters *qing zhen* that one encounters wherever the people known as Hui are found. The importance of this concept initially caught my attention in 1982 while in China as a language student at Beijing University. One of the first Hui with whom I became acquainted came to my room but refused a cup of tea I offered. The cup, he said, was not "pure and true enough" (*bu gou qing zhen*). He explained that he did not want to drink from the same cup or eat with the same utensils that formerly may have been used by someone who had eaten pork; the residue might still be on the cup, no matter how often or how well I had washed it. I later discovered that this

Imam at prayer, Jiaxing Mosque, Zhejiang. April 1984.

person was a member of the Communist Party, a well-educated urbanite, and although he frequently attended the local Haidian-district mosque, he was a self-avowed atheist.

During the rest of the summer in Beijing, I began to notice the characters *qing zhen* on restaurants, food shops, bakeries, ice cream stands, candy wrappers, mosques, Islamic literary works, and even on packages of incense produced in the Dachang Hui Autonomous County just east of Beijing. It became clear to me that the concept expressed by these Chinese ideographs meant more to the Hui than the absence of lard or pork. It had become, in the Geertzian (1968, p. 79) sense, a "sacred symbol" marking Hui identity and thus provides a good starting point for this study of Hui ethnicity.

Wherever the Hui have traveled, both in and outside of China proper, this concept of *qing zhen* has followed them. In Los Angeles, there are at least four Muslim Chinese establishments serving *halal* Chinese food. The largest one, in Rosemead, is known in English as the China Islamic Restaurant and in Chinese is called "The Pure and True Ma Family Restaurant" (*Qing Zhen Ma Jia Guan*), run by a Hui immigrant family from Taiwan. Most Chinese restaurants in the Muslim Middle East are run by Hui and are *qing zhen* restaurants. In Kirghizia and Kazakistan of Soviet Central Asia, where Hui fled after the failure of their mid-nineteenth-century rebellions and established themselves in close-knit communities, the title of *qing zhen* is found on all of their restaurants and food stands, but written in the Dungan Cyrillic script that they have adapted over the years. In Bangkok, I was surprised to find a small Islamic restaurant run by Hui immigrants from Yunnan, whose name was "*Chien Jan*," a Thai transliteration of *qing zhen*, reflecting Southern Chinese and Thai pronunciation.

Donald Leslie (1972, p. 102) suggests that *qing zhen* might have originated with the Chinese Jews and referred to Judaism in many of their ancient inscriptions. Beijing's East Mosque (*Dong si*) is the earliest structure referred to as a *Qing Zhen Si* in 1447, the twentieth year of the Ming Emperor Zheng Tong (Ma Shouqian, 1979, p. 156). The early eleventh-century Arab-style mosque in Quanzhou was known as the *Qing Jing Si* (Pure and Clean Mosque), and the Islamicist, Yang Yongchang (1981), gives several examples of mosques with Purity and Truth in their early titles. In his etymological study of the term, the prominent Hui historian Ma Shouqian (1979) concludes that before the Yuan dynasty, *qing zhen* referred loosely to both Islam and Judaism, but by the Ming dynasty its meaning was generally restricted to the religion of the Hui people.

The Chinese etymological dictionary, *Ci Yuan* (1982, (3), p. 1817), traces *qing zhen* to a Tang dynasty expression: "Pure and True lacks desire, it is everything that cannot change" (*qing zhen guayu, wanwu bu neng yi ye*). Ma Fuchu (1851–1874), the Yunnan Hui scholar who first translated the Qur'an into Chinese, defined *qing zhen* in terms of Confucian ideals when he wrote: "To deny oneself is pure, to restore propriety is true" (*keji zhiwei qing, fuli zhiwei zhen*). Here we see the two complementary but distinct uses of the term. Ma Fuchu explicitly tied the Islamic concept of *qing zhen* to traditional Confucian principles expressed in the phrase: "Denying oneself and restoring propriety" (*keji fuli*; see Gladney & Ma, 1989).

Hui scholars in China today generally suggest *qing zhen* denotes "clean and authentic" (*qingjie zhenshi*), emphasizing both the sanitary and authoritarian aspects of the term. Matthews (1931, p. 166) translates *qing* as clear, pure, and lucid. A Beijing "sanitation worker" or "street cleaner" is known as a *qingjie gongren*. *Qing jiaotu* is the Chinese gloss for the Christian "Puritan." Matthews (1931, p. 36) informs us that *zhen* refers to what is true, real, unfeigned, and genuine. "Authenticity" or "truthfulness" is generally rendered as *zhen shi xing*. Vernon Fowler (1987, p. 41), in an interesting, recent etymological study of the term *zhen*, concludes that the graph appears in early sacrificial texts related to "ritual cooking." It is noteworthy that early Muslim attempts to elucidate the foreign term "Islam" with Chinese script should turn to ideographs that connote ritual purity and sacrificial authenticity.

The concept of *qing zhen*, I argue, reveals two aspects of Islam in China central to Hui community interests and self-understanding: purity (*qing*), in the sense of ritual cleanliness and moral conduct; and truth (*zhen*), in the sense of authenticity and legitimacy. This wider meaning of *qing zhen* goes beyond the Arabic term *halal*, as *qing zhen* is sometimes translated, for it involves much more than ritually prepared food according to Islamic dietary prescriptions. The concept of *qing zhen* governs all of one's life. The Arabic term *tahára* ("ritual or moral purity") is perhaps a better translation for this all encompassing concept, but the Jewish term "kosher" would be more familiar with Western readers. Keeping kosher, however, is much more restrictive than the *qing zhen* requirements and it is thus not the best translation. For the Hui, the two aspects of *qing zhen*, purity and truth, define important tensions in their identity: Islamic moral purity and the authenticity of ethnic ancestry, lifestyle, and heritage. In China, the Hui have always been ritually and perhaps morally suspect, not merely because of their foreign origins—there have been many foreigners easily assimilated into Chinese society without developing ethnic, enduring, social collectivities—but perhaps, more fundamentally, due to their avoidance of those objects, such as pork, that have been a fundamental part of the elementary structure of Chinese ritual and food presentations (Thompson, 1988). Yet, as Julia Kristeva (1980) has so acutely described, there is a basic powerfulness, even horror, related to defilement and impurity that goes beyond social structure. It strikes at the core of one's self and ontology. There is something more fundamental than food proscription at stake here: The Hui's defining and ordering of their world into one that is pure and true turns the tables on Chinese society. It reverses the Durkhemian (1915, pp. 52–57) polarities of what is sacred and profane in China, making the Hui the *pure* community that rejects Chinese ritual values and the *true* believers who follow the one God above all others.

The concept of *qing zhen* is so central to Hui ethnoreligious concern that it has become the very confession of their faith. The monotheistic formula—that there is no God but Allah and Muhammad is his Prophet—is known in Arabic as the *Shahadah*; to the Hui, it is known in Chinese as the *Qing Zhen Yan*, the very words of *qing zhen*. It is not surprising that the early Muslims settled on the concept of *qing zhen* to translate the meaningfulness of Islam for Muslims living in Chinese society. Significantly, they could have settled on Chinese translations of "submission," "obedience," or "faithfulness," that are arguably closer to the original meaning of Islam. They also did not simply transliterate the technical term until recently. Instead, the combination of *qing* and *zhen* seemed to capture and express their deepest concerns as Muslims living in the Chinese world. "Pure" reflected their concern to morally legitimate themselves in a Confucian society preoccupied with moral propriety and order. "Truth" and belief in the "True Lord" (*Zhen Zhu*) distinguished them as monotheists in a land where polytheistic belief and practice predominated. There is clearly a subtle irony here, as in China the Han have typically looked down on the Hui as dirty, larcenous, and immoral. While the Hui, by their choice of translation, portray their ethnoreligious identity as more "pure and true" than the Han. The different ways Hui have sought to adapt their ethnoreligious identity—their ideas of a pure and true lifestyle—to the various sociopolitical contexts of China have led to a wide diversity of Hui identities and Islamic orders in China, as well as influencing the nature of their conflict and interaction with the Chinese state.

FROM NAME TO CLAIM: IDENTIFYING THE HUI

It is clear that the Hui have exercised some degree of originality and flexibility in interpreting their understanding of Islam to a Chinese audience and thus have sought interpretive control over their internal understanding of Islam. Externally, however, the state has traditionally labeled their faith simply as the "religion of the Hui" (*Hui jiao*). While archaeological evidence has revealed that Muslim peoples traded and settled in China since the very advent of Islam, there was no consistent term in Chinese to refer to these peoples and their religion until the thirteenth century. The rise of this term and its institutionalization as the accepted ethnonym for one people is intimately bound to the increasing power of the state in China and its authority over the naming of social entities. According to Bernard Cohn (1987), the power of the British colonial authorities to conduct a census and institutionalize labels and castes in India contributed to the "objectification" of their cultures and identities.

It is not that these social labels did not exist in some form prior to their institutionalization by the state in China. People referred to themselves as Huihui, believed in the Hui religion, and lived ethnically distinct lives. However, naming by the state, legislating who was and was not ethnic, then quantifying the numbers of certain groups, solidified them and gave them a social life unknown before.

The early Nationalists (and later Communist Party leaders) argued that only by counting and categorizing their population, as the Western nations did, could they begin to compete in the age of nation-states and engender a national movement. As early as the seventh century, Tang-dynasty historians documented the presence of large groups of foreign merchants dwelling in the southeast coastal communities of Canton (Guangzhou), Xiamen, and Quanzhou.[1] Among these foreigners there were increasingly large numbers of mainly Persian and Arab Muslims who were grouped with the other foreigners as *Fan Ke* ("barbarian guests"). As they settled and took on local spouses, their offspring became known as *Tusheng Fanke* ("autochthonous" or "native-born barbarian guests"). Ma Shouqian (1989) reports that during this early period the foreign Muslims rarely interacted with non-Muslim Chinese outside the marketplace and Islam was of little interest to local officials. Islamic religious activities were described in Tang and Song texts simply as the worship of other spirits (*shen*), ghosts (*gui*) and even heaven (*tian*). Ma reports early terms for

Islam such as the "Law of the Arabs" (*Da shi fa*), the religion of the Celestial Square (*Tian Fang Jiao*), and Muhammadanism.

The Chinese term *Hui* or *Hui jiao* for the Hui people or Islam in China did not gain widespread usage until the Yuan dynasty, when large populations of Central Asian Muslims began to migrate to China under Yuan dynasty administration. The Mongols, under Khubilai Khan's leadership, were the first to make an official, legal hierarchical distinction between four kinds of peoples in China: The Mongols were at the highest level of society; next were the *se-mu*, or other foreigners, that included other Central Asians, Europeans, and Muslims, known as the *Huihui*; then came the *Han* people, which included not only Northern Chinese, but also Koreans, Khitans, and Jurchen; and at the lowest end were the *Nan*, or "southern" people, the Chinese populations in the south, including the Cantonese, Fujianese, and others, who were the "least desirable and least trustworthy group" (Rossabi, 1988, p. 71).

The term that was later adopted as the modern Hui ethnonym derives from a medieval Chinese transliteration for the Uygur people (*Huihu or Huihe*). The term *Huihui*, or *Huijiao*, was used to generally refer to all Muslim and Islam people in China, no matter what their ethnolinguistic background, until the modern era. It received its first official institutionalization under the Nationalist government. More specific terms were often employed by locals to distinguish between various Muslims, thus in Xinjiang, *Chan Hui* ("turban Hui"), literally referred to those Muslims who wore wound cloths on their heads, like the Uygur. Other more specific ethnonyms included *Wei Hui, Dongxiang Hui, Sala Hui*, and even *Han Hui*, which referred to those Hui who were more culturally close to the Han (Pillsbury, 1976, p. 45).

Djamal al-Din Bai Shouyi, the famous Hui Marxist historian, was the first to argue persuasively that "Islam" should be glossed in Chinese as "*Yisilan jiao*" (Islam), not the Hui religion (*Hui jiao*) (Bai, 1951). In a chapter entitled "The Huihui People and the Huihui Religion," Bai (1951) argued that even though Hui are descendants of Muslims and have inherited certain Muslim cultural traditions such as pork abstention, they do not all necessarily believe in Islam. "Muslim" is different from "Hui person" (*Hui min*) and one should not use the term *Hui jiao* ("Hui religion") but "Islam" (*yisilan jiao*). He argued that the Hui believed not in their own religion, but in the world religion of Islam, and therefore are Muslims in faith. In ethnicity, they are the Hui people not Hui religion disciples. In Marxist terms, Bai identified a process of the indigenization of a world religion, in this case Islam, to a local context, which for the communities now known as the Hui had been going on for 1,200 years. Muslim groups identified by Chinese linguists with supposedly their own language derived their ethnonym from their language family; in this way the Uygur, Kazak, Tadjik, Uzbek, Kirgiz, and Tatar were identified. In this, the Chinese were heavily influenced by the 1920s Soviet identification of these peoples in Soviet Central Asia (Connor, 1984, p. 53ff).[2] Bai Shouyi went on to identify the Muslim peoples not distinguished by language or locality as a catch-all residual group known as *Hui min*, not *Huijiao*. Thus, the official category of the Hui was legitimated, and one might even say invented, so far as the legal definition of who is considered Hui is concerned.

In Taiwan today, the term *Hui* still continues to refer to all Muslim peoples and Islam is often referred to as *Hui jiao*, though this usage is opposed by some Hui (Pillsbury, 1973, p. 45). The refusal to recognize the Hui as a separate nationality in

Tibetan Mosque, near Jokhang Temple, Lhasa. February 8, 1985.

Taiwan, but instead as a religious group—the believers in the Hui religion (*Hui jiao tu*) rather than members of the Hui ethnic group (*Hui minzu*)— is intimately tied to different policies in both states, as we shall see later. These contrasting policies and ethnonyms play an important role in the construction of Hui identity on both sides of the Taiwan Strait.

After the founding of the People's Republic, many of these Muslim peoples received specific ethnonyms, leading to the creation or recognition of 10 Muslim nationalities in China: the Hui, Uygur, Kazak, Dongxiang, Kirghiz, Salar, Tadjik, Uzbek, Baonan, and Tatar (see Table 2.1). Other Muslims in Tibet, Mongolia, Yunnan, and Sichuan, who were smaller in number and did not have a language of their own, however, were merely grouped with the Hui as one nationality.

In general, the Communist government has used the ethnonym "Hui nationality" (*Hui minzu*) to refer to those Muslims who do not have a language of their own but speak the dialects of the peoples among whom they live, as opposed to the other nine Turkic-Altaic and Indo-European Muslim language groups. In China, I rarely heard Hui refer to themselves as *Huijiao tu* (Hui religion disciples) and only occasionally heard *Huijiao*. Instead, Hui generally preferred "*Hui min*" or "*Huizu*" (Hui nationality) and sometimes "*Huihui*" in rural areas. Urban Hui and intellectuals often use the Chinese renderings for "Islam" (*Yisilan jiao*) and "Muslim" (*Musilin*), and even "*Mumin*" (Muslim people). Urban Hui often found the term *Huihui* to be offensive, and slightly demeaning, connoting rural origins. Other terms used to refer to the Hui include *Dungan* in Soviet Central Asia and *Xinjiang* (Dyer, 1979), *Panthay* in Southeast Asia and Yunnan (Yegar, 1966), as well as *Hanhui, Huihui, Khojem, Khalkhas,* and, most frequently, "Chinese Muslims" (Sinor, 1969, p. 47). The Hui are often referred to as the "Chinese Muslims" because of their speech and other cultural similarities to the Han

TABLE 2.1
MUSLIM NATIONALITY POPULATIONS IN CHINA, 1982 AND 1990 CENSUS

Ethnonym	Location	Languages	1982 Population	1990 Population	Percent Growth
Hui (Dungan)	All China, esp. Ningxia, Gansu, Henan, Xinjiang, Qinghai, Yunnan Hebei, Shandong	Sino-Tibetan	7,219,352	8,602,978	19%
Uygur	Xinjiang	Altaic (Turkic)	5,957,112	7,214,431	21%
Kazakh	Xinjiang, Gansu Qinghai	Altaic (Turkic)	907,582	1,111,718	24%
Dongxiang	Gansu, Xinjiang	Altaic (Turkic)	279,397	373,872	34%
Kyrgyz	Xinjiang, Heilongjiang	Altaic (Turkic)	113,999	141,549	24%
Salar	Qinghai, Gansu	Altaic (Turkic)	69,102	87,697	27%
Tadjik	Xinjiang	Indo-European	26,503	33,538	27%
Uzbek	Xinjiang	Altaic (Turkic)	12,453	14,502	16%
Bonan	Gansu	Altaic (Mongolian)	9,027	12,212	35%
Tatar	Xinjiang	Altaic (Turkic)	4,127	4,873	18%
Total Muslim minority populations			14,598,654	17,597,370	26%
Total minority populations			67,295,217	91,200,314	35%
Total Han majority populations			940,880,121	1,075,470,555	10%

Note. Name(s) of group based on most commonly used and Chinese *pinyin* transliterations.
Sources. Renmin Ribao, "*Guanyu 1990 nian renkou pucha zhuyao de gongbao*" [Report regarding the 1990 population census primary statistics], 14 November 1991, p. 3; Dru C. Gladney, *Muslim Chinese: Ethnic Nationalism in the People's Republic*, 1991, p. 21. Note that Muslim population estimates in China are based on the official census nationality categories, which do not include religion. Non-Muslim nationalities, such as the Han, may include believers in Islam, just as the "Muslim Nationalities" may include those who do not believe in or practice Islam.

than the Turkish-speaking Muslims; however, this term is inappropriate and misleading because, by law, all Muslims in China are citizens of the Chinese state and thus Chinese. The Hui, in this respect, are no more *Chinese* than the Uygur or Kazak. However, through more than 1,200 years of intimate contact with the Han majority, and other peoples that they have lived among, the nature of the Hui as a people at the least is exceedingly complex, and at most, questionable.

THE PROBLEM: WHO ARE THE HUI?

The wide diversity found within Hui communities and the various ways different Hui have sought to resolve the tension of maintaining a "pure and true" lifestyle in

Chinese society has often obfuscated their identity. According to the official nationality census and literature in China, the Hui people are the third most populous of
China's 55 recognized minority nationalities who altogether comprise almost 9% of
the total population. The sociocultural uniqueness of the Hui can be readily seen by
briefly examining their wide distribution, dispersed population, manifold administrative units, occupational diversity, linguistic variety, and cultural complexity.

Wide Distribution

The Hui are the most widespread minority, inhabiting every region, province, city,
and more than 97% of the nation's counties. Incredibly, the 1982 census revealed
that there are Hui living in 2,308 of 2,372 counties and cities across China (Population Census, 1987, p. xvi). This substantiates the popular Hui conception that they
are "spread widely and concentrated narrowly" (da fen can, xiao ji zhong). It is
noteworthy that while the Hui may represent a small fragment of the population in
most areas (with the exception of Ningxia), they often make up the vast majority of
the minority population in Han dominated areas (see Table 2.2). In Anhui, only
one-half of 1% of the provincial population are Hui but they represent more than
97% of all the minorities. This is also true for most of China's cities where the Hui
are the main urban ethnic group (such as Beijing, Shanghai, and Tianjin).

In border areas where most of China's minorities are concentrated, the Hui are
also numerous, but they only represent a small proportion of the minorities. For example, in Yunnan, the southwest province bordering Burma and Vietnam, the Hui
are the eighth largest minority group (behind the Yi, Bai, Hani, Zhuang, Dai, Miao,
and Lisu), but they only represent 4.2% of the minority population, and 1.3% of the
entire provincial population. It is conventionally thought that China's Muslim minorities are concentrated in the northwest corner, near Soviet Central Asia. The Hui
minority, however, are mainly spread throughout China's Inner Asia (see Fletcher,
1979). This region is at the juncture of four distinct cultures, the Central Asian, Tibetan, Mongolian, and Chinese (Han) and encompasses a vast area including Xinjiang, Ningxia, Gansu, and Qinghai that has been justifiably referred to as China's
"Qur'an belt" (Barnett, 1963, p. 182).

Dispersed Population

With a population of at least 8.6 million, according to the 1990 census, the Hui are
the most numerous of the 10 nationalities recognized by the state as adhering to
Islam as their nationality religion (see Figure 2.1).

According to the 1990 census (Renmin Ribao, 14 November 1990, p. 23), the
total population of the 10 Muslim nationalities in China is 17.5 million (refer to
Table 2.1). However, the census registered people by ethnic group, not by religion,
so the actual number of Muslims is still unknown and the local figures I have collected range widely from the census reports.

While total Muslim population figures have been hampered by the lack of a
category for religion in the 1990 census, a minimum of 15 million and a maximum
of 20 million seem the most reasonable estimates for total Muslim population.
More wide-ranging population figures of as many as 40 million or even 50 million

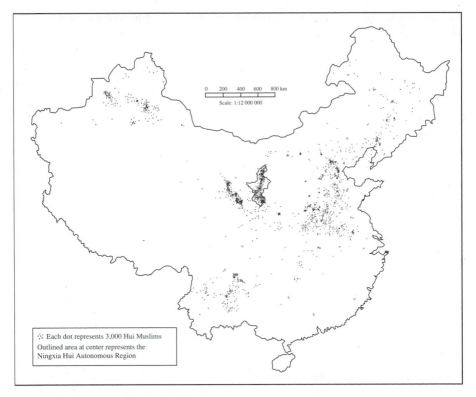

0   200   400   600   800 km

Scale: 1:12 000 000

∴ Each dot represents 3,000 Hui Muslims
Outlined area at center represents the
Ningxia Hui Autonomous Region

Figure 2.1   Hui Muslim Minority Distribution

Muslims among the Hui alone in China (Chang, 1987, p. 73; Winters, 1979, p. 58) appear to be influenced by similar political concerns that in the earlier part of this century led people to purposively inflate Muslim population in China (see Pills-bury, 1981b).[3]

Manifold Administration

As the most widespread and second most numerous of China's minority nationali-ties, the Hui have more autonomous administrative units assigned to them than any other minority, including one autonomous region, two autonomous prefectures, and nine autonomous counties, as well as numerous autonomous townships that only re-cently have been established (see Table 2.3 and Figure 2.2 on p. 36).[4]

While the Hui have their own Ningxia Autonomous Region, they are only one-third of its population, with the Han in the vast majority. Merely one-sixth of the total Hui population is concentrated in their only autonomous region. By contrast, 99.8% of the Uygur population live in Xinjiang Uygur Autonomous Region and the vast majority of Tibetan, Zhuang, and Mongolian populations are concentrated in

TABLE 2.2
DISTRIBUTION OF THE HUI MINORITY, 1982

Municipality Region or Province	Population	Percent of Total Population	Percent of Hui in China	Percent of Minorities in Area
Ningxia	1,235,207	31.6%	17.1%	99.3%
Gansu	950,974	4.8%	13.2%	61.4%
Henan	727,146	0.9%	10.0%	91.3%
Xinjiang	570,788	4.3%	7.9%	7.3%
Qinghai	533,750	13.7%	7.4%	34.7%
Yunnan	438,883	1.3%	6.1%	4.2%
Hebei	418,853	0.8%	5.8%	49.2%
Shandong	389,506	0.5%	5.4%	95.5%
Anhui	254,602	0.5%	3.5%	97.3%
Liaoning	239,200	0.7%	3.3%	8.2%
Beijing	184,693	2.0%	2.5%	57.3%
Inner Mongolia	169,096	0.9%	2.3%	5.6%
Tianjin	142,847	1.8%	1.9%	87.2%
Heilongjiang	126,427	0.3%	1.7%	7.8%
Shaanxi	118,389	0.4%	1.6%	89.0%
Jilin	110,673	0.4%	1.5%	6.0%
Jiangsu	103,822	0.1%	1.4%	94.1%
Guizhou	100,058	0.3%	1.3%	1.3%
Hubei	70,516	0.1%	0.9%	3.9%
Hunan	67,205	0.1%	0.9%	3.0%
Shanxi	51,585	0.2%	0.7%	81.1%
Shanghai	44,123	0.3%	0.6%	89.0%
Fujian	31,060	0.1%	0.4%	12.4%
Guangxi	19,279	0.05%	0.3%	0.13%
Guangdong	10,849	0.01%	0.15%	1.02%
Sichuan	10,000	0.01%	0.13%	0.27%
Zhejiang	9,435	0.02%	0.13%	5.85%
Jiangxi	7,926	0.02%	0.1%	35.85%
Tibet	1,788	0.094%	0.02%	0.099%
Total:	7,138,680	1.45%	98.3%	10.73%

Source. 1982 Census; *Minzu Tuanjie,* 1984.

their autonomous regions. Surprisingly, after Ningxia and Gansu, the third-largest population of Hui is found in Henan Province, in central China. Their sixth-largest concentration is in Yunnan (see Table 2.2).

Occupational Specialization

In addition to the wide distribution of the Hui across China, there is also extensive economic and occupational diversity found among the Hui, from cadres to clergy,

TABLE 2.3
HUI AUTONOMOUS ADMINISTRATIVE UNITS

Province or Region	Autonomous Administrative Unit	Founded
Ningxia	Ningxia Hui Autonomous Region	1958
Gansu	Linxia Autonomous Prefecture	1956
	Zhangjiachuan Autonomous County	1953
Xinjiang	Changji Autonomous Prefecture	1954
	Yanqi Autonomous County	1954
Hebei	Dachang Autonomous County	1955
	Mengcun Autonomous County	1955
Qinghai	Hualong Autonomous County	1954
	Menyuan Autonomous County	1953
Guizhou	Weining Yi, Hui and Miao Autonomous County	1954
Yunnan	Weishan Yi and Hui Autonomous County	1956
	Xundian Hui and Yi Autonomous County	1979

Source. Zhongguo Shaoshu Minzu, 1981, pp. 587–593.

Figure 2.2   Hui Autonomous Administrative Units

TABLE 2.4
OCCUPATIONAL STRUCTURE OF MUSLIM MINORITIES IN CHINA IN PERCENT, 1982

Occupation	Hui	Uygur	Kazakh	Dongxiang	Kyrgyz	Salar	Tadjik	Uzbek	Baoan	Tatar	All Ethnic Groups
Scientific technical staff	5.75	4.25	11.25	1.0	7.0	3.25	5.75	17.25	1.5	23.5	4.0
Administration	1.75	0.75	2.0	0.25	1.5	0.75	2.75	3.75	2.25	4.5	1.0
Office and related workers	1.75	1.0	2.0	0.25	1.75	0.75	2.0	3.25	0.75	4.25	1.0
Commerical workers	3.5	1.5	1.25	0.25	0.75	0.75	0.5	10.75	0.5	5.25	1.25
Service workers	4.0	1.5	1.5	0.25	1.0	0.75	0.75	6.5	0.5	4.5	1.25
Farming, forestry, fishing and animal husbandry	60.75	84.0	74.5	96.75	84.0	90.5	85.75	31.5	92.25	38.5	84.0
Production and transport	22.25	7.0	7.5	1.25	4.0	3.25	2.5	27.0	2.25	19.25	7.5
Others	0.25	—	—	—	—	—	—	—	—	0.25	—

Source. Adopted from *Population Atlas,* 1987, p. 28.

rice farmers to factory workers, school teachers to camel drivers, and poets to generals. Hui have occupied a wide variety of economic niches throughout the history of China. Most of these were related to their Islamic restrictions in diet and hygiene, leading them to take up such occupations as restauranteur, innkeeper, shepherd, cavalryman, caravaneer, butcher, tanner, tea trader, jeweler, interpreter, and clergyman. In the north, the majority of Hui are wheat and dry-rice agriculturists, while in the south they are primarily engaged in wet-rice cultivation and aquaculture. In urban centers, the majority are employed in common labor and industry. Since the collectivization campaigns of the 1950s, most Hui were prevented from engaging in the small, private businesses that were their traditional specializations. Nevertheless, Table 2.4 reveals that the Hui continue to be occupied in trade and commerce. In contrast to the Uygur, 84% of whom are primarily involved in the production of agriculture and husbandry, only 60.7% of the total Hui population is engaged in such occupations. It is significant that the census revealed 29% of the Hui are involved in the occupations of service, commerce, production, and transport, more than any other ethnic group in China, including the Han. However, these figures do not begin to take into account the many private and part-time small businesses that are now dominating the local village business economies, in which the Hui play an active part.

Linguistic Variety

The Hui are distinguished from the other nine Muslim nationalities in China by the fact that they do not have a language of their own, but speak the dialects of the other ethnic groups with whom they live, mainly the Han. Thus, in the past, they have been inaccurately labeled as the "Chinese-speaking Muslims" (Lipman, 1987, p. 112). However, among those recognized by the state as Hui, there is extremely wide linguistic variety. These include Hui in non-Han majority areas who have adopted the language, dress, and customs of their minority neighbors, such as the "Tibetan-Hui" (*zang hui*) in Lhasa, Tibet; the "Mongolian-Hui" (*meng hui*) of Alashan district, Inner Mongolia; the "Dai-Hui" in Xishuangbana; and the "Bai-Hui" in Eryuan county, both in Yunnan (Ma Weiliang, 1986). When I spoke in Almaty with the Dungan of Soviet Central Asia, who call themselves *Hui min* (Riftin, 1989), we spoke in a hybrid Gansu dialect that combined Turkish and Russian lexical items, which had been written in Cyrillic for more than 30 years (see Dyer, 1979; Mair, 1989). These Muslims are culturally indistinguishable from the minority group with whom they live, but they identify themselves as Hui and are recognized by the state as members of the Hui nationality.

In one Bai (Minjia) nationality village north of Erhu Lake in Dali prefecture, I interviewed five Hui women who were training to become Imam. They wore traditional Bai dress and spoke only the Tibeto-Burman Bai language, yet they were studying Arabic and Islamic doctrine under a woman Imam from their village. Bilingual in Bai and Mandarin, this woman had studied for 5 years in a Hui mosque in southern Yunnan.[5] It is significant that in order to receive further Islamic training beyond her village, this woman had to go to a predominantly Hui area, where there were no Bai people. Most of these Hui say that they fled to the Bai concentrated area north of Dali city after the failed Panthay Muslim uprising (1855–1873) led by the Hui hero, Du Wenxiu. They say that they gradually assimilated to Bai culture in the last 100 years. One village elder, however, described an origin myth, where the Hui in that village descended from the "Black cloth" early Turkish-speaking Muslims who settled there under the Tang or perhaps Yuan dynasties (see Yokoyama, 1988).

The "Tibetan Hui" are a community of about 6,000 Muslims living in Lhasa who speak Tibetan, wear Tibetan clothes, and worship in a mosque that is decorated with Tibetan floral designs and carpets. Their mosque is one of two mosques left in the city after the Chinese occupation and suppression of the Tibetan uprising in 1959. At that time, another community of "Kashmiri" Muslims, who came from the northern Pakistani–India border region of Kashmir, fled *en toto* with the Dalai Lama. I was told that there was only one household of "Kashmiri Hui" left in Lhasa. Xue Wenbo, the late Hui intellectual, who conducted 2 years of research among the Hui in Tibet after he was sent there with the People's Liberation Army in 1951, argued that "the majority of them are Sichuanese, a minority are Western Shaanxi Hui, and a few are from Gansu, Qinghai, and Yunnan" (Xue, 1986, p. 148). He suggests that most fled to Tibet after the failed nineteenth-century rebellions. During several interviews in February 1985, I was impressed at how distinct they regarded themselves from the other Hui traders in Lhasa. At any one time, there are from 20,000 to 30,000 Hui merchants from Ningxia, Gansu, and Qinghai working primarily in Lhasa, as well as the other major trade centers throughout Tibet (Tibet Academy of Social Sciences Interview, 1985). The local "Tibetan Hui" did not interact with these traders, whom they regarded with suspicion, and preferred to marry their children to other Tibetans, instead of their coreligionists from outside Tibet.

Hui carpet trader from Gansu, Jokhang Temple market, Lhasa. November 18, 1995.

In Yunnan, I attended the ordination service, at the well-known Wukeng Mosque in the Weishan Yi and Hui Autonomous County, of an acolyte who called himself a Hui from Hainan Island. He had traveled almost a thousand kilometers from Hainan Island to study under a famous Hui Hajji in southwestern Yunnan on the Burmese border. At the time, his brother was studying at the national madrassah in Beijing, sponsored by the China Islamic Association. When I visited one of two Muslim villages along the southern coast of Hainan Island in January 1984, the local Imam said, in Mandarin, that his people were Hui. However, in their own Malayo-Austronesian language, Pang Keng-fong (1992) has found that they call themselves *Utsat*, which simply means Muslim. It is significant that while speaking Mandarin, the national language, these people call themselves Hui, and they send their sons to faraway Hui religious centers in Yunnan and Beijing to obtain the necessary training in order to become Imam.

Three other identified Muslim groups, the Dongxiang, Baonan and Salar, located primarily in the Hexi corridor of the Gansu-Qinghai Tibetan plateau, did not

Tongxin Great Mosque, Huhehot, Inner Mongolia. October 3, 1983. Taken from the top of the minaret. Note the Mongolian architectural style.

derive their ethnonyms from the Soviet Central Asian model but were decided on by the Chinese state. Each of these groups speak a combination of Turkic, Mongolian, and Han Chinese dialects and are thus defined mainly by locality. For example, the Dongxiang (East Township) derive their name from the eastern suburb of old Hezhou (Linxia) where they were concentrated. The question remains, however, why these groups received their separate identifications when other groups such as the Mongolian, Tibetan, Bai, and Hainan Muslims are all identified as Hui. They did not receive separate identities despite their divergent localities and languages. Their populations are not insignificant enough to warrant refusal as a distinct nationality, as the Baonan only numbered 9,027 in 1982 and the Tatar only 4,127. Chinese-minority publications proudly proclaim the recognition of such insignificant groups as the Hezhe, despite their only possessing a population of 300 at the time of the revolution and 450 reported at the time of their identification in 1953, with a 1982 population of 1,476 (Zhongguo, 1981, pp. 57–68; Banister, 1987, pp. 322–323).

All of these seemingly multiethnic peoples, the Bai, Tibetan, and Hainanese Muslims, are registered as Hui by the State Commission for Nationality Affairs and are considered members of the Hui nationality. Just as the Cantonese, Shanghainese, Fujianese, and other non-Mandarin speakers are registered as Hui, so these groups do not have their own ethnonym, or legal separate ethnic status. Unlike the Dongxiang and Baonan peoples in Gansu, these Hui peoples are counted by the state simply as Hui. Interestingly enough, after living for 30 years under this policy, despite their linguistic diversity and multicultural background, they themselves claim membership to the same Hui ethnic group as other Hui in China and they often quoted to me the popular phrase: "All Hui under Heaven are one family" (*Tianxia Huihui shi yi jia*).

Islamic Diversity Among the Hui

In addition to geographic, economic, cultural, and linguistic differences, the Hui also subscribe to a wide spectrum of Islamic belief. The variety of religious orders within Hui Islam represent a long history of reforms and Islamic movements that resulted from interaction with the Islamic world. The earliest Muslim communities were descended from the Arab-, Persian-, Central Asian-, and Mongolian-Muslim merchants, militia, and officials who settled along China's Southeast Coast and in the Northwest in large and small numbers from the seventh to the fourteenth centuries. Generally residing in independent small communities clustered around a central mosque (*danyi jiaofangzhi*), they became known as the *Gedimu* (from the Arabic *qadîm* for "old"). They followed the traditional Sunni, Hanafi Islam (Feng, 1985). With the exception of the 26,000 Tajik nomads of the Pamir mountains in southwestern Xinjiang, the vast majority of Muslims in China are Sunni. Few Hui I spoke with in the northwest knew the difference between Shi'i and Sunni, even though the Iran–Iraq war was at its height during my fieldwork and in the daily news.[6]

The isolation of these individual Gedimu communities, and their thin dispersion throughout China, reveals the importance of trade and migration history among the Hui. Although the early origins of the Hui can be traced to the descendants of migrants from the Southeast along the "Spice Route," and from the Northwest along the "Silk Road," it is interesting that the major concentrations of the Hui are no longer in those border areas. After Gansu and Ningxia, Henan Province contains the third-largest concentration of Hui. Hui villages can be found throughout China, especially evident along the main transport nodes of the Yellow River in the north, and the Burma Road in the south, revealing the traditional Hui proclivity for exploiting trade opportunities. Iwamura Shinobu's (1948) perceptive analysis of the Inner-Mongolian Hui communities in Huhehot and Baotou revealed that the vast majority of them were populated with Hui native to central and southern China— not Mongolia—who left poorer areas to engage in business and seek opportunities in the new frontier. James Millward (1989, p. 45) persuasively documents that almost all interior wool collection and transshipment agencies in the northwest were taken over by Hui after the problems of taxation, banditry, and warlord politics led the previously foreign-owned companies to return to the safer enclaves of Tianjin. It is not surprising, therefore, that we find the major wool-trade towns and cities during the heyday of wool trade in the early Republican period continuing to be populated with many Hui communities.

Sufism did not begin to make a substantial impact in China until the late seventeenth century. Like Sufi centers that proliferated after the thirteenth century in other countries (Trimingham, 1971, p. 10), many of these Sufi movements in China developed socioeconomic and religiopolitical institutions built around the schools established by descendants of early Sufi saintly leaders. The institutions became known in Chinese as the *menhuan*, the "leading" or "saintly" descent groups.[7]

The important contribution that Sufism made to religious organization in China was that the leaders of mosques throughout their order owed their allegiance to their *shaykh*, the founder of the order who appointed them. These designated followers were loyal to the leader of their order and remained in the community for long periods of time, unlike the Gedimu Ahong, who were generally itinerant, not well connected to the community, and less imbued with appointed authority. Gedimu mosque elders were loyal to their village first and connected only by trade to other communities.

Many Sufi reforms spread throughout northwest China during the early decades of the Qing dynasty (mid-seventeenth to the early eighteenth centuries). Increased travel and communication between Muslims, both east and west, during the eighteenth century had great influence on Muslims from West Africa to Indonesia, and not least of all, on China's Hui Muslims (see Voll, 1982, pp. 33–86; Rahman, 1968, pp. 237–260). Exposure to these new ideas led to a reformulation of traditional Islamic concepts that rendered them more meaningful and practical for the Hui Muslims of that time. Sufi orders were gradually institutionalized into such forms as the *menhuan*.[8] Only four orders maintain significant influence among the Hui today, what Claude Pickens (1942), as a Protestant missionary in Northwest China, first discovered as the four *menhuan* of China: the Qadiriyya, Khufiyya, Jahriyya, and Kubrawiyya (see Ma Tong, 1983; Yang, 1989). While these are the four main *menhuan*, they are subdivided into a myriad of smaller *menhuan* and branches along ideological, political, geographical, and historical lines (see Gladney, 1987a; 1996, pp. 385–392).

In the early decades of the twentieth century, China was exposed to many new foreign ideas and, in the face of Japanese and Western imperialist encroachment, sought a Chinese approach to governance. Intellectual and organizational activity by Chinese Muslims during this period was also intense. Increased contact with the Middle East led Chinese Muslims to reevaluate their traditional notions of Islam. Pickens (1942, pp. 231–235) records that from 1923 to 1934 there were 834 known Hui Muslims who made the *Hajj* (pilgrimage) to Mecca. In 1937, according to one observer, more than 170 Hui pilgrims boarded a steamer in Shanghai bound for Mecca (Anonymous, 1944, p. 127). By 1939, at least 33 Hui Muslims had studied at Cairo's prestigious Al-Azhar University. While these numbers are not significant when compared with pilgrims on the *Hajj* from other Southeast Asian Muslim areas, the influence and prestige attached to these returning Hui *Hajji* was profound, particularly in isolated communities.

Influenced by contacts with the Middle East, Wahhabism flourished in China, and a more conservative "Muslim Brotherhood" (*Ikhwan al-Musilim*, known in Chinese as the *Yihewani*) was established (see Lipman, 1994). Following strict Wahhabi practice, Yihewani mosques are distinguished by their almost complete lack of adornment on the inside, with white walls and no inscriptions, as well as a preference for Arabian-style mosque architecture. This contrasts sharply with other Chinese-style mosques in China, typical of the "old" Gedimu, whose architecture resemble Confucian temples in their sweeping roofs and symmetrical courtyards (with the Xi'an Huajue Great Mosque as the best example). The Yihewani also proscribed the adornment of their mosques with Arabic, especially Chinese, Qur'anic texts and banners, whereas this is the most striking marker of Sufi mosques and

Entrance to Masjdid (prayer hall), Huhehot mosque, Inner Mongolia. October 3, 1983. Note the "reverse swastika" Buddhist symbol embedded in the parallel Qur'anic quotations in Khufic script on either side of the door.

worship centers in the Northwest, whose walls are often layered with calligraphy and unique Hui-style art.[9]

Because of their emphasis on nationalist concerns, education, modernization, and decentralized leadership, the order has attracted more urban-intellectual Muslims. The Yihewani are also especially numerous in areas like Qinghai and Gansu, where they proliferated during the Republican period under the patronage of Hui warlords. Many of the large mosques and Islamic schools rebuilt with government funds throughout China in the late 1970s and early 1980s tend to be staffed by Yihewani Imam.

While the total population of the various Islamic associations in China has not been published, Yang Huaizhong (1989) writes that of the 2,132 mosques in Ningxia Hui Autonomous Region, 560 belong to the Yihewani, 560 to the Khufiyya, 464 to the Jahriyya, 415 to the traditional Gedimu, and 133 belong to Qadiriyya religious-worship sites (some of which include mosques). The most comprehensive estimate given for Hui membership in Islamic orders throughout China is by Ma Tong (1983, pp. 477–482). Out of a total of 6,781,500 Hui Muslims, Ma Tong records that there are 58.2% Gedimu, 21% Yihewani, 10.9% Jahriyya, 7.2% Khufiyya, 1.4% Qadiriyya, .5% Xidaotang, and .7% Kubrawiyya.

ETHNICITY THEORY AND HUI IDENTITY

Despite the wide cultural and religious diversity of Hui communities discussed earlier, several theories have been advanced to explain how the Hui regard themselves as an ethnic group and why the state chooses to recognize them as such. These theories may be grouped under three main approaches: the Chinese–Stalinist, the culturalist–primordial, and the circumstantialist–instrumentalist. After briefly discussing these theories and their limitations when applied to the Hui, a fourth approach is proposed that arguably interprets more adequately the unity and diversity of Hui identity.

Identifying the Hui: The Chinese–Stalinist Approach

As described in chapter 1, after the People's Republic of China was founded in 1949, the state embarked on a monumental endeavor to identify and recognize as nationalities those who qualified among the hundreds of groups applying for national minority status. Groups qualified for recognition if they could meet the Stalinist criteria of the "four commons": a common language, locality, economy, and cultural makeup.

Despite their clear failure to meet the Stalinist criteria for recognition, the Hui were among the first minorities to be recognized. Most Chinese publications that discuss Hui ethnic identification tend to see them in a situation similar to those of the Manchu (Man) and She minorities who have lived for such a long time among the Han majority that they have lost their own language and many cultural distinctives (See Fei, 1981, p. 62; Huizu, 1978; Ma Yin, 1984, p. 9). Historical records document that these minorities once spoke a common language different from the Han and because they maintain some cultural distinctives, they are recognized as minorities in a historical application of the Stalinist criteria. While this may be true of the Manchu and the She minorities, it does not adequately account for the identity of the Hui. The Hui claim to be descendants of foreign Muslim merchants, militia, and officials who came to China in large numbers from the seventh through fourteenth centuries and later intermarried with the local Han populace. These foreign residents did not speak a single language—they spoke either Persian, Arabic, Turkish, or Mongolian—and there is no record that the foreign languages of these early Muslim ancestors was adopted by their Hui descendants later than the Ming dynasty.

While Qur'anic Arabic is used in Hui-Islamic ritual, it has never served as a common language for communication. Hui do use certain Persian and Arabic loan words (known as *Huihui hua*) that are unintelligible to Han, but these in no way constitute a separate language. Of course, to the Hui themselves, these distinctive non-Han expressions of speech, while not constituting a separate language in any sense, continue to serve as important markers of ethnic identity. I have been in many public market situations in the Northwest where Hui easily identified other Hui in a group of people bargaining, just by listening to their speech. In setting the price among themselves, Hui will often use Arabic or Persian numbers that the Han do not understand before announcing in Chinese what the price is to the Han buyers. For this, and other entrepreneurial practices, Hui have been traditionally denigrated as the *zei Huihui* "larcenous Hui people."

Defining the Hui: The Culturalist Approach

It is evident that ethnic identification in China relies on an analysis of a group's cultural traits and history. This approach is similar to what Naroll (1964) and other Western scholars have carried out and later termed the "culture unit" or "historical–idealist" model. These culturalist studies of ethnic phenomena have understood ethnic groups to be units of the population distinguished by their loyalties to certain "primordial" traits (Geertz, 1973) acquired at birth, including such cultural features as language, religion, economy, place of origin, and biogenetic physical features. This model has also been described as the "cookie-cutter" model in that it suggests that the world might be divided into discrete shapes and even colors along cultural and physical lines, such as language, religion, physique, and skin color (or race). In this approach, ethnic change is seen as the attrition or alteration of these core cultural traits. Discussion in this approach is generally limited to cross-cultural comparison of these discrete "culture units" or their traits, and often overlooks such important issues as "ethnogenesis" (how new ethnic groups form), interethnic relations, and the social organization of ethnic groups.

The identity of the Hui is problematic under a model that emphasizes cultural criteria. If we examine the Hui with reference to the four Stalinist criteria we find the following discrepancies: The Hui do not share a common language, but speak the dialect of the area where they live; they do not live in a common locality, but are distributed throughout China in rural and urban areas, in large and small concentrations; they do not share a common economic life, as their employment ranges from peasant farmers, to small business people, to government cadres; and finally, they do not share a common psychological makeup or culture, as there are Hui who maintain traditional Islamic customs, Hui who are atheist Communist Party members, and many young, urban Hui who have ceased to follow any Islamic customs traditionally associated with being Hui.

It is evident that more factors are involved in the state's recognition of the Hui people than language, economy, locality, or culture. Cultural factors alone are inadequate to consistently distinguish the Hui as a minority people. In addition to linguistic distinctives, Fei (1981, p. 77) emphasizes the historical background of a group for determining nationality status. If the historical descent of modern Hui from foreign Muslim ancestors is considered a crucial determinant in their identification, then it becomes important to ask why the Southeastern Hui lineages were so late in being recognized. No other Hui group in China can lay claim to as much historical evidence for descent from foreign Muslims as the Ding, Guo, and Jin lineages of Fujian province. If historical tradition is the basis for ethnic identification, then these Hui have more claim to nationality status than other more conservative and religious Hui in the northwest, who have little written record of their foreign Muslim ancestry. Yet, because most of these individuals no longer practice Islam, it becomes problematic to think of them belonging to a nationality whose only shared characteristic is that they are Muslim and speak Chinese.

Finally, the inclusion as Hui of the previously mentioned Muslims who culturally belong to the Tibetan, Dai, Bai, Yi, and Mongolian peoples certainly indicates that the Hui category could not be based on Stalin's four criteria. In this, and every ethnic identification decision, political factors came into play. It was expedient to enlist the Hui's and other ethnic's support at the very founding of the People's Republic. Clearly, a cultural theory of ethnic identification, whether the Stalinist or culture unit approach, is inadequate to account for the Hui as a distinctive ethnic group, with their historical continuity and wide diversity. The leaders of the Chinese Communist Party had other reasons for accepting some groups such as the Hui, and rejecting others, such as the Chuanqing Blacks or the Sherpas.

Shifting Hui Boundaries: The Circumstantialist Approach

In response to a "culture unit" approach that portrays ethnic identity as defined by a distinct set of cultural traits, an alternative theory focuses on the socioeconomic and political circumstances influencing a group's identity. This "circumstantialist" (Glazer & Moynihan, 1974, p. 37) or "functional–ecological" (Gates, 1981) model sees ethnicity as a dependent variable, created and controlled by a combination of external instrumental interests and strategies, investing it with potential for action and mobilization. Ethnicity, portrayed as "reactive," is regarded as dependent on such explanatory factors as the environment, economics, politics, and class (see Barth, 1969). Culture, central to the earlier "culture unit" paradigm, is now treated as tertiary to ethnicity. Cultural symbols are seen as justifying interest groups and often are easily manipulated to rationalize identity.

Pillsbury (1973, p. 63ff; 1976, p. 3) found this situational approach to ethnicity most useful in her detailed study of Hui in Taiwan who migrated from divergent ecological and socioeconomic circumstances throughout China. In her analysis, Pillsbury (1973, p. 222) concentrated on the "emergence, maintenance and disintegration of boundaries between Hui and Han and on the ultimate question of acculturation and assimilation." Pillsbury (1973, p. 67) finds continued identity but acculturation to Han customs among the "Hui-Hui." In a more recent study, Pang (1992) has also suggested a "boundary maintenance" approach is the most helpful way to understand Hui relations with Li and Han on the island province of Hainan in the South China Sea.

While a circumstantialist approach has helped to isolate the phenomenological and practical usage of ethnicity in social situations, when taken alone it has serious limitations. This is particularly the case when applied to the Hui. Ethnic identity is not always instrumental; it often possesses a power of its own that the actor may or may not be able to use to their own advantage. A circumstantialist view fails to account for the central place that these powerful, enduring ideas of identity—what Shils (1967, p. 135) terms "primordial" loyalties—have for the Hui in China, as well as for other ethnic groups. Michael Fischer (1986, p. 195) describes the "id-like" power of ethnicity, the paradoxical sense that ethnicity is something reinvented and reinterpreted in each generation by each individual, something over which he or she lacks control. Ethnicity is not something that is simply passed on from generation to generation, taught and learned; it is something dynamic, often unsuccessfully repressed or avoided. It can be potent even when not consciously taught; it is something that institutionalized teaching easily makes chauvinist, sterile, and superficial, something that emerges in full—often liberating—flower only through struggle.

A further limitation of this functionalist approach is the assumption that ethnic identity is a matter of rational choice that actors are free to assume, discard, or manipulate in their efforts to construct or cross "ethnic boundaries." Worsley (1984, p. 246) argues that a situational approach removes the ethnic groups from the field of power and social relations. An approach that assumes ethnic identity is primarily utilitarian fails to account for the fact that ethnic groups often have little control over their identification by others. Government policy in many cases determines who is defined in ethnic terms and the state often dictates who may register as such. This is particularly true for China where one's "nationality" is stamped on one's passport and not easily manipulated.

Finally, these three theories fail to make a distinction between a group's subjective self-perception of itself as an ethnic group and the state's role in objectifying that identity, through conferring nationality status, or contesting the group's ethnicity by refusing recognition. There are many cases of groups in China who perceive of themselves as ethnic, and seek nationality status, such as the Chinese Jews, Sherpas, Khmer, Ku Cong, and Deng peoples, yet whom the state has continued to deny. It is this dynamic interplay between self- and state-definition and contested identities that is crucial to our understanding of ethnic nationalism in China.

Toward a Relational Theory of Identity

Barth's "circumstantialist" approach has helped us to understand how identity, ethnic or otherwise, is manipulated and altered under varying socioeconomic and political situations. It has been less useful in clarifying the persistence of ethnicity, the attachment a group has to a certain idea of common identity and loyalty. Charles Keyes (1979; 1981) has argued persuasively that this primordial loyalty stems from a group's basic agreement on and attachment to an idea of shared descent, which constitutes the basis of an ethnic group's identity. Yet, these loyalties only become explicit, salient, and empowered in the context of social relations—in relational interaction with certain sociopolitical contexts. Just as the "self" is often defined in terms of the "other" (Rosaldo, 1984, p. 137), so ethnic groups coalesce in the context of relation and opposition. Similarly, Marcus and Fischer (1986) have argued that cultural identity is established through a process of social and political "negotiation," which continuously changes depending on relations of power and hierarchy. In a relational approach to ethnicity, social relations of power become the focus of attention, while taking seriously both the symbolic and instrumental aspects of ethnicity, its enduring and mutable nature.[10]

Bringing the State Back In

Keyes and others have emphasized the interactive process of ethnic adaptation involved in making shared ideas of ethnic identity salient for changing social contexts, and I have argued that through relational interaction with certain others, people define and redefine themselves. However, we must not forget that for the Hui in China, and many other ethnic groups today, government policy plays a privileged role in the socioeconomic arena, exerting a tremendous influence on ethnic change and identity. In expansive nation-states faced with the task of administering macroregions inhabited by competing minority nationalities, the importance of power relations and shifting government policy in influencing ethnic identity must be further explored (see Nash, 1989). In China, nationality status marks one group from another and is stamped on one's identity card. Like class, nationality in China objectifies social relations and modes of production, in that some minorities are given certain privileges and encouraged to maintain cultural and economic niches. In China, one may regard oneself as a member of an ethnic group, such as the Chinese Jews, but unless that group is recognized as a minority nationality by the state, one is denied the privileges accorded to certain minorities, such as the allowance to have more than one child and purchase lamb cheaply. Conversely, even if one does not regard oneself as ethnic, but is a member of a nationality designated by the state, such as the Manchu, one may be stigmatized by an identity stamped on one's work card that is unwanted. This may be especially onerous during radical periods, as when Manchus were singled out as being feudal remnants of the oppressive Qing empire.

The interaction between ethnic and national identity has led to the invention of some identities, the resurgence of others, and the loss of many. Though it was once thought that ethnicity would quickly fade in authoritarian Marxist–Leninist states like China or Russia through sinicization or Russification campaigns that sought to wipe out ethnic difference as another manifestation of feudal class distinctions, the recent resurgence of ethnic identities along national lines, some of which were once thought artificial or imposed by the state, calls for more dynamic interpretations of identity in these nation-states. The Hui case makes an important contribution to our understanding of the relational nature of ethnic identity and state policy.

Dali mosque, interior view of Mihrab, or niche indicating direction toward Mecca, Yunnan. February 25, 1985. Note the parallel Qua'anic quotations in Khufic script on either side of the niche, as well as the Chinese characters for longevity and prosperity.

The Ethnogenesis of the Hui: From Muslim to Minzu

Official histories and minority nationality maps to the contrary, before their identification by the state in the 1950s, the Hui were not a *minzu*, a nationality, in the modern sense of the term. Like many other groups, the Hui only emerged in the transition from empire to nation-state. The people now known as the Hui are descended from Persian-, Arab-, Mongolian-, and Turkish-Muslim merchants, soldiers, and officials who settled in China from the seventh to fourteenth centuries and intermarried with Han women. Largely living in isolated communities, the only thing that some, but not all, had in common was a belief in Islam. Until the 1950s in China, Islam was simply known as the "Hui religion" (*Hui jiao*)—believers in Islam were *Huijiao* believers. Until then, any person who was a believer in Islam was a "Hui religion disciple" (*huijiao tu*). One was accepted into Hui communities and mosques simply by being a Muslim. After the fall of the last empire and the rise of nationalism in the first half of this century, the Hui emerged as one of several nationalities militating for recognition. Through a relational process of self-examination and state-recognition, the Hui emerged fully as an ethnic group, a *minzu*, only after their institutionalization by the state. Not that the Hui previously had no ethnic consciousness. Rather, prior to state recognition, Hui ethnic identity was localized and less fully articulated. Hui related to each other as fellow Muslims, not as *minzu*. Now that Hui ethnic identity has been legitimated and legalized by the state, the Hui are beginning to objectify their identity, to think of themselves and relate to each other in interreferential, national terms.

Ordination service for 20 new Imams, Weishan mosque, Yunnan province. February 28, 1985. Note the Southeast Asian architectural style of minaret in background.

Hui in China, no matter where one travels, now refer to themselves as the Hui people (*Hui minzu*). Hui are generally offended in China when asked if they believe in *Hui jiao*, the Hui religion, as they take great pride in being members of a world religion, the international Islamic *Umma*. Sometimes, however, less-informed members of the community slip into old habits. I was amused when one of my Hui colleagues who was present at an interview corrected a wheat farmer and sideline rope maker in Wuzhong, central Ningxia: "No you are not a 'Hui religion disciple' (*Huijiao tu*)," he reprimanded, much to my consternation, "you are a 'Hui person' (*Hui min*). Hui believe in Islam (*Yisilan jiao*), not their own Hui religion." I was even asked, at times, if I was a *Meiguo Huihui* (an "American Hui") when locals mistook me for a Muslim, since, they reasoned, only a Muslim would be interested in Hui history. Nevertheless, the label "Hui nationality" is beginning to stick, particularly as participation in the ethnic group carries with it important practical benefits. These labels are becoming more and more accepted by the people as inclusive ethnonyms, stimulating further communication, exchange, and interreferentiality between the Hui communities.

Despite the continued diversity that we have seen among these communities, a process of ethnogenesis has also brought them closer together, through dialogue with state policy and local traditions. Nationalization, as noted by Benedict Anderson (1991, pp. 41–49), is assisted by the acceptance of the label "Hui," increased "pan-Hui" interaction and mandatory education in special state-sponsored Hui schools. The Hui, of course, desire more political power through larger numbers and they are beginning to argue for and experience the national unity of their people.

THE UNITY AND DIVERSITY OF HUI IDENTITY:
FOUR COMMUNITIES IN FLUX

For the purposes of this study's argument regarding the diverse nature of ethnic identity in the Chinese nation-state, I settled on four Hui communities that provide revealing examples of the widely divergent expression of Hui identity and its recent adaptation to the contemporary Chinese social context and power relations. These communities should be viewed as case communities, not complete ethnographies of certain villages or places. These communities are presented as exemplary of Hui identity in different contexts and the data utilized was drawn from other similar communities as supportive material.

The wide diversity of ethnic identity found among Hui Muslims in China led me to focus my research on four disparate communities: a mosque-centered Naqsh-bandiyya Sufi village in the northwest, a northern suburban village, an urban worker ethnic enclave in Beijing, and a lineage community on the southeast coast. Thus, I conducted fieldwork in both urban and rural, northern and southern, Islamic and tra-ditional Chinese folk-religious communities in an attempt to examine the broad spectrum of ethnic identity across the breadth of the modern nation-state. I noted a similar range of ethnoreligious diversity as Clifford Geertz (1968) observed in his comparison of Moroccan-scripturalist fundamentalism and Indonesian "syncretis-tic" Islam, which he argued existed by necessity in "two countries, two cultures"— yet I found even more varied identity among Muslims defined by the Chinese state as a *single* national minority.

The Northwest Hui identity is described in chapter 3 with reference to Na Homestead (*Najiahu*), one village that I am most familiar with, in Ningxia Hui Au-tonomous Region, and in many ways typical of mosque-centered Hui communities in Northwest China. The issue of marriage within isolated Hui communities in rural Han-dominant areas throughout Central China is a paramount problem for Hui con-cerned with the perpetuation of their identity. Marriage endogamy among Hui, some from distant communities, is an important strategy these Hui use to preserve and express the purity of their descent from foreign ancestors. This issue is dis-cussed in chapter 4 with reference to Chang Ying, a suburban Hui village east of Beijing. The dispersion of Hui across China is due partly to their traditional procliv-ity for engaging in long-distance trade and small business operations that are linked to urban centers and market centers. Like the Jews of Eastern Europe prior to the Second World War, the Hui are the main urban-ethnic minority in almost every major city and town in China. In chapter 5, the question of the identity of urban Hui is discussed, with reference to the Niujie ("Oxen Street") community in Beijing. Fi-nally, chapter 6 explores the identity of one community in southeastern China who are arguably the least "Hui" in China, in that few of them are Muslims or follow Is-lamic dietary restrictions. Nevertheless, this last community struggled to become recognized as members of the Hui nationality and has experienced tremendous eth-nic revitalization in recent years.

In these four communities studied the discussion centers on how Hui identity is rooted in local, shared ideas of descent based on accepted texts and rituals. The rele-vance of Hui identity for each case is discussed with respect to its expression in the local social context, in the attempt to show how Hui identity makes a difference in

A Sufi Dao Tang (or Tekke) belonging to the Qadiriyya Sufi order, Hezhou City (Linxia), Gansu. April 1985. Note the women and men at prayer together.

the lives of the Hui in each community—how it affects their lifestyle, work, marriage, and social relations. Finally, the relational emergence of new Hui identities and government policies through the interaction of local identities with the state in each social context is analyzed.

Much of this study attempts to understand ethnographically who the Hui are and the role they play in modern Chinese society, as well as the government's dealings with them. The preceding proposed approach to ethnicity is analyzed with regard to its power to adequately interpret Hui ethnoreligious expression in each case. Unlike most ethnographic reports that tend to describe an isolated village community frozen in time, apart from changing sociopolitical realities, these four Hui communities are examined in the political–economic context of their recent history and the People's Republic of China today. These four Hui communities represent processes or "types" of Hui ethnoreligious identity that help us to understand the kinds of Hui identity and community interests throughout China.[11] While no particular community or individual will be representative of the whole, this spectrum of expression illustrates the issues that often confront each community and individual in that particular context.

A Spectrum of Ethnoreligious Expression

First, at one end of the spectrum there are highly concentrated communities of Hui, especially in Northwest China, where religious identity is the most salient aspect of Hui identity. In these communities, to be Hui is to be Muslim, and purity (*qing*) de-

Qadariyya Sufi Imam at the "Great Tomb" complex, Hezhou City, Gansu, indicating Arabic inscription, "He who looks upon the Muhammad's saint, looks upon Muhammad." October 1988.

rives from the individual's moral and religious integrity. At the other extreme, one finds southeastern Hui lineages for whom Islam is almost totally irrelevant and Hui identity is entirely based on genealogical descent from foreign Arab ancestors: To be Hui is to be different in ancestry than the Han, and authenticity (*zhen*) is based on the truth of one's ancestry. Between these two extreme expressions of identity one finds urban Hui communities for whom identity is a mixture of ethnic ancestry and religious commitment in varying degrees. While Islam continues to be meaningful to most of these Hui, and to some more than others, the mosque generally has ceased to be a locus of religious authority and cultural activity, replaced by more secular organizations, such as the restaurant, school, or voluntary association. Finally, a fourth type are those traditional communities of isolated Hui villages in Han majority areas where the mosque continues to maintain its central role in the affairs of the community, but for whom issues of religious authority and orthodoxy are less important than more practical concerns such as marriage and social cohesiveness.

While these communities are portrayed as types along a spectrum of expression, they are not intended to suggest that this scheme has any predictive value for ethnic change. The discussion focuses on how the Hui express their identity in different contexts due to widely divergent historical, ecological, socioeconomic, and political factors, and the intention is not to suggest any stage or developmental scheme.

In my interviews in more than 400 Hui households throughout China, I always asked: "What is the difference between Han and Hui?" In Na Homestead, and other similar Hui communities throughout Ningxia, Gansu, and Qinghai, I almost always received the response: "Hui believe in Islam. Han believe in Buddhism or Marxism." In these areas, both Han and Hui tended to couch their differences in religious discourse. When I interviewed a Han who lived in the almost all-Muslim village of Na Homestead, he said: "Hui and Han have different religions. We eat pork, they don't." Among Hui lineages outside Quanzhou, the response was generally: "We are Hui because we are descended from foreign Muslims." Differences were perceived genealogically. In urban areas and Hui communities in central and southern China, I often heard: "Hui are different because we have different customs than the Han, we don't eat pork." Here, cultural practice epitomized ethnic difference. In rural northern villages, they told me: "We are Hui because our parents are, and we maintain the *qing zhen* life." For these isolated communities, not only was practice important, but its perpetuation through association and intermarriage was a central issue.

These responses indicate the wide variety of Hui self-understanding and ethnic ascription. Arguably, expressions of ethnic identity and interpretations of *qing zhen* will also differ between these communities. Though there is much variety of ethnic expression, the shared idea of descent from common ancestors is the root that grounds Hui identity in a shared ethnoreligious tradition. While it might be plausible to argue that these communities and individuals are so different that they are not ethnic, they nevertheless think they are and believe they share something in common with other Hui, no matter how different. This feeling becomes institutionalized and legitimated by the state, which in relational fashion, leads to a further expression, even invention, of ethnicity. Genealogical or historical evidence to the contrary, this common self-perception of descent from related ancestors forms the basis of a meaningful ethnoreligious identity that continues to maintain "All Hui under Heaven are one family."

Notes

[1]For excellent introductions to the early history of Islam in China, see especially Donald Leslie (1986); Jonathan Lipman (1981); Ma Qicheng (1983). Morris Rossabi (1979) provides a seminal introduction to the complex history of Inner Asia; for Inner Asia in general, see Denis Sinor (1969), and for pre-thirteenth century, see his recent definitive edited volume, *The Cambridge History of Early Inner Asia* (1990). For overviews of Islam in China, see Aubin (1986); Gladney (1993a; 1995c); Israeli and Goodman (1994).

[2]Connor (1984, p. 53) quotes the following statement by Stalin in 1923 that revealed his early intention of passing on their nationality policy to China: "We must here, in Russia, in our federation, solve the national problem in a correct, *a model way,* in order to set an example to the East, which represents the heavy reserves of our revolution" (emphasis in original).

[3]For a discussion of the high degree of accuracy for the 1982 Chinese national census, see Banister (1987). While there is underreporting among Hui, and several groups have been admitted in recent years previously unrecognized as Hui (see chapter 3), a figure of no more than 10 million Hui, and from 15 million to 20 million Muslims seems the best estimate.

[4]I translate Chinese administrative terms in the following manner, arranged according to administrative size: *sheng* (province), *qu* (region), *shi* (city), *shiqu* (city district), *xian* (county), *zhen* (town), *xiang* (township), or *gongshe* (people's commune), *dadui* (brigade), *cun* (village), or *xiaodui* (team). Confusion arises in that the commune system was in the process of returning to a village system during my fieldwork, and government administrative units (e.g., *zhengshi cun* or *xingzhen cun* "official village") do not necessarily conform to natural traditional units (e.g., *ziran cun* "natural village").

[5]Female Imam are very unusual in Northern China and I only encountered them in Yunnan (see chapter 4). They lead the women in prayer, never the men, and are responsible for mosque administrative duties. Among the Yihewani (see below) in Qinghai and Gansu, I encountered many girls enrolled in the local Islamic schools learning Arabic, though it was unclear whether they aspired to be formal Imam. For a history of Yunnan's Hui Muslims, see Ma, 1992.

[6]Aside from perhaps a few remaining cultural influences deriving from the large communities of Persian Muslims in the earliest period of Islam in China, there is no institutionalized Shi'ism among the Hui. There is at least one Shi'i community among the Uyghur in Khotan and the majority of the Persian speaking Tajik are Shi'ite. Nevertheless, cultural and political contacts are strong between China and Iran.

[7]*Menhuan* is the Chinese technical term describing the socioeconomic and religious organization of Sufi brotherhoods linked to the "leading descent line" of the Sufi founder, extending through his appointees or descendants to the leader himself and from him to Muhammad. For a more detailed discussion, see Gladney (1996a, pp. 36–60; Jin (1984). Sufi factionalism and *menhuan* conflicts are described in fascinating detail in a novel by a Hui Muslim, Zhang Chengzhi (1990), who also wrote the novel upon which Tian Zhuangzhuang's popular film, *Horsethief,* was based (see Gladney, 1995a).

[8]Early twentieth-century Western travelers in Northwest China were struck by the nonreligious political nature of some of these *menhuan,* which were instrumental in organizing many of the large and small Hui rebellions. Lattimore (1950, p. 185) observed: "Different religio-political families—in the name, characteristically, of different sects of Islam—began to struggle against each other both for hegemony as between Moslems and for control of external relations as between Moslems and Chinese." The sociopolitical role of these *menhuan* has been the main focus of Chinese historians, especially during the 1950s land-reform campaign when large *menhuan* landholdings were expropriated as allegedly belonging to feudal landlords. The most controversial victim of this critique was Ma Zhenwu, the Naqshbandiyya Jahriyya Shagou branch leader in Ningxia, whose vast holdings were confiscated in 1958. After dying in prison in 1960, he was posthumously rehabilitated in August 1983, which led to more open study of these groups. (See the October 1958 document, "Chinese Moslems Expose the Crimes of Ma Chen-wu" in MacInnis, 1972, pp. 167-175.)

[9]This special art form that combines floral Arabic calligraphic Qur'anic content with Chinese form is unique to the Hui and begs further study. An initial paper has been presented on the subject (see Fletcher, Alonso, & Chorbachi, 1989), but much work needs to be done on this extraordinary combination of Eastern and Central Asian aesthetics.

[10]Elsewhere, I have more fully developed this theory in terms of "relational alterity" (see Gladney, 1996b). This approach can also be understood in terms of dialogic theory (see Gladney, 1994c; 1996b, pp. 27–60).

[11]This is similar to Weber's use of "ideal types" for the purposes of comparative analysis. Weber never reified society nor compared society as wholes, but always contrasts cross-cultural institutions within them, such as law, marriage, religion, and so on. Typology, for Weber, was a means of focusing on what is "typically important in the historical realization of religious ethics. This is important for the connection of religions with the great contrasts of economic mentalities" (Weber, 1963, p. 37).

3 / Ethnoreligious Resurgence in a Northwestern Sufi Community

I had heard of rising Islamic "fundamentalism" among the Hui, but did not become personally aware of resurgent religious activism until I visited Na Homestead, in Ningxia Hui Autonomous Region in October 1983. My first awareness of the changing Hui–Han social dynamics in Na village from a discussion with one of the Han villagers in Team One. Wang Xiaohua, a young mother who constantly fidgeted to keep an obnoxious piglet from escaping her courtyard while we talked in the gateway explained:

> Since 1979, we have had less and less social contact with the Hui in the other teams. There are no problems between us, but the Hui are more devout (*qiancheng*) now and less willing to come to our homes and visit or borrow tools. We raise pigs in our yards and eat pork, so they are afraid it will influence their religion (*yingxiang tamende jiaomen*).

Like many conservative Northwest Hui, most Na villagers have become more conscientious of Islamic purity (*qing*) through attention to dietary restrictions. In order to preserve the *qing zhen* lifestyle, conservative Hui who visit Han homes at the most accept sunflower seeds or fruit when offered by their host. When Han come to their homes, Hui offer them tea from a separate set of cups that the family itself does not use, lest the family *qing zhen* utensils become contaminated. Hui are also free to offer Han prepared dishes of lamb and beef, but the Han cannot reciprocate. Gradually this imbalance of obligation leads to less and less contact. Increased scrupulous attention to the culturally defined notions of Islamic purity—especially in a culture that traditionally places high priority on extending social courtesies—has begun to increasingly limit Hui–Han social interaction.

This is not surprising. Careful Hui attention to this tradition maintains the purity–impurity power reversal in which Han, who can never fully reciprocate Hui hospitality by offering them social presentations of food in return, are placed in an inferior power relation to the Hui. As Marcel Mauss (1967, p. 10) so eloquently described, "the thing given is not inert," and Hui refusal to receive Han gifts places them in a position of moral superiority, though they may occupy a socially inferior and marginal position in the socioeconomic and ethnic context of Northwest China.

Na Homestead (*Najiahu*), in Ningxia Hui Autonomous Region, is in many respects typical of other Hui Muslim communities throughout the Northwest. A collection of adobe-mud houses clustered around a central mosque, Na Homestead has been

Na Homestead Great Mosque, Ningxia Hui Autonomous Region. Note the cemetery in the foreground and the Hui Muslim at prayer. October 12, 1984.

the site of an Islamic resurgence in recent years. As several visitors to other Northwestern Muslim communities have noted, Islamic conservativism has become more pronounced among the Hui since 1979 (Barnett, 1993, p. 174; Burns, 1986, p. 4). This rising radical, even fundamentalist, emphasis on Islamic purity (*qing*) among Hui communities has caused concern among local government cadres.

This chapter argues that, especially in Northwestern China, Hui ethnic identity is inseparably identified with an Islamic tradition handed down to them by their Muslim ancestors. Hui identity in the Northwest is more than an ethnic identity; it is ethnoreligious, in that Islam is intimately tied to their self-understanding. Recent reemergence of the meaningfulness of Islam and stress on the requirements of a decidedly Islamic *qing zhen* lifestyle represent a return to Northwestern Hui ethnoreligious roots. In this regard, an examination of Na Homestead reveals some of the expressions of this Northwestern Hui ethnoreligious identity, as well as its recent transformation in the midst of rapid socioeconomic change. A close analysis of salient Hui institutions, rituals, and texts reveals that a state policy that seeks to make a clear distinction between religion and ethnicity is based on an inadequate understanding of Hui identity. The resurgence of Islamic practice and conservativism in Na Homestead, under recent liberalized policies, illustrates the important relevance of Islam in this context. The interaction of Na ethnic identity with recent liberalized government policies has also led to important changes in the expression of that identity and in the reformulation of local nationality policies.

A FUNDAMENTALIST REVIVAL IN NA HOMESTEAD?

Na Homestead is part of Yongning County, Yang He Township, 15 kilometers south of Yinchuan City in central Ningxia.[1] Traveling south on the main north–south highway linking Yinchuan with Wuzhong City and southern Ningxia, one finds a dirt road leading off to Na Homestead at the main intersection of the Yongning county seat. Separated from the intersection by 3 kilometers of fields, Na Homestead is a somewhat isolated, formerly walled community of mud houses clustered around a central mosque (*qing zhen si*). The sloping eaves of the mosque rising up above the flat-roofed houses are visible from the road, providing a striking visual contrast with other surrounding communities.

This compact collection of households is comprised of nine teams that are almost 100% Hui, a rarity in central and northern Ningxia where Hui are thinly distributed among the majority Han population (see Table 3.1). Yongning County is only 12.9% Hui, a relatively small minority in contrast to neighboring Lingwu County in the southeast, which is 46.9% Hui, and southern Jingyuan County, which is 96.8% Hui (the highest concentration of Hui in one county in China, see Figure 3.1).

Just north of the all-Hui community in Na Homestead, separated by about 2 kilometers of fields, is another collection of households belonging to the village administratively and containing two teams (Team One and Team Eleven) of mixed Han and Hui. All 22 households (264 people) of the Han families belonging to Na Homestead are located in this smaller community, separate from the nine all-Hui teams. Based on 1984 statistics, Na Homestead is comprised of 767 households, with a total population of 3,871. There are 745 Hui households, amounting to more than 95% of the population. More than 60% of the Hui in the village are surnamed Na.

Religious Revitalization in Na Homestead

The rise in religious activity and conservativism in Na Homestead stands in stark contrast to the closed mosques and restricted religious behavior common elsewhere in China since the 1958 Religious System Reform Campaigns (*zongjiao zhidu gaige*). Frequent Na villager participation in mosque ritual is also noticeably different than the lack of popular participation in urban mosques in northern and southern China. In those areas—with the exception of holidays where large turnouts of the Hui community are becoming common—mosques are generally frequented only by a few bearded old men sitting on benches and sunning themselves while awaiting the next call to prayer. Not so in Na Homestead.

The Hui of Na Homestead are associated with the Khufiyya brotherhood, a popular Sufi order in Ningxia that developed from a branch of the Naqshbandiyya introduced through Central Asia in the seventeenth century (see chapter 1). Yet, Na villagers, like many Khufiyya in Ningxia, do not subscribe to the Islamic order that venerates the descendants of Sufi saints. Hence, they resemble an isolated mosque-centered Gedimu community that maintains Sufi forms of ritual. Although they regard themselves as Khufiyya, Na villagers are not connected to the other Sufi Khufiyya networks extending throughout Northwest China. This is not unusual in

TABLE 3.1

POPULATION OF THE HUI NATIONALITY IN NINGXIA HUI AUTONOMOUS
REGION BY CITY AND COUNTY, 1983

County or City	Total Population	Hui Population	Percent of Hui Population in County	Percent of Regional Hui Population in County
Jingyuan	82,464	79,823	96.797	6.3
Tongxin	218,967	172,906	78.96	13.5
Haiyuan	249,672	170,732	68.38	13.4
Xiji	316,298	156,477	49.47	12.3
Lingwu	184,289	86,424	46.95	6.8
Guyuan	377,634	154,875	41.01	12.1
Pingluo	234,375	71,511	30.51	5.6
Pengyang	186,334	52,636	28.25	4.1
Helan	159,953	37,337	23.34	2.9
Yinchuan	371,250	69,636	18.76	5.5
Qingtongxia	188,362	26,510	14.07	2.1
Yongning	156,504	20,282	12.95	1.6
Shizuishan	301,957	32,422	10.74	2.5
Taole	19,017	1,842	9.68	0.1
Longde	162,572	13,233	8.13	1.0
Wuzhong	217,704	12,081	5.55	9.4
Yanchi	121,741	3,274	2.69	0.3
Zhongning	180,778	4,463	2.47	0.3
Zhongwei	251,329	1,924	0.76	0.3
Total:	3,983,198	1,276,388	32.04	100.00

Source. 1983 Regional Census.

northern Ningxia and other areas where the Khufiyya have become more decentralized. While they are thus not closely connected to other Khufiyya orders, their Sufi background continues to influence daily life and ritual.

One wintry morning, I arose from my warm *kang*[2] to the call for prayer (heard throughout the village) at 6:00 A.M. and walked over to the mosque. In this season,

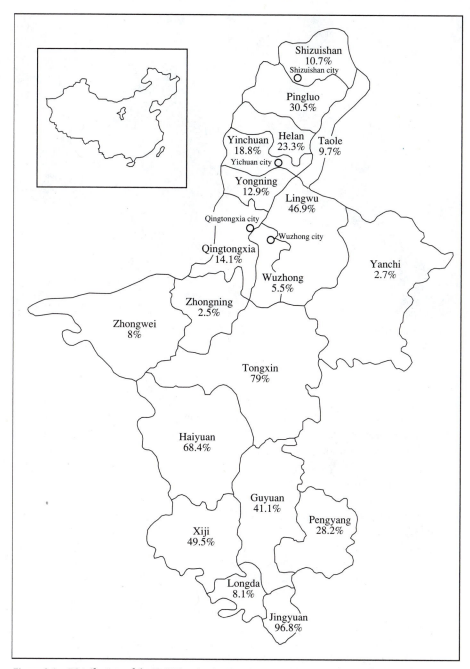

Figure 3.1   Distribution of the Hui Minority in Ningxia Hui Autonomous Region by Percentage of County

the ground is frozen and the temperature hovers around 13 to 14 degrees below zero (centigrade). I was surprised to find the large prayer hall full of men when I arrived.

A "Great Reading" of the entire Qur'an in one sitting, divided into 30 chapters and read simultaneously. Na Homestead Great Mosque, January 5, 1985.

On any weekday morning, at least 150 people kneel at prayer on the hard floor of the mosque an hour before dawn. As the service began, two or three stragglers came running up, hastily donning fleece-lined coats over their bare backs and removing their boots as they entered the prayer hall so as not to be late. They prayed in unison on the bare concrete floor for the duration of the 30- to 45-minute service, some of them kneeling on lamb pelts or on small carpets purchased from a Zhejiang factory that makes the colorful rayon, Islamic-style prayer mats sold throughout the northwest. Because of the sermon, the main prayer on Fridays (*zhuma ri*) generally lasts more than an hour. This differed markedly from mosques in other parts of China where latecomers straggled in at the last minute, knowing they could always "make up prayers" (*bu li*) later.

One official count of attendance on a Thursday morning in January 1985 recorded 141 worshipers, including 31 worshipers between 14 and 50 years of age (Wang, 1985, p. 7). On Fridays, an attendance of up to 500 worshipers is not unusual (13% of the village), with an average of 100 to 200 praying at least once in the mosque during the week. On holidays, the whole village, including women and children, turns out. While some say that participation has not yet reached 1950 levels, this is still perceived as a new peak (*gaofeng*) of religious activity among the Hui since 1949.[3] During the Month of Ramadan in 1984, the mosque reported that one-third of all households had at least one member who took part in the fast. I have also visited concentrated Hui areas such as Linxia Hui Autonomous Prefecture, Gansu Province, and southern Ningxia where 100% of the villagers above the age of 12 (for boys) or 9 (for girls) fast. The level of participation in the fast among Na villagers is still considered rather high in a predominantly Han area.

Mosque income (*sifei*) derived from offerings (*nietie*) has also risen dramatically. According to the mosque's own careful accounting records, in the 2 years I studied the mosque it averaged more than 20,000 yuan ($6,700 U.S.) annual income from offerings. Based on an outside study, over a 4-month period during 1984 and 1985, offerings of grain produce, goods, or money totaled 8,997.23 yuan (about $3,000 U.S.). An economic survey of expenditures of 113 Hui households in Na Homestead revealed that the average amount given to the mosque was 47 yuan per household, or 8.40 yuan per person in 1984 (Wang, 1985, p. 7). If this average is applied to the entire Hui community of the village, then the mosque's total income last year was well over 32,500 yuan ($10,833 U.S.). The money supports the staff of seven Ahong, including one "teaching" or head Ahong (*kaixue ahong* or *jiaozhang*), and four student Ahong (*halifat* from *khalifa*, "successor," or *manla*, from *mullah*), and the daily upkeep of the mosque.[4] Offerings are given during the three main religious holidays and to individual Ahong when they read the Qur'an at weddings, funerals, and naming ceremonies. Amounts given at funerals by the family to guests and to the mosque ranges from 100 to 1,000 yuan. As much as 2,500 yuan has been reported when the status of the deceased was extremely high.

On one holiday celebrated in Na Homestead, the "Prophet's Day" or "Muhammad's Birthday" (*Shengji*) on December 7, 1984, I witnessed offerings brought by children and adults in bags of flour or rice and in fists full of money. A group of mosque officials dutifully registered each offering according to amount, name, and team number. Gifts totaled 3,000 kilograms of wheat, 2,500 kilograms of rice and 300 yuan ($100 U.S.), equal to approximately 3,313 yuan ($1,100 U.S.). None of the donated money is required for the restoration of the mosque building (*qianliang*). The mosque has received more than 90,000 yuan ($30,000 U.S.) from the State Nationalities Affairs Commission since it was identified as a national monument in 1981. Dating from the Ming dynasty's Jia Jing period (1522–1567), it is the oldest remaining mosque in Ningxia.

Donations to the mosque come from a village considered fairly poor by neighboring village standards, with an average annual income of 300 yuan (about $100 U.S.) per household.[5] The average per capita annual income in Yongning county in 1982 was substantially higher, 539 yuan according to the Population Census Office (1987, p. 206). Poor households (*pinkun hu*) occupy 2% of the village (Zhu, 1985, p. 6). Mosque income, however, does not necessarily reflect total giving per household. A study of 17 households from three different villages belonging to different Islamic orders found that out of an annual average income of 96.67 yuan, 8.96 yuan (9.26%) was given to religious concerns in 1980.[6]

The Ascendence in Qur'anic Education

A decrease in public school enrollment and an increase in children studying the Qur'an in private *madrassah* attached to local mosques is another phenomenon that has local cadres concerned. This growing interest in pursuing religious education has not yet reached large proportions among the Hui in Na Homestead, as only 10 school-age children were not attending public school in 1985. Instead, they are studying the Qur'an at home privately. There are four officially permitted *manla* in the village. In more heavily populated Hui areas, however, this is becoming a more noticeable trend. In Guyuan County, Jiefangxiang (Liberation Township), in 1984, only 12 out of 104 school-age children in the village were attending school, and 27 of those not in school were studying the Qur'an in the mosque.

When asked about their reluctance to send their children to school, Na Homestead parents expressed doubts about the value of learning Chinese and mathematics. "It would be much more useful," I was told by one mother, "for our children to learn the Qur'an, Arabic, and Persian." If a child excelled, he or she might become a *manla*, and eventually perhaps an Ahong. Their status in the village would be much higher than the average middle-school or even high-school graduate, as would their income (estimated at 100 to 500 yuan a month for a well-known teaching Ahong). Children who are in poor health are often kept at home to study the Qur'an. In large families with more than one son, generally one child is encouraged to study to become an Ahong. Although the government officially allows each mosque to support from two to four full-time *manla*—who should be at least 18 years old and junior middle-school graduates—many younger children study at home without official approval.

Ningxia, as the only autonomous region for China's Hui Muslims, tends to monitor Ahong training and religious practice more closely than other areas where Hui are concentrated. In Yunnan's Weishan Yi and Hui Autonomous County, several mosques had more than 20 resident *manla* studying under well-known Ahong. In Gansu's Linxia Hui Autonomous Prefecture, at the South Great Mosque there were more than 130 full-time students. In Linxia City's Bafang district, where most of the Hui are concentrated, there were at least 60 full-time *manla* in each mosque. Mirroring the spiritual importance of Mecca and the centrality of theological learning of the Iranian city of Qum for China's Hui Muslims, Linxia's famous mosques and scholars attract students from all over China.

The Rise in Islamic Conservativism

The increasing conservatism of the Hui in Na Homestead is apparent to any visitor. Smoking and drinking are now prohibited in the village for the simple reason that "the elders are against it" (*laoren fandui*). When pressed as to their reasons, the elders invariably refer to the dictates of maintaining a pure (*qing zhen*) lifestyle according to Islamic prescriptions. According to the local store clerk, few people buy cigarettes anymore. Smoking and drinking were commonplace in the village during the Cultural Revolution. The clerk now keeps only a few bottles of low alcohol content "champagne" (*xiangbin jiu*) under a back shelf for rare occasions when outside cadres need to be entertained. When young men want to drink or smoke, they go outside the village to the Yongning county seat or to Yinchuan City.[7] It came as quite a shock to the elders of this village when visited by a foreign Arab Muslim "friendship delegation" in August 1983 to discover that these dignitaries, dressed in flowing robes and fluent in Qur'anic Arabic, lit up their cigarettes immediately after the prayer in the courtyard of the mosque. Hui villagers still complained bitterly about the event, but it did help to disillusion many regarding the "holiness" of Arab and other Middle Eastern Muslims.

While only the older women wear the head covering (*gaitou*) associated with the Muslim custom of *purdah*,[8] younger Hui admit that male–female interaction is much more restricted than in neighboring Han villages (Zhang, 1985, p. 11). Men and women rarely work together in the fields and the majority of marriages are arranged through introductions. In a survey of 50 newly married young couples, only eight (16%) met their partner on their own, without an intermediary. The average courtship period was less than 5 months for 76% of the couples surveyed (Zhang, 1985, pp. 11–12). While some younger Hui complain about this conservatism, change in the near future appears unlikely. In fact, "modern" marriage practice has continued to decline since the high point of male–female "free love" (*lianai ziyou*) encouraged during the Cultural Revolution. The only "love match" I knew of took place between a local Na villager who had met his bride while studying for 2 years at a vocational training college. One of a handful to receive higher education above the middle-school level, the case of this young intellectual was anything but typical.

When I asked several Hui villagers if there was anyone in their team who did not believe in Islam (*buxinjiao de huizu*), I was always told that they did not know of anyone. By contrast, in urban areas such as Yinchuan, the capital of Ningxia region, Hui youth often openly discuss their belief in Marxism or secularism and the lack of relevance of Islam for their lives (for unbelief in Taiwan see Harrell, 1974a). Several have told me that they believe in neither Marxism nor Islam, but in "individualism," or in only "making money." This attitude is even more prevalent in cities such as Beijing and Shanghai where urbanized Hui youth are becoming attracted to Western ideas (see chapter 6). One Shanghai Hui youth married to a Han woman told me: "Buddhism is for peasants, Islam is for old Huihui, and Christianity is for those interested in the West."

Perhaps of greatest concern to local party officials in Ningxia is the lack of participation in the local party apparatus and the "problem of party members who believe in religion" (*dangyuan xinjiaode wenti*). There are 63 party members in Na Homestead, representing only 1.7% of the total population. Of those 63 party members, 22 publicly worship at the mosque and say they believe in Islam. Three of these believers go to mosque five times daily and one has officially quit his party membership in order to become an Ahong. Many of these Muslim party members have at one time been a team-level chairman, and four have been brigade (*da dui*) vice-party secretaries in the past. When I asked one Hui state cadre, who openly prayed at the mosque in another city, about this contradiction he rationalized, "I believe in Marxism in my head, but I believe in Islam in my heart." Mason (1922, p. 7) remarkably reported a similar explanation offered by Confucian Hui officials in the Qing dynasty:

> It may be added that military officials in the Manchu times were not altogether exempt from certain ceremonies of worship at temples; but Moslems seem to have made a compromise with conscience and went with the rest; one said to me long ago in Szechwan that though his bodily presence was there, and he shared in the prostrations, his heart was not there, so it didn't matter!

Local cadres give many reasons for religious behavior among Hui party officials. In Na Homestead, it is explained that 80% entered the party in the 1950s and are too old and uninvolved with party affairs (Wang, 1985, p. 9). As they grow older, these veteran party members are becoming more interested in religion. Yet, we may also note that no one has been admitted to the party in Na Homestead since October 1976.

THE ETHNORELIGIOUS ROOTS OF NA IDENTITY

When I made my first visit to Na Homestead during a short 1983 trip through central Ningxia, I was immediately presented with the story that the Na villagers like to tell about their ancestry. This origin myth was often repeated to me throughout 1984 and 1985:

> We are all Muslims in this village. Most of us are surnamed Na. The Chinese character for "Na" is not in the classical book of Chinese surnames, and this proves that we are descended not from Han Chinese but from a foreign Muslim from the west. Our ancestor was none other than Nasredin, the son of Sai Dianchi (Sayyid Edjell), the Muslim governor of Yunnan under the Yuan Dynasty. Nasredin had four sons, and those sons changed their names to Chinese under the Ming government's ethnic oppression policy. The four sons adopted the surnames "Na, Su, La, Ding" corresponding to the four Chinese characters that made up his name. This is why so many Northwest Huihui in the Ming dynasty had these surnames. The son surnamed Na moved to this place and had five sons, of which we still have five Na leading lineages (*men*) in the village. There is also a Na Village in Yunnan Province, Tonghua County, where some of our relatives live.[9]

Based partly on historical records and partly on oral traditions that may or may not be accurate, this story is nevertheless critical for understanding Na self-understanding. The ability to trace ancestral origins to the five leading Na lineages is an important aspect of personal status in Na Homestead. Those surnamed Na are buried together in one part of the large cemetery connected to the mosque and village. The cultural reckoning of their descent from an ancestor who was not only foreign, but also Muslim, is critical for Na self-identity.

The Na have maintained this cohesive identity over centuries of interaction with Han neighbors and in the face of prolonged, oppressive, local government policies and socioeconomic instability. Na villagers are proud that their ancestors participated in Ma Hualong's Northwest Hui rebellion (1862–1877). They say they only surrendered to the Qing army general, Zuo Zongtang, after 3 months of siege by two of his commanders, with more than 12,000 troops. They often mentioned to me that Ma Hualong's birthplace, Jinji, and gravesite, Dong Ta, are within 40 kilometers of Na Homestead. While Zuo Zongtang's commanders spared most of the men because they surrendered, the Hui say many of his soldiers carried off their women to Henan. According to some elders, the Sichuan general, Wang Tuan, and his army fought them for more than 3 years but were never able to enter the walled village. During a conflict in the 1920s with the local Han warlord, Sun Dianying, Na villagers resisted his efforts to incorporate them into his domain. When many of the Na men were inducted into the large standing army of the Ningxia Hui warlord, Ma Hongkui, Hui women in Na Homestead refused to marry men outside the village. Unmarried girls wore their hair up, so that Han men would think they were married and not approach them (*mei bianzi, mei hanzi,* "no ponytails, no men"). One Ahong, they say, even agreed to marry a young girl to a chicken, so that she would not have to leave home. Ethnic independence and a proud tradition of Muslim self-reliance during periods of adversity are reflected in these stories.

After 1949, Hui ethnoreligious identity was profoundly influenced by political campaigns that discouraged "local nationality chauvinism" (*difang minzu zhuyi*) in favor of "nationality unity" (*minzu tuanjie*). Liu Keping, the first Hui Chairman of the Ningxia Hui Autonomous Region, in a *Beijing Daily* speech, criticized minority groups with "separatist ideas" who desire "the right of self-determination" or "independence." There was concern that the Hui in Ningxia might become influenced by Tibetan separatist movements and seek to turn the newly established Ningxia Autonomous Region into their own "Israel" (see Barnett, 1960, pp. 29–32). During the 1958 Religious System Reform Campaign (*zongjiao zhidu gaige*), most of Ningxia's smaller mosques were closed in order to concentrate worship in larger mosques. As the largest and oldest in the area, the Na Homestead mosque was not closed and remained the main mosque in the area until the advent of the Cultural Revolution in 1966. In the mid-1950s, Na village had been recognized as an autonomous Hui village (*Najiahu Huizu zizhixiang*). However, with the 1958 drive to establish communes in the countryside, Na Homestead was incorporated as Chaoyang Brigade of the Yongning County Yanghe Commune. It was not renamed Na Homestead and recognized as an official village (*xinzheng cun*) of Yang He Township until 1983. Since many of the religious restrictions imposed on Muslims in China began with these campaigns in the late 1950s, and were not lifted until the 1979 reforms, many Hui referred to this period as the "20 lost years" instead of the "10 lost years" (*shinian haojie*) that is generally restricted to the Cultural Revolution.

A cadre from another area told me that at a 1960 Northwest Region United Front meeting, several cadres outside Ningxia advocated a policy of requiring Hui to raise pigs. This was in response to Chairman Mao's call during the Great Leap Forward for every household to raise pigs, the perfect "fertilizer factory," reflected in the following saying: "The more pigs, the more manure, the more manure, the more grain, the more grain, the greater contribution to our country." Hui who were reluctant to raise pigs risked criticism for feudalist ideas and refusal to answer Mao's call.

Despite resistance by some local cadres who were later accused of "local ethnic chauvinism" (*difang minzu zhuyi*), by 1966 at least 10 Hui households in Na Homestead were raising pigs. Most of these were cadre activists who volunteered. Some Ahong in other villages also volunteered to show their support for the party. These were later disparagingly called "policy Ahong" (*zhengce Ahong*) and recently have been rejected by many Hui as unqualified to be religious leaders.

Na villagers say that many people became sick and died in the village during the time when they were forced to raise pigs. Hui regard pigs as dirty and unhealthful animals. For the Hui, they embody the antithesis of *qing zhen*. A neighboring Han villager told me that many of the Hui who raised pigs did not take care of them well, and, consequently, many of the animals died prematurely. One Hui villager recounted a familiar story of the dilemma of having to feed the pig or face criticism. He would look at the animal and say: "Oh you black bug (*hei chongzi*, a Hui euphemism), if you get fat, you will die. If you get thin, I'll die!"

By 1966, during the Cultural Revolution's "smash four olds" (*posijiu*) campaign, the mosque was closed and the Ahong worked in the fields with the production teams.

Other local Ahong often returned to their original homes. Na Youxi, head Ahong of the neighboring *Xinzhaizi* ("new stockade") mosque, left to join his relatives in northern Ningxia, where he worked in a store. I was told that no local youth took part in the Red Guard activity of that time. The mosque was converted to a county ball-bearing factory, and although it was reopened for prayer in 1979, the factory was not relocated until 1981. By 1982, open participation in mosque affairs had resumed. Throughout this stormy period, the Hui in Na Homestead maintained their ethnic identity and there were no cases that I could find of people attempting to deny or conceal their Hui heritage.

The Recurring Texts of Na Ethnoreligious Identity

Recurrent rituals play an important role in reaffirming and maintaining a group's ethnic identity.[10] In the life of Hui villagers in Na Homestead these rituals are frequently and regularly reinforced. They have become a part of the daily practice of communal life (see Bourdieu, 1977, p. 16). On the third day after the birth of each child, every Na villager invites the local Ahong to come to the home, read the scriptures, and give the child a Qur'anic name (*jingming*). Usually based on Arabic or Persian, such Muslim names as Muhammad, Yusuf, Usiar, Dawud, Salima, and Fatima are often heard around the Hui household.[11] Chinese names, or *Hanming* (Han nationality names) are used for official purposes and in school (sometimes referred to as *xiaoming*, literally, "school name"). After the naming ceremony, a large feast and *nietie* are provided for the Ahong and guests.

At weddings, every Hui family invites the Ahong to come to the bride's home, read the scriptures, and then accompany her to the new home. At one of the weddings I attended, the Ahong arrived with the bride at about 8 o'clock in the morning. The father and mother of the groom came out of the house into the yard and everyone gathered for the reading of the special Qur'anic text reserved for weddings (*nikaha*). The Ahong first addressed a series of questions (*yizabu*) to the father of the groom, interestingly enough, and not to the groom himself. "Are you the father of this boy?" "Do you agree to the marriage with this girl?" "Do you guarantee that their children will be raised as Muslims?" Following the father's affirmative replies, the Ahong turned to the groom and asked him to quote the *Shahadah*. The groom then proclaimed the monotheistic formula (*qing zhen yan*) in fluid Arabic, "There is no God but Allah, and Muhammad is his prophet." The Ahong then recited the scripture and signed their marriage certificate, at which time the guests repaired to the groom's home for a large feast.

The Hui not only regularly reaffirm their group solidarity through rites of passage to themselves, but it behooves them to demonstrate their unique ethnic separation from the outside Han world. Thus, the Islamic content of the rituals becomes particularly powerful. Perhaps underscoring the responsibility of the parents and elders for maintaining ethnoreligious tradition, male guests were seated in the main room of the house, with the Ahong and several elders on the *kang* in the front, while the groom and his friends waited on the tables. It is the responsibility of the elders and the whole community to make sure ethnoreligious identity is impressed on each new generation. Thus, marriage and parenthood—the increasing of the community—are indivisible actions that must receive sanction through Islamic ritual that stresses the purity of their identity.

Hui Sufi member of the Jahriyyah order, near Na Homestead. November 10, 1984. Note the six-pointed hat and trimmed beard.

Funerals are a significant part of Na community life, insuring that ethnoreligious identity is crucial in death as well as life. Membership in the community does not end with the cessation of breath. Death ceremonies do not terminate after the funeral, which must take place within 3 days after death (Hui use the Buddhist term *wuchang*, "impermanence," not the normal Chinese term *chushi*). Important commemoration rituals take place on days 7, 14, 21, 40, 100, and years 1 and 3 after the death date. At one 21-day commemoration ritual (*jinqi* or *sanqi*) for a 92-year-old man, there were separate prayers and banquets at the older and younger sons' homes. The prayer began when the Ahong sat down on the *kang* in the front of the younger son's house. A semicircle of other Ahong and village elders was formed around him, facing the gathered men. The women packed into the back room of the house or stood outside and participated in the prayer. Several people who could not fit into the small room, crowded with more than 100 men, knelt on the ground in the freezing weather outside. The prayer began with a loud chanting of the *Shahadah* in unison, then a recitation by the assistant head Ahong (whose voice was stronger than the 77-year-old head Ahong) of several passages of scripture with others joining, and a final chanting of the *Shahadah* by all present, including the women.

Although the Na villagers are members of a Khufiyya Sufi order, they do not practice the silent *dhikr* traditionally associated with the Khufiyya. When the Khufiyya order was first introduced to China it was known for promoting the silent *dhikr*, as opposed to the later Jahriyya order, known for the vocal use of the *jahr* in remembrance. However, like many Khufiyya members in north and central Ningxia, the Na villagers now practice an oral *dhikr*. Local historians suggest that the interesting combination of Jahriyya and Khufiyya ritual practices among the Na may result from their participation in Ma Hualong's Jahriyya-led uprising (1862–1876), after they had already been Khufiyya for many generations. As a result, when they pray in unison at certain rituals, the *dhikr* is vocally expressed out loud.

At this ritual, they chanted the *Shahadah* in a rhythmic cadence unique to their Khufiyya order. The last syllable of the *Shahadah* receives special stress while participants raise their voice and sway their bodies rhythmically side to side. It is from this movement among Sufi Hui that their religion became known in earlier accounts as the "shaking head religion" (*yaotou jiao*; see Pillsbury, 1973, p. 174). As I sat in the rear, wedged between several older men, I had no choice but to be swayed back and forth with them. I tried to accustom my ears to the loud chanting that went on for 15 to 30 minutes. It was always under the control of the lead Ahong, and occasionally "primed" by worshipers when the reciting began to die down in intensity. After some duration, the lead Ahong intoned a sort of "mm" sound and the service ended. As the men departed, each received a small donation (*dajiawangren*) of about two to four *mao* (7 to 13 cents), while several stayed for a nine-course banquet.

Following the meal, the entire ceremony was repeated in a more elaborate and lengthy fashion at the older brother's home. Mourners also chant the *dhikr* at funeral ceremonies (*zhenazi*). There, men remove their shoes and kneel in orderly rows behind the deceased, whose body is placed on a mat on the ground and wrapped in a white shroud. After the recitation of remembrance, the body is carried by hand from the mosque environs where the ceremony is performed to the gravesite. At one funeral I attended in Xining, the men carried the body for more than 50 kilometers from the mosque to the "Public Hui Graveyard" (*Hui Gong Mu*) in the mountains behind the city. The rest of us went by truck. At the grave site, to the accompaniment of several readings or recitations of Qur'anic suras, the body is lowered into the earth in the shroud without a coffin, whereupon most of the community present assist in replacing the soil.

I subsequently learned that the prayer and funeral ceremony for this 92-year-old man in Na village were more elaborate due to his venerable age and standing in the community. Well over 1,000 yuan in *nietie* were distributed to those attending. By contrast, another man was given a very simple funeral while I was there. One older man complained: "Only 250 yuan was distributed to guests." He explained that this particular individual was not well cared for by his family, nor very religious. He was often left alone in a room and died at the comparatively young age of 60. "No wonder he died young," one villager told me, "it's like repairing old pants. If you just keep patching them rather than caring for them or getting new ones, when winter comes they won't last." Consequently, fewer than 100 villagers attended his funeral, the others displaying their disapproval by lack of attendance.

Hui often say that longevity is the result of Allah's blessing (*Zhenzhu baoyou*) for a devout *qing zhen* life. They attribute their good health to their maintaining Islamic dietary restrictions and attention to personal hygiene. Hui say they are cleaner than Han because they must engage in the "small wash" (*xiao jin*) five times a day before prayer, and the "complete wash" (*da jin*) every Friday. Hui are proud to note that, though the Hui are only one-third of Ningxia's population, the 1982 census revealed 21 of the 23 centenarians in Ningxia Region were Hui (*Ningxia Pictorial* 1984)—veritable proof of the benefits of living a pure *qing zhen* life.

Wang Zixiao is held up by the Na Villagers as an example of God's blessing. At 101 years old, Wang Lao still regularly prays at home even though his legs are too weak for him to go to the mosque. The walls surrounding his warm *kang* are covered with Arabic texts and flowery Islamic paintings containing Qur'anic verses arranged in traditional Chinese *duilian* style. His wife lived to be 113 years old, and his eldest son is 86. His mother was a Han woman who converted to Islam at marriage and the children were raised in a strict Muslim household. When I asked Lao Wang what his secret was for longevity, he responded: "good religion" (*jiaomende hao*). The Hui in Na Homestead feel that Allah rewards a *qing zhen* lifestyle with health and longevity. Religious devotion is critical to this understanding of *qing zhen*, where purity (*qing*) exemplifies the authenticity (*zhen*) of one's religion.

Along with rituals that take place at important stages of the Hui life cycle, Islamic holidays interrupt the normal course of the agricultural year. In addition to the Ramadan and Corban festivals, Na village Hui celebrate the Prophet's Day, or Muhammad's birthday, as well as Fatima's birthday. When I attended the all-day Fatima festival, I was surprised by the turnout of the entire village for the event. The men attending the festival entered the mosque and knelt for prayer in the front with their shoes off, while the women and children assembled in the back of the mosque. The presence of women and men together in a mosque anywhere in the Muslim world is rare and China is no exception. This allowance was perhaps due to the fact that the mosque was under construction and the place where the women stood was not yet repaired and well behind the men. There are no women's mosques in Ningxia and only one women's prayer room that I know of, located in the Yihewani "South Great Mosque" in Wuzhong City. While the women wore shoes and many of their heads were uncovered, they continued to recite the scriptures in unison.

The Ahong, elders, and several young *manla* were the last in a procession to enter the mosque. They were seated in a circle at the front, around low tables on which they had placed the Qur'an, divided into 30 separate chapters. After a short sermon (*hutubai*) on the significance of the Prophet's birth, the men divided up the chapters and simultaneously read the entire Qur'an (*yuanjing* or *da nian*). The Ahong later explained that this was so the entire village would receive the benefit of being present when the whole Qur'an was read, since most of them could only recite memorized Qur'anic texts and could not read it. Young *manla* who learn to read the Qur'an are often employed by villagers to read portions of it at the graves of their ancestors. They are thus accorded high status in the village. Hence, several of the young *manla* were seated at the head of the mosque in front of the entire village to read the Qur'an, along with the other elders and Ahong. As the worshipers left the mosque they were given traditional Hui pastries, "fragrant oil cakes" (*youxiang*), with a slice of boiled mutton on top.

The Cultural Organization of Na Identity

The cultural organization of space in Hui villages and homes also distinguishes them from their Han neighbors. Hui homes are often decorated with brightly painted mirrors depicting Mecca or Medina, as well as ornate Qur'anic calligraphic drawings and paintings in Chinese and Arabic. These mirrors and texts are generally placed where Han traditionally would have their ancestral altars. Hui homes, like those of the Han, are usually open to the south, but for the Hui there is generally no communication or doorways linking the side homes of the sons with the central hall of the parents. Hui claim that this reflects a more conservative perspective because the women are more secluded from their in-laws. The gates of Hui homes are less ornate than Han and not fixed according to *fengshui* (geomantic) principles. Hui also say their homes are cleaner than Han houses. Unlike most Han, the Hui usually do not allow domestic animals, such as dogs or chickens, into the home. Hui often set aside places in the home for ritual washing and some even build separate, small prayer rooms for the women to use. Hui pay scrupulous attention to order and cleanliness in their homes.

The central location of the mosque in virtually every Hui village marks its importance as the focal point of the village in ritual and social organization. Han temples, by contrast, are traditionally located wherever the *fengshui* determines it best suited, which may place it either within or well outside the village. Those who maintain Han temples are not necessarily regarded by the locals as leaders or integral to the affairs of the village. The Ahong in a Hui village, however, are regarded as the primary actors. They must approve every marriage and are intimately acquainted with the villagers' lives. Most Ahong are regularly invited to Hui homes for meals on a revolving basis (*chuanfan*). The Ahong also assist in resolving conflicts. For example, I witnessed the intervention by a Na village Ahong in a dispute over the construction of a water pipe that one villager thought was being installed too close to his yard. If the pipe broke, the spillage would ruin his grain storage. As the argument escalated to the point of violence, several villagers ran to get the Ahong to help settle the matter. When the Ahong arrived, the dispute calmed down considerably.

Unlike their Han neighbors, Hui often build their graveyards either adjacent to or within the confines of their village. This land is held in common by the community and often frequented by the villagers for regular prayer and meditation. In Na Homestead, an average of four to eight individuals went to the graveyard (*shangfen*) every day to pray, with 30 or more visitors on Friday. Someone from the extended household made at least one trip a week to the graveyard. Hui do not believe in ghosts and gods like their Han neighbors and are not afraid of the graveyards at night. A popular Hui folk saying is: "When on the road the safest place for Hui to sleep is the Han graveyard; the ghosts won't bother us because we don't believe in them, and local Han bandits won't bother us because they are too afraid of the ghosts." In his book, *Under the Ancestors' Shadow*, Francis L. K. Hsü (1967, p. 196) relates that in the religious cosmology of Han villagers (actually, they were Bai; see Yokoyama, 1988, p. 2), the Hui's ancestral spirits were neither feared nor welcomed: "They do not influence the West Towner's relations with the other world at all." Hence, Han, and in this case Bai villagers, did not object to the close proximity of a neighboring Hui village's graveyard. Desecration of graveyards and tombs was one Red Guard activity in Hui areas during the Cultural Revolution that led to major and minor confrontations throughout China.

The role of the graveyard among the Hui and the influence of the ancestors buried there resembles the place of traditional temples dotting the Taiwan countryside (Weller, 1987, pp. 37–42). Women often take their daughters to these temples, seeking otherworldly help in having sons or resolving financial problems. Miracles also are known to occur in the vicinity of these folk Chinese shrines and they influence the natural powers of the earth, bringing good weather and fruitful harvests (compare Sangren, 1987). Local communities may adopt non-lineage ghosts and historic heroes as patron deities over time (Harrell, 1974). Similarly, among the Hui, especially well-known deceased religious leaders or *Hajji* are often honored with local tombs (*tu gongbei*) that are patronized in a similar way as these traditional Han temples. Deceased Sufi saints are built more elaborate tombs and shrines (Gladney, 1987a). The value attached to these local symbols has often been viewed as a threat to the state. While Hui do not have any known institutionalized practice of geomancy with professionals skilled in selecting sites for buildings and graves, it is interesting that many of these graves are placed in a similar location. Many Hui graveyards and tombs are placed on the side of a hill with a stream or plain below. The most notable example is the graveyard and *gongbei* complex at North Mountain, in Linxia, Gansu. Following their own Islamic customs, Hui arrange their graves on a north–south axis, with the entrance to tombs almost always to the south. The body lies with the head to the north, the feet to the south, and the face turned west, toward Mecca.

THE SOCIOECONOMIC CONTEXT OF NA IDENTITY

Shared ideas and rituals illustrate the solidarity of the Hui community and the important role the texts of their faith play in defining ethnic identity. The texts become particularly meaningful during periods of intense socioeconomic change. The years since 1979, not to mention the "10 catastrophic years" (*shinian haojie*) of the Cultural Revolution, have called into question the relevance of Islam and the nature of Hui identity in Na Homestead. Hui identity has also been expressed and altered by interaction with recent government policies and renewed participation in the market place under the private responsibility system.

Na Homestead has 5,036 mu (805.7 acres) of land under cultivation, planting mainly rice, winter wheat, sorghum, and some fruit from a few orchards. Average land per person is 1.37 mu (.21 acres), and 6.95 mu (1.1 acres) per household, somewhat less than in neighboring Han villages. Average grain yield per mu in Na Homestead is about 200 kilograms, less than the regional average of 238 kilograms. Important shifts in the involvement of the local labor force since the private responsibility system was introduced in 1979, however, reveal significant socioeconomic change. These changes in the labor force reveal a significant decline in collective activity and power since the dismantling of the commune, as documented elsewhere in China (see Lardy, 1986, pp. 99–102; Shue, 1984). Chance (1991, p. 153), in a study of a rural village also on the outskirts of Beijing, notes similar power shifts in the transition from collectivist to market economy. In 1978, 27.8% of the village population was involved in the labor force. However, by 1984 that figure had grown to 49.6% of the village, reflecting similar pre-1950 levels (see Table 3.2).

Agriculture and husbandry, industry and construction, and small sideline enterprise (such as cottage industries, private shops and food stands, transportation and service industries) are the three main industries. A significant change in sideline

TABLE 3.2
CHANGE IN LABOR FORCE IN NA HOMESTEAD SINCE 1950

Year	Population	Labor Force		Agriculture and Husbandry		Industry and Construction		Private Enterprise	
		N	%	N	%	N	%	N	%
1950	2,004	985	49.0	607	61.6	55	5.6	175	17.8
1978	3,378	937	27.8	760	81.1	162	17.3	15	1.6
1984	3,871	1,921	49.6	1,439	74.9	175	9.1	307	16.0

Source. Adapted from Zhu, 1985, p. 3.

industries has absorbed much of the increased labor. While only 1.6% of the labor force was involved in these small enterprises in 1978, involvement increased to 16% by 1984, slightly less than the 1950 levels of 17.6%.

In the 113 households studied, 60 people are engaged in sideline businesses, representing 19% of the labor force. In 1978, only one person was involved in food-related small business, and no one from the village was involved in service or transportation. By 1984, however, 85 people were in the food trade, 26 in the service industry, and 24 in transport (Zhu, 1985, p. 4). In terms of the small food industry, eight households opened small restaurants in Yanghe Township with several others selling *yang zasui*—a traditional Hui spicy stew made from the internal organs of sheep. This surpassed the reported four households who operated small restaurants before 1950 (Zhu, 1985, pp. 1, 3).

Participation in the free market and the private responsibility system has also encouraged Hui in Na Homestead to increase their planting of vegetables and cash crops, significantly higher than 1978 levels (see Table 3.3). While agricultural income derived from cash crops in 1984 was only half as much as 1957, it was more than three times that of 1978 before the responsibility system was instituted in Na Homestead. Before 1949, Hui proclivity for growing cash crops in this area was noted by Fan Changjiang. He observed that the opium produced by Han and Hui peasants in the Yanghe area was of a very high quality, but the Han could not make much of a profit from it. The Han smoked too much of it themselves and were too weak to gain financially from it. However, the Hui did not smoke opium and their fields produced 120 *liang* per mu whereas Han fields yielded only 70 *liang* per mu (Fan, 1937, p. 312).

Economic Values and Na Entrepreneurship

Some Hui complain that they have no alternative than to engage in small business, because the land they have been allotted is too little or unproductive. Since the nineteenth-century Hui rebellions, the Hui in Shaanxi, Gansu, and Ningxia were often forced to live in areas that Han avoided, with steep mountains and saline flatlands. While attempts to redress many of these inequities were made during the Land Reform campaigns of the early 1950s, some Hui feel that they still have poorer land than Han and are thus compelled to be more interested in business. On his 1980 tour

TABLE 3.3
GRAIN, VEGETABLE, AND CASH CROPS IN NA HOMESTEAD SINCE 1957

Year	Percent Land Planted With Grains	Percent Agricultural Income From Grain	Percent Land Planted With Cash Crops	Percent Agricultural Income From Cash Crops
1957	61.7	33.5	38.3	66.5
1978	91.0	89.6	9.0	10.4
1984	82.2	66.8	17.8	33.2

Source. Adapted from Zhu, 1985, p. 5.

of southern Ningxia's Guyuan District (six counties) where the Hui are most con-centrated (occupying 45.7% of the total population in Guyuan, 49.1% of Ningxia Region's total Hui population), Hu Yaobang remarked that this area was China's most impoverished region. In 1983, the State Council set up a special committee to encourage economic development in Guyuan District, Ningxia, and Longxi and Dingxi Counties, Gansu.

Despite the poverty of northwestern China where they live, the Hui from Na Homestead are playing an important role in the local free market economy. The Hui operate 70% of the new restaurants, food stands, and private sales stalls in the nearby Yongning county seat market area, even though they constitute only 12.6% of the population. The Hui from Na Homestead own most of the stands. They also participate in the central free market in Wuzhong City, 30 kilometers south. There, Hui merchants make up more than 90% of those doing business, in a city that is 95% Han. Most of the Hui come into the city to do business from outlying Hui vil-lages such as Dongfeng Township, which is 95% Hui. This active entrepreneurial participation is an important aspect of Hui ethnoreligious identity. As one Han peas-ant from Na Homestead remarked, "The Hui are good at doing business; the Han are too honest and can't turn a profit. Han are good at planting, Hui at trade."

Only 2% of households in Na Homestead were *wanyuan hu* in 1985, reporting an annual income of more than 10,000 yuan. While not a large percentage com-pared to some areas in China, it is unusual in a fairly poor Hui area. The prestige and influence of these *wanyuan hu* is significant. Na Jingling, the most successful of Na Homestead's new entrepreneurs, made his fortune setting up a popsicle (*bing-gun*) factory in 1982. A former mechanic for the commune, he and his brother have now moved into the transportation and construction business. They have recently entered into a contract with two other investors to build an "Islamic" hotel in Yinchuan City at a cost of 1.4 million yuan. The hotel will feature a restaurant and shopping facilities with "Arabic" architecture. "We want a real Hui hotel," his brother said, "not like other Hui restaurants in town where you aren't sure if it's *qing zhen*."

Recent economic prosperity among rural Hui, as a result of favorable govern-ment policy and Hui entrepreneurial abilities, has lead to increased support for reli-gious affairs. Na Jingling, for example, wants to use his profits to help the Hui in Ningxia, support the mosque, and build a "really *qing zhen*" Islamic hotel. Other

Hui *wanyuan hu* have told me that because Allah is responsible for their new found wealth under the new government policies, they should devote some of their profits to promoting Islam and mosque construction. Red posters on the walls in every mosque clearly list by name and amount who has given to the construction projects, with names of these *wanyuan hu* and their donations prominently displayed. More wealthy Hui sometimes complained to me of the pressures brought to bear on them to contribute to the mosque.

LOCAL GOVERNMENT POLICIES AND NA IDENTITY

Ningxia Hui Autonomous Region was established in 1958 with its present boundaries redrawn in 1976. Since its founding, Hui throughout China have taken an active involvement in its leadership and civic affairs. While the First Party Secretary of the Region has always been Han, the Chairman of the People's Government (*renmin zhengfu*) has always been Hui. Four of the five current vice-chairmen are presently Hui. Concerned to involve different Hui Islamic leaders, the government is represented by influential members of several religious orders. One regional Vice-Chairman, Hajji Ma Tengai, was the acknowledged *murshid* of the Banqiao branch of the Sufi Jahriyya order. The leader of the Shagou Jahriyya branch from Lanzhou was a Vice-Chairman of the Regional Chinese People's Political Consultative Conference (CPPCC).

Greater religious freedom is evident throughout the region in the rapid rebuilding of mosques that were either closed or destroyed during the "smash four olds" campaign of the Cultural Revolution and the 1958 Religious System Reform Campaign. The government has spent large sums of money to rebuild and restore famous mosques in Na Homestead (90,000 yuan), Tongxin (800,000 yuan), and Yinchuan's Southgate Great Mosque (more than 1 million yuan). Hui are allowed to rebuild mosques in almost every village where they existed before 1949, as well as in newer areas where Hui have become concentrated. As a result, there are now more mosques in Ningxia than before 1949—almost one in every Hui village.

The shifting religious landscape in the northwest is a direct result of recent nationality reforms that have had an important impact not only on the Hui, but on the Han majority as well. Many of Ningxia's recently rebuilt 2,132 mosques are visible from the window of the bus as one travels the main arterial from Yinchuan to Jingyuan. On one trip in 1985 I counted well over 100 mosques on either side of the road. While many of these mosques were under construction on my first trip through central Ningxia in 1983, there were few Han temples noticeable. As a response to the rapid rebuilding of Hui mosques, Han have become actively engaged in rebuilding their temples and many of them were visible along the highway in 1985. The Han were able to effectively argue the validity of rebuilding their *Mazu* and *Tudigong* temples since the Hui had already built their mosques. It is arguable whether the Han would have been granted the privilege if the Hui were not first able to exploit the opportunity. One Han villager in Qingtongxia said, "The Hui get to rebuild their temples, why can't we? Their temples rise up and block our wind–water alignments (*darao fengshui*), and the gods are angry that only the Hui spirits have temples built to them."

Education

In addition to allowing from two to four students (*halifat*) to train privately in each mosque, the government has approved and funded two Islamic Schools (*yixueyuan*) in Yinchuan and Tongxin. In the late 1980s, the government established a large Islamic seminary and mosque complex outside the West Gate of Yinchuan, near Luo Village. The Number Two Northwest Nationalities Institute was established in 1984 to raise the educational level of Hui in Ningxia. A special one-year preparatory course for Hui students (*minzu yubei ban*) at Ningxia University was established to raise Hui students to college level. There are Hui high schools in Yinchuan, Lingwu, Tongxin, and Guyuan, as well as numerous Hui primary schools. The curriculum of these schools is the same as Han public schools, using materials published by the Education Bureau. The main difference of these Hui public schools is that entrance requirements for middle schools and colleges are lower for Hui, and no pork is served in the student cafeterias.

Birth Planning

The Hui minority in Ningxia follow a "one-two-three" policy: allowing one child in the city, two children in the countryside, and three children in mountainous or desert areas. In 1985, a law was promoted that minorities with populations above 1 million in urban areas would have to follow the birth planning policies of one child only. In general, however, the Hui are often allowed to have at least one child more than their Han neighbors. This leads to much resentment among Han, who often feel that the Hui are just the same as they and should not be given any advantages.

In rural areas where population is sparse, Hui have been known to have even more than their allotted number children. One man from a village outside Guyuan told me his wife was pregnant with her ninth child. However, with the support of the Ahong and use of the mosque for disseminating policy, birth planning has been judged relatively successful among most Hui. Infractions by the Hui tend to be judged more lightly than among the Han. I knew of one Hui village chairman with three sons and another child on the way in early 1985. A Hui villager north of Yinchuan had three daughters and was officially allowed to have one more child in order to see if he might have a son. He began spending every morning in the mosque praying for a son.

Perhaps because of this flexibility among the Hui, I heard of no female infanticide in Na Homestead or elsewhere in Ningxia. Hui villagers claimed that their Han neighbors practiced it and said they occasionally found female infants in the fields. Hui youth are permitted to get married 2 years earlier than Han, allowing Hui girls to marry at age 18 and boys at 20. I encountered several Hui weddings, however, where the bride was between the ages of 14 to 16 years old.

International Islamic Exchange

The Ningxia government is interested in promoting closer ties with foreign Muslim countries to foster economic development. Ye Zhikun, the director of the region's economic commission, stated: "Ningxia, the home of Chinese Muslims, expects loans from Arab countries to help develop foodstuffs and light industrial goods for the Muslim world" (*China Daily*, 1984a, p. 2). The government has sponsored several economic and "Muslim Friendship" delegations to the Middle East to correspond with the Hajj, with the delegations including important religious leaders and well-known Ahong fluent in Arabic (see Gladney, 1994b). Delegations of foreign Muslim government and religious leaders have been hosted by Ningxia and escorted to visit historic mosques in Yinchuan, Na Homestead, and Tongxin. Hui "Muslim Construction Teams" formed by collectives and encouraged by the government have been sent to Third World Muslim nations on state development projects. While many of the workers are Han, several leaders are Hui and some translators are Hui trained in the Islamic schools. The son of the current leader of the Jahriyya Shagou branch, trained in Arabic at Beijing's Foreign Language Institute, spent 2 years (1984–1986) in Yemen as the translator for a Chinese development project. He sought the roots of China's Naqshbandiyya Sufism in Yemen where it is thought Ma Mingxin studied in the seventeenth century (see Fletcher, 1975).

Now that Hui are becoming increasingly exposed to the Islamic world through visiting delegations and returning work teams or Hajji, their awareness of the Islamic world is changing significantly. The Tongxin-mosque Halifat wear colorful silk turbans sent to them by friends and relatives working in the Middle East, or given to them by visiting Muslim delegations. While the government hopes for development assistance and increased trade through improved Middle Eastern relations, many delegations are only interested in supporting religious development through mosque and madrassah reconstruction. In the spring of 1986, an Arab visitor to the Central Mosque in Yinchuan wrote out a check for $10,000 U.S. to assist its restoration and expansion.

Ethnoreligious Tourism

While the government is conscious of these unexpected results of its program, for the sake of improved international relations and the earning of foreign exchange currency, it continues to promote travel to Islamic holy sites in China. Public prestige in historic Islamic sites has led to a growing interest on the part of local cadres in developing "Muslim tourist attractions" in places like Na Homestead. While the mosque leaders are still not supportive of the idea, economic interests are beginning to prevail. Construction was begun in 1986 on an "Islamic Hotel" (*yisilanjiao binguan*) featuring Arab and Islamic architectural motifs. Na villagers do not want their mosque to become a tourist site like the "South District Mosque" in Yinchuan, which sells tickets at the gate to visitors interested in seeing the new Arab-style complex built with government funds in 1982. The government's encouragement of tourism, to foster better relations with Middle Eastern Muslim nations, is an important factor influencing the ethnic identity of Na villagers, who are beginning to conceive of themselves in more international religious terms.

Notes

[1]Najiahu, which I translate "Na Homestead," is a brigade (*dadui*) belonging to Yanghe Commune (*gongshe*). Now that Yanghe has become a township (*xiang*), Na Homestead can be considered a large village, comprised of 11 teams (*xiaodui*). For a more extensive analysis of the village, see Gladney, 1992b.

[2]A *kang* is an adobe bed with reed mats on top under which a smouldering fire is kept to warm the bed. It is kept lit throughout the day and night in order to keep the entire room warm and upon which the family, especially the women and elderly, spend the entire winter days working and socializing. At night, the whole family sleeps side by side, and in my case, my *kang* was kept so hot that I had to keep rolling over at night to keep from burning. As a result, the family members sleeping next to me had to keep rolling as well.

[3]A 1964 report collected by the county "United Front Office" (*tongzhanbu*) claimed that in 1954 over 200 were worshiping at the mosque five times daily, 9.5% of the total Hui population, whereas present participation stands at only 80 worshipers, 4.7% (cited in Wang, 1985, p. 8). The population of the village has almost doubled since that time (see Table 3.2).

[4]As elsewhere in Central Asia, in Hui villages, any elder who possesses advanced Islamic knowledge (*Ahlin*) or who can read the Qur'an is generally recognized as an Ahong (Imam). Among the traditional non-*menhuan* Gedimu or Khufiyya, the "teaching" (*kaixue*) Ahong is recognized as the preacher (*woerzu*) and responsible for delivering the main Friday sermon (*hutubai*). The mosque is generally administered by a committee (*siguan weiyuanhui*) that replaced the traditional "three leader system" (*sandaozhi* or *zhangjiao zhidu*) in 1958, after the Democratic Reform campaign (*minzhu gaige*)—among the Jahriyya, the term *zhangjiao Ahong*, for the teaching Ahong, is preserved. The assistant to the teaching Ahong is now known as the *zhangxue Ahong*; the mosque administrator in charge of daily affairs is the *si shifu* or *si guan zhuren*. The teaching Ahong among the Gedimu and Yihewani is often transferred (*sanxue*) to another mosque after an average of 3 years. An elder with minimal Islamic knowledge is known as a "second Ahong" (*er Ahong*) or even, "primary school Ahong" (*xiaoxue Ahong*).

[5]The only available figures on Ningxia for the average wage of workers in state-owned units was 936 yuan per year and in collective-owned units was 646 yuan per year in 1982 (State Statistical Bureau, 1983, p. 488). This does not reflect rural income, which averaged about 400 yuan according to most areas I surveyed. Compare also Mackerras, 1994b.

[6]The study revealed that individual giving among six households in a Gedimu village averaged 7.52%, among six households in a Jahriyya village averaged 11.99%, and among five households in a Yihewani village averaged 9.34%.

[7]On one occasion, when several young men in the village and I were celebrating the departure of one of the villagers to go off to college with one of the bottles of incredibly sweet "chocolate champagne" (*chakelei xiangbing jiu*) the Imam walked in to say farewell. The young men, who openly drank and smoke in the nearby township, dove for cover and blamed me (the only non-Muslim present) for supplying the liquor.

[8]Hui women's head coverings (*gaitou*) veil the hair, forehead, and neck, but leave the face exposed. In heavily-populated Hui areas, particularly among communities influenced by the Yihewani such as Linxia, Gansu, and Xining, Qinghai, almost all women over 12 years of age wear them. While it is not a consistent practice in every area, young unmarried women often wear green, married women tend to wear black, and older women wear white, generally after their husbands die or their grandchildren are born.

[9]For more information on Sayyid Edjell, the Bukharan Muslim governor of Yunnan, Sichuan, and Shaanxi during the Yuan dynasty and his son, Nasredin, see Armijo-Hussein (1989). Note also in this legend the failure to mention the Han co-villagers in Teams One and Eleven.

[10]For an analysis of the role of body and ritual in the 1989 Tianamen student protest, see Gladney, forthcoming.

[11]Ekvall, 1939, p. 19, traveling outside Hezhou (Linxia), reports: "...so for that night we stopped in a little Moslem world. The children were called I-si-mer (Ismael), Fa-ti-mai (Fatima), Er-pu-tu (Abdul)."

4 / Chang Ying: Gender, Marriage, and Identity in a Hui Autonomous Village

"Out of ten Hui families, nine are related."

— Hui proverb

> It is thus the same with women as with the currency the name of which they often bear, and which, according to the admirable native saying, "depicts the action of the needle for sewing roofs, which, weaving in and out, leads backwards and forwards the same liana, holding the straw together." (Claude Lévi-Strauss, 1949, p. 479)

"Only 11 stops on bus number 342 from Red Temple (*hongmiao*) station, Chang Ying Hui village is not far from Beijing," a local Hui friend told me. "Just get off at the first *qing zhen* restaurant. If you see the small mosque at Xiao Guanzhuang, you've gone too far." Such are the ethnic signposts marking the way to Chang Ying Hui Autonomous Village, as described by a Hui Niujie resident. He often visits his wife's relatives who live in this village, one of many satellite suburban villages on the outskirts of Beijing (see Figure 4.1).

Chang Ying is located just 15 kilometers east of Beijing on the main road to Tongxian, Dachang Hui Autonomous County, and Tianjin. I was never prepared for the long lines and crowded buses that turned the short distance into a 2-hour ordeal. Chang Ying villagers are undaunted by this situation, however, regularly making the arduous trek into the city to peddle wares, buy sundries, and even report to work in one of the many small factories that ring Beijing's perimeter. At Guanzhuang, the closest bus stop to Chang Ying, hundreds of bicycles parked tightly together—deposited after a 2-kilometer ride from the village—witness the close connections that Chang Ying villagers maintain with Beijing and with the world outside their concentrated Hui village. These connections are critical to local Hui identity.

It is this chapter's thesis that the social world of Chang Ying Hui villagers is vitally influenced by their ethnoreligious identity. Interaction with the outside world for the Hui in Chang Ying is more restricted than for neighboring Han villages, and at the same time, more wide-ranging. This is illustrated by the intensive and extensive marriage networks maintained by Hui villagers. William Skinner (1965, p. 32; 1971) has persuasively argued that the world of the Chinese peasant—once thought

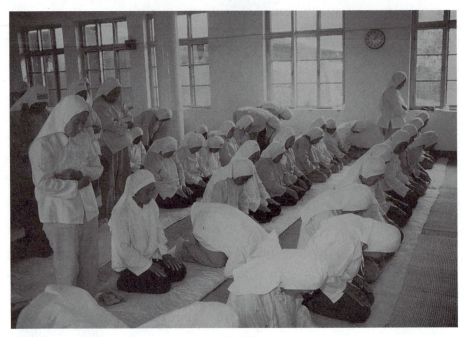

Chang Ying Muslim women at prayer. December 15, 1983.

to be bound by the local village—is at least as large as the standard marketing area, and tied vertically into a nested hierarchy of intermediate and central marketing centers. William Lavely (1991), in an extensive survey of a rural "marriage market" in Sichuan, has further proposed that marriage networks indicate interaction with a world even larger than the standard marketing center.

Hui ethnic identity has direct bearing on the boundaries of their social world. Indeed, the marriage network maintained by the Hui in Chang Ying indicates that their social world may be much smaller than that of the Han, discretely bound by the confines of the village and production team. Yet, it also may be more far-reaching. When Hui marry outside of the team or village, their networks extend to distant Hui areas that are far beyond the areas where Han villagers would normally consider finding a spouse or sending a daughter. Hui develop networks with these distant Hui villages in order to maintain their ethnic identity.

In response to the problem of maintaining their ethnic identity, while ensconced in Han-dominated areas, the Hui practice strict ethnic endogamy. For these Hui, ancestral heritage and ethnic identity is expressed through endogamy, which is marriage within a particular group in accordance with custom or law. While cultural traditions such as the pork taboo are important for urban Hui identity, the equal importance of the idea of endogamy for the ethnoreligious identity of the Hui was expressed well in the following statement made by a Beijing Hui intellectual: "There is a 'Great Wall' separating us Hui from the Han; we do not eat pork and we do not give them our women."

Ethnic identity is often preserved and expressed through mate selection. Charles Keyes (1979, p. 5) suggests that the nature of ethnic identity is shaped by the structural oppositions of interacting ethnic groups, often expressed in marriage exchange. This is clearly the case for the Hui in Chang Ying. Their marriage practices are

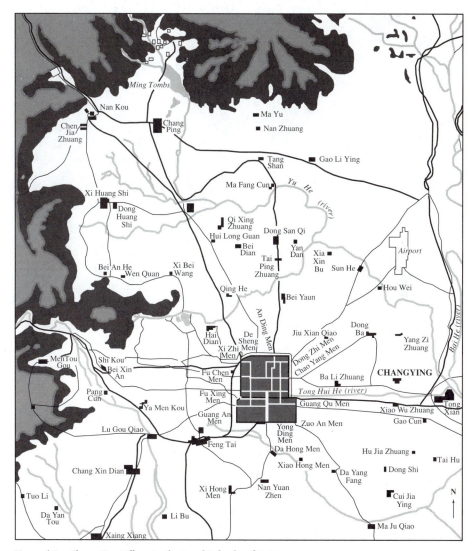

Figure 4.1   Chang Ying Village in the Rural Suburbs of Beijing

influenced by and reveal much about Chang Ying villagers' ethnoreligious identity. The persistence and high rate of endogamous marriages within the Hui village are one of the main strategies that Hui in isolated northern villages rely on to maintain their community. Fluctuations in government policies have also influenced Chang Ying marriage practices and ethnic identity. By considering the importance of marriage as practice, not as ritual, to the Hui villagers in Chang Ying, we gain insight into the relevance of their Hui identity in the context of a northern suburban village.

At the same time, gender in a Hui Muslim village is strongly influenced by ethnic and religious identities, and it shall be seen from this chapter that the Hui Muslim woman's world is both smaller and larger than her Han woman counterpart's social world. Institutions such as the "woman's mosque" (detailed later) in the village, a strong tradition of trading, and wide marriage networks throughout

Young Muslim women in green and black head coverings (gai tou). *Hezhou City (Linxia), Gansu. June 1985.*

the nation mean that Hui women are connected both to their village and to the larger world, perhaps even more so than Han women. This goes against certain theories that have been advanced about the limitations placed on women by Islam and religious seclusion (see Fernea, 1965; Mernissi, 1987).

ETHNOHISTORICAL ORIGINS OF A HUI AUTONOMOUS VILLAGE

Chang Ying *Huimin xiang* is a former brigade (*dadui*) of Shuangqiao Commune, located in the Chaoyang District (*shiqu*) of Beijing Municipality. Beijing Municipality is administratively comprised of 18 districts and counties, of which Chaoyang is the easternmost district. Chaoyang District has a population of more than 1.5 million, with Shuangqiao Commune comprised of 20,000 residents. In 1984, Chang Ying Brigade had 8,350 residents (2,200 households), comprised of 11 production teams (*shengchandui*).

Teams numbered One through Eight are clustered tightly together and are 95% Hui, consisting of 5,020 residents. This represents the greatest concentration of Hui in one village throughout the Beijing suburban area, and one of the largest Hui villages in the North China plain. There are also three, almost completely Han, production teams (Shilibaocun, Wuliqiaocun, and Gongzhufencun) under the administration of Chang Ying Brigade, but separated from the eight Hui teams by 1 to 2 kilometers of fields and canals (see Figure 4.2). In 1984, 85% of the households in Chang Ying Brigade were Hui and 15% were Han. Five percent of the households within the eight Hui teams are Han, but these Han no longer eat pork or raise pigs, in deference to their numerous Hui neighbors.

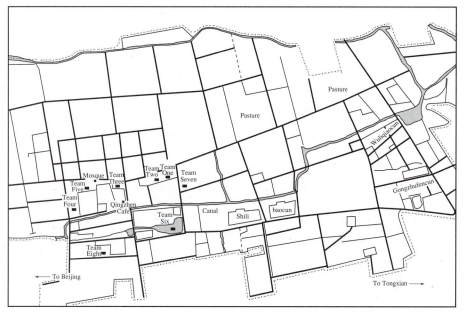

Figure 4.2   Chang Ying Hui Village

The Han who live within the eight mainly Hui teams of Chang Ying Village are the only Han that the Hui will entertain with their own eating utensils. Han who visit from outside the Hui teams are provided with a special set of bowls, cups, and chopsticks that the Hui never use. The sense of coherence within these eight Hui teams is such that the villagers exclusively refer to them when they mention Chang Ying Village. The three Han teams are always called by their proper village names. The grouping of these 11 production teams under the single administration of the Chang Ying Brigade, changed to Chang Ying Hui Autonomous Village (*Huimin xiang*) in 1986, is thus an artificial one—a fact that is substantiated by the marriage survey data. Hence, in this chapter, Chang Ying Village refers to the eight Hui teams and Chang Ying Brigade refers to the administrative unit that includes all 11 Hui and Han teams.

Ethnic Coherence and Chang Ying Identity

Chang Ying Village has a long history of Hui ethnic independence and resilience. It has been known as a concentrated Hui village in northern Hebei since before incorporation into Beijing Municipality after the 1949 revolution. Even Hui villagers in Na Homestead in Ningxia told me they had heard of Chang Ying. In 1956, Chang Ying was recognized as a *Minzu xiang* (nationality village), but during the Cultural Revolution this label smacked too much of local ethnic chauvinism and was changed to Chang Ying Brigade. As a result of liberalized government policies and intensive lobbying by Chang Ying Brigade leaders, it was recognized as a Hui Autonomous Village (*Huimin zizhi xiang*) in 1986.

Hui village ethnohistories that I collected were unclear as to ancestral origins prior to four or five generations ago. Most Hui said they migrated to the Chang Ying area from Shandong, but beyond that they only knew that their ancestors were Muslims who came from the West (*xiyuren*). As with many northerners, genealogical records are scarce and the few geneaologies found in the village were destroyed during the Cultural Revolution. For these Hui, their ancestral home is Shandong. Beyond that, there was not much interest in or knowledge of their earliest ancestors, except for the fact that they were Hui Muslims. This contrasts to southeastern Hui lineages for whom descent from foreign Muslim ancestors is the most salient aspect of their identity.

Despite having settled the area during the Yuan dynasty and having prospered under the Mongols (twelfth and thirteenth centuries), the Hui in the area endured abject poverty in the twentieth century due to the limited village farmland in Hui possession. Hui admit that, over the years, their original land was let out and then sold off to Han who were more adept at agriculture. The Hui preferred to engage in trade and transport with Beijing. By 1949, more than 40% of the land was in the hands of five Han households. After land reform, the government distributed a fairly equal proportion of the land to both Hui and Han. There is now more than 8,600 mu of land in Chang Ying (1.02 mu per person), with 6,000 mu devoted to rice and 1,260 mu planted with vegetable cash crops.

Chang Ying Traditions of Rural Entrepreneurship

With the recent economic reforms, Hui have once again begun to leave the land in favor of engaging in private business and small-scale industry. Very few Han are involved in sideline enterprises, but active Hui participation has significantly increased their income. This is similar to Na Homestead, where the Han basically left small trade to the "crafty Hui," who they say are better at it. In 1980, average per capita annual income among the Hui was 145 yuan per year. By 1984, average income had risen to more than 400 yuan, with many workers in small-scale factories earning more than 1,000 yuan a year. This results from a substantial increase in participation among the Hui in small-scale industries and sideline enterprises. Many of these Hui have returned to the small enterprises that their families had engaged in before 1949.

Of the 3,000 laborers in Chang Ying, 1,000 work in small factories, including a cotton spinning factory (300 workers), a car repair factory (200 workers), an air conditioner factory (100 workers), and a clothing factory (100 workers). Many of these laborers are women, who frequently travel outside the home to work, and never wear a veil when they are outside of the village. There are also 30 households involved in a fledgling dairy industry, having purchased more than 150 milk cows in the last 5 years. This is a new enterprise for the Hui in Chang Ying. Prior to 1949, no one in the village had raised any livestock except for sheep and horses. The milk is sold to a nearby Chaoyang District processing plant. Demand for the milk has grown with the recent substantial increase in Beijing residents' consumption of dairy products. Twenty households raise chickens as a sideline industry, and there are 10 *getihu* (individual economic households) engaged in various small enterprises. Nine households sell *shaobing* (pastries) and one household opened a small seven-table *qing zhen* restaurant in the village, the *Deshun Guan* ("The Obedient to Morality Cafe"). The father had run a cafe in the village until 1956 when he became a factory worker. Ever since the first week, when the son opened the cafe in July

1984, they have averaged a 25% profit margin. A new *geti* restaurant was established around the corner in 1986.

Except for the larger restaurants, most of these private *geti* (small enterprises) are unregistered, due to their temporary sideline nature, as well as the desire of the entrepreneurs to avoid taxation. While government statistics estimate that only 0.6% of economic enterprise is private in China, and thus not very significant, at the local level I found it to be otherwise. These small-scale entrepreneurs are changing the socioeconomic horizons of every village I entered. State statistics can never reveal the impact these businesses are having on these villagers, because as their income and registration are, in general, far underreported.

Religious Traditions and Chang Ying Female Identity

Like many other rural Hui, Chang Ying residents say that they enjoy engaging in small business as an expression of their ethnoreligious heritage. They also feel responsible to give back part of their income to the mosque, in appreciation for Allah's assistance. Mosque participation and influence in the village are important aspects of Chang Ying life, but not as vibrant as I found in more conservative northwestern Hui villages. Average Friday attendance is about half that found in Na Homestead (7.9% in Chang Ying versus 13% in Na Homestead).

Chang Ying was quite unique in that one-third of those at prayer are generally women, who gather in their own small room southeast of the main prayer hall that is connected by an intercom system. Although in north China public participation of women in prayer is generally rare and women mosques (*nu si*) are few, their participation in Chang Ying religious life is strong. Half of the 650 individuals (12.9% of the village) who fasted during the month of Ramadan in 1984 were women. I found even more participation in Yunnan, where there were many trained women Imam and separate women's mosques. While Alles (1994) claims these women are full-fledged "Ahong" or "Imam," the issue here is whether they have any authority over men. Since they clearly do not, it is clear that "Ahong" or "Imam" here should be taken in its more general sense as "one possessing advanced Islamic knowledge" or training, and does not imply institutionalized authority beyond the sphere of women. Nevertheless, it is significant that women in China have such organized authority, training, and separate prayer halls or mosques among themselves.

The issue of whether a prayer hall (*libai tang*) exclusively reserved for women is actually a "woman's mosque" (*nu si*) is really a matter of semantics, since often mosques in China are referred to as "prayer halls" (*libai tang*). The real issue is whether the women are organized independently of the man's mosque and if their mosque is considered independent. Usually, women's prayer halls are adjacent to the main mosque, as in Chang Ying, or women are given a curtained section or outlying room of the main prayer hall in which to pray. But I have heard of at least one totally independent women's mosque in Henan that is nowhere near a mosque that includes men (Arthur Barbeau, personal communication). Maria Jaschok (personal communication) has suggested that the 1994 International Women's Conference in Beijing did much to galvanize Muslim women organizations nationwide in China and this may lead to increased Muslim women activism, either in social welfare programs or even in new mosque building. The existence of extensive women's Islamic educational training and active women's organizations in the

Hui woman at prayer in her home "prayer closet." Wuzhong, Ningxia Hui Autonomous Province. October 12, 1983.

mosques in Yunnan and Henan suggests that this has a long history in China, and is worthy of further study. This is quite significant given the fact that there are no such independent "women's mosques" nor the institutionalized ordination of women in the rest of the Islamic world.

In the more conservative Muslim areas of the Northwest, women are more restricted from public participation in ritual and leadership (see Cherif, 1994; Halfon, 1994). It was explained to me by many Northwest Hui that the reason their women are not allowed more participation in public ritual and leadership is that Hui women's blood is not considered pure. As one Na Homestead villager explained: "Our women carry Han blood in them, since so many of our ancestors have intermarried with the Han and brought in Han women, we do not allow women to take part in funerals or other public rituals."

On the rare occasions when Hui men do bring in Han women as spouses in the Northwest, there seems to be less concern with their religious conversion than with their willingness to "lead a Hui life" and bring their children up in the ways of *qing zhen*. In order to do this, and in keeping with tradition, women were often ritually cleansed prior to marriage, through the drinking of soda water (said to clean the large intestine) or the consuming of teas that had burned Qur'anic texts dissolved in them. While I never witnessed this, and was told it happened less in recent years in the Northwest, it was a tradition often discussed, which reveals Hui concerns with ritual and moral purity, particularly where women are concerned.

In Chang Ying, the issue of unpurified blood was not as great an issue for the people and the women said the men also had Han blood. There was, of course, concern with pork pollution, but since few intermarriages took place, it was not an on-going concern. Barbara Pillsbury (1976) has argued that this notion of "blood ethnicity" for the Hui in Taiwan is a strong factor in their identity. As I have not found the Hui consistent in their responses, it is difficult for me to draw any conclusions. It may be that where emphasis on blood ethnicity is strong, Hui women's participation in religious activity outside the home will be more strictly curtailed (see also Pillsbury, 1978).

Chang Ying's seventeenth-century mosque is staffed by two local Ahong, and from five to ten students. One Ahong had studied in Beijing's Niujie and Dongsi mosques before 1949 and the other had studied in mosques in Ma Dian and Tianjin. Three out of a group of ten Halifat were recently selected to continue their studies at the Beijing Dongsi Mosque. Except for the Ahong, villagers knew nothing about the various Hui Islamic orders—so critical to Northwestern Hui identity. Some know that they are Gedimu and that other Ahong in Beijing are trained differently than theirs. Since distinctions in Islamic orders are of no concern to the villagers, they maintain frequent contacts with both Yihewani and Gedimu Ahong and Halifat from Beijing.

Before 1949, there were five mosques in Chang Ying, including two women's mosques. Four small mosques were converted to nursery schools in 1958 during the Religious System Reform campaign, leaving the one remaining large mosque (refer to Figure 4.2). The present mosque became a factory in 1966 at the start of the Cultural Revolution and reopened in 1982. During that entire period the Ahong continued to meet secretly with many of the local Hui and chanted the scriptures (*nianjing*) whenever it was requested of them. While most chanting takes place in Hui homes today, at that time caution required them to meet privately at the grave-yard. During the "destroy four olds" campaign, each production team was required to run a pig farm.

The Ahong recognizes that, except for holidays, few young people come to the mosque. This does not mean that they do not believe in Islam or disrespect the tradi-tions of their ancestors, he assured me, but that they are just too busy. Most of them smoke and drink outside their homes, but none are known to have violated the lo-cally accepted norms of *qing zhen*. While all the Hui in the village continued to maintain traditional Hui Islamic funeral customs—very elaborate in Chang Ying—less than half have invited the Ahong to read at their weddings since 1979. Inter-marriage with Han, as we shall see, is still extremely rare.

Local Policies and Ethnic Resurgence

Chang Ying was reconstituted as a Hui Autonomous Village in 1986. Village lead-ers expect many benefits to accrue from this new status, including increased control over local planning and development policies, further jurisdiction over tax revenue disbursement, more representation by Hui in township and district policy meetings, and greater flexibility in meeting local needs. In early 1986, the municipal govern-ment and State Commission for Nationality Affairs financed the building of a large *qing zhen* restaurant that is equipped to entertain and eventually house foreign Mus-lim guests. Chang Ying is only 12 kilometers from the Beijing Sanlitun diplomatic district and is often visited by foreign Muslim delegations interested in the mosque and rural Muslim life. The mosque regularly accepts requests to slaughter sheep and cattle ritually for foreign Muslims. This contact is encouraged by the district and municipal leadership and will continue to have a growing influence on the Chang Ying Hui villagers.

Minority policies promulgated since 1979 in Chang Ying have also had an im-portant influence on the Hui. Nationality policies have allowed each couple to have two children under the minority family planning policy. Benefits for nationalities also include the providing of extra ration coupons for Chang Ying factory workers. Now that Chang Ying has become an autonomous village, they have more control over village administrative decisions and dispersal of local tax revenues. They are still under the administration of the Shuangqiao Township, Chaoyang District gov-ernment, but they have more flexibility in planning and application of policies than other non-autonomous villages.

The most important stress has been placed on raising the educational level of Hui villagers. In 1958, more than 90% of the Hui were found to be illiterate. By contrast, almost all of the children above the age of 10 in the neighboring Han teams could read. The commune had to send in outside accountants to handle the brigade paperwork for the Hui. By 1980, there were eight Hui college students from the village, 650 high-school students, 3,000 middle-school students, and 3,000 pri-mary-school students. The municipality and district government donated 300,000 yuan to build a Nationality Primary School (*Minzu xiaoxue*) in Chang Ying, with the plan of making it into a cultural center for all the Beijing suburban villages to emulate. The faculty are paid a higher wage than other primary schools and there is twice the budget for the children's meals and snacks. Out of 647 students, 85% are Hui, a proportion higher than any other nationality school in Beijing. The faculty are 30% Hui; 95% of the first class entered middle school, and 50% of the first class tested into high school.

There are still problems to overcome, however. The Hui principal said that Hui parents do not value education as much as do the Han. They would rather have their children help out with the family sideline enterprise. The brigade government has developed special training programs to help families realize the importance of a public education. One of the issues that the local officials have yet to address, however, is the nature of education for these Hui. The Imam mentioned that while desire for Han learning was low, many of the younger Hui were quite motivated in studying Islamic history and Qur'anic languages. The party secretary countered that this was not regarded as education by the state and therefore could not be encouraged by state schools. It was part of religion, according to him.

One of the most difficult questions I had to ask in China was one regarding education. The way to pose the question in Chinese is, literally: "What is your cultural level?" (*nide wenhua chengdu duoshao*). "Culture" here refers only to learning in state-sponsored schools and literacy in Chinese characters. I still remember asking this question to an elderly Hui Hajji in Hezhou, who answered that he "had no culture." This Islamic scholar had spent 12 years living in the Middle East, was fluent in Persian, Arabic, and a master of the Islamic natural sciences. Efforts to integrate "nationality general history" (*minzu changshi*) into the state school curriculum do not even begin to address this issue of pervasive Han chauvinism. It may be a strong factor that keeps Hui children from wanting to attend mainly Han schools.

GENDER, MEMORY, AND ETHNORELIGIOUS MARRIAGE TRADITIONS IN CHANG YING

During interviews with Hui married women in Chang Ying, I became accustomed to the response that their natal home was within Chang Ying Village, and that they were generally born in the team in which they were still residing or in one of the other seven nearby. This was consistent with what I found in other Hui villages such as Na Homestead: The wives and daughters-in-laws generally married in patrilocally from another household within the team, or from a Hui household in a village nearby; daughters married out to a household in a Hui village that was near their original home.

Every so often, however, I would be surprised to find that a daughter-in-law had come to Chang Ying from a distant Hui village in Shandong or a daughter had married out to a Hui family as far away as Ningxia. When I told Niujie Hui residents that I was interviewing Hui in Chang Ying, I found several with relatives there. Finding a Hui spouse is not a major issue in the Northwest, where Hui are numerous. Religious issues, such as which Islamic order one's mate must belong to, often supersede ethnic concerns. Intermarriage with Han is almost inconceivable for these Hui. In urban areas, on the other hand, intermarriage with Han is resisted in some Hui communities like Niujie, but is an accepted eventuality in Shanghai and Guangdong. Along the Southeast Coast, Hui lineages are concerned more with maintaining lineage continuity than with finding a Hui spouse or preserving ritual *qing zhen* purity.

Unlike the Hui in the Northwest or in Southeastern lineages, for Hui living in pockets of isolated Hui communities amid Han majority areas (*zaju huimin diqu*), finding an appropriate Hui spouse can be a difficult task. It is a pressing issue for Hui who wish to preserve their ancestral traditions and maintain their Hui community. Intermarriage with Han is almost nonexistent in these areas, but locating a Hui spouse may be challenging—especially if one does not want to marry the boy next door. The patterns Hui have established and the networks they have developed to solve this problem tell us much about Hui identity. Like the weaving of the vine that holds the straw roofs together in Lévi-Strauss' analogy, the movement of Chang Ying women has much to do with the continuing ethnoreligious coherence of this Hui community.

Hui Marriage Practice in Chang Ying

I conducted a marriage survey of Hui women in Chang Ying Village over the summer of 1984. This was an appropriate time because most Hui marriages, like those of their Han neighbors, take place during the spring festival, so that the majority of marriages through 1984 could be included. With the help of the Chang Ying village leadership, a total survey of all living Hui women related to the most senior male in the family was conducted. Both women in Chang Ying and those who had left the village as a result of out-marriage or migration were included. Unmarried women were also included in order to provide a base for follow-up study. I tried to survey all of the Hui families in the village with as many members present as possible, since the study relied not on household registers but on their memories of living women relatives, and women tend to disappear from family oral histories.

Perhaps as a result of the patrilineal and patrilocal Chinese tradition that the Hui maintain, I found that many women were forgotten over the years. In several of my earlier interviews, when I asked how many children were in the household, the parents would respond by naming only the sons. Married daughters would often be omitted and sometimes totally lost track of if they had married out more than 10 years earlier. This revealed much about Hui social hierarchy within the family and across gender lines.

There are 799 families in the marriage survey drawn from the eight Hui teams of Chang Ying Village. This represents all of the known Hui women from three generations related to these eight teams, the Hui village of Chang Ying Brigade. Randomly selected data from 200 families have been analyzed, amounting to 1,131 women, among whom 796 were ever-married.[1]

Village leaders told me that *tongyangxi* or minor marriage (see Wolf & Huang, 1980), in which an adopted daughter is raised and later married to a son, was never practiced among the Hui in Chang Ying, so all marriages are adult marriages. No data were collected on divorced, widowed, or remarried women who do not exceed 5% of all women in the village. The survey was focused on the movement of women so these changes in marital status are not significant for the study. Uxorilocal marriages was very rare. Couples that marry within the team live so close to both the husband's and the wife's original homes that it is more convenient to reside virilocally, and uxorilocality is generally avoided within the team.

No Hui for Han: Intermarriage in Chang Ying

There were only two Han women who married into Chang Ying out of the 546 women surveyed, both of them married to Hui men within the last 8 years. Chen Guizhen, a Han from the Chaoyangmenwai Nanxiaojie district in Beijing, wedded the youngest of Wang Yuming's two sons in 1981. After she moved into her husband's household in Team Eight, she continued to commute to a factory in the Chaoyangmenwai district near her natal home. The other Han woman is a factory worker who married a Hui soldier from Chang Ying while he was stationed in her home in Wenzhou, Zhejiang. They now live there together.

Intermarriage between Hui women and Han men from outside Chang Ying is virtually unknown. The Ahong and village elders could not ever remember having heard of such a case. There are a few cases of Hui women marrying Han men from within the eight teams, but even these incidents were opposed by most villagers. In 1956, for example, a Han man from within the eight Hui teams married a local Hui woman. Even though this man had previously accepted Hui dietary restrictions and religious practices, most of the Chang Ying villagers were still adamantly opposed to the wedding. After a prolonged dispute involving the entire village, the marriage was allowed to take place on the condition that the husband converted. He did so, and is now registered as a Hui.

Officially, Han conversion to Islam at the time of intermarriage with a Hui should not involve a change in ethnic registration. However, all Han I knew of who had intermarried with Hui before the 1982 census were registered as Hui. Since the census, these spouses are no longer allowed to change their ethnicity, whether they convert or not. They should be known as Muslim Han (*xinyang yisilanjiao de Hanzu* or *Hanzu Musilin*). I often asked throughout China whether a Han who believes in Islam could become a Hui. Hui workers and farmers always agreed this was possible. Only cadres and intellectuals were inclined to deny the possibility. On the contrary, when I asked if Hui could lose their ethnicity through atheism or violation of *qing zhen*, not one Hui said that it would be possible. Such a person would merely be known as a "bad Hui," never a Han. This reveals that Hui rarely make the distinction between ethnicity and religion, and, according to most Hui, ethnic change is unidirectional: Han can become Hui, but Hui cannot become Han.

Ethnic Endogamy in Chang Ying Village

During my first visit to the mosque, the Ahong told me that before 1949 he had performed most of the weddings and thus knew where most of the women came from and went to. Even though many young people no longer have a traditional Hui wedding with the Ahong present, he is still cognizant of current trends. Many parents consult with the Ahong when they have questions about the suitability of a marriage. When a local match cannot be found, Ahong can also ask other Ahong from distant mosques if there are any appropriate unmarried youth. Thus, the Ahong are a good place to begin one's study of marriage exchange in any Hui village.

The Ahong said that before 1949, more than 60% of the women married within Chang Ying Village, 10% of the remainder married within the commune, and about 10% married to or from Beijing. Now, however, with recent enforced policies restricting urban migration, there are few Hui marriages between Chang Ying and

TABLE 4.1
MIGRATION IN MARRIAGE TO AND FROM CHANG YING VILLAGE,
1922–1984, BY DESTINATION OR PROVENANCE

Destination or Provenance	Out-Marrying (Daughters)		In-Marrying (Wives)	
	N	%	N	%
Within team	84	33.6	98	17.9
Within brigade	89	35.6	188	34.4
Neighboring brigade	25	1.0	55	10.0
Neighboring commune	4	1.6	11	2.0
Neighboring district or county within 40 kilometers	11	4.4	55	10.0
Distant county beyond 40 kilometers	1	0.4	93	17.0
City	36	14.4	46	8.4
Total:	250	100.0	546	100.0

Note. Figures for marriage in and out of the team are unequal because not all the women in the survey have been tabulated yet. It is assumed that once all of the women are accounted for, within team and brigade exchange of women should be equal. The survey was also only conducted on the Hui families in Teams One through Eight, so instances of intermarriage with the three Han villages within the brigade are not recorded. Hence, women from the eight Hui teams who came from or went to the three Han teams in marriage would be recorded, but no women from the three Han teams would be included if they were exchanged with the Hui teams. This would also account for imbalance in the figures at the brigade level.

Source. Family survey.

Beijing. Instead, there has been an increase in marriage with the rural Hui from neighboring Dachang Hui Autonomous County. From before 1949 until now, mosque records indicate that the vast majority of Hui women marry within Chang Ying Village. This was substantiated by my survey (see Table 4.1). The data are arranged in a hierarchy of place and distance so that we can see if women are moving from within the team and the brigade (essentially all-Hui), the commune, the district, or farther out.

The most striking feature revealed by Table 4.1 is the high incidence of marriage within the brigade and teams. More than 33% of the daughters who married out of their present family into a neighboring family stayed within the same team; 17.9% of wives married into their current family from another family within the same team. Adding brigade and team marriages together, we find they account for more than 79.2% of out-marrying daughters, and 52.3% of in-marrying wives. This is almost twice that found in similar surveys conducted among Han villagers.[2]

As this survey relies on the memories of the families interviewed, early out-marriages might tend to be under reported. Assuming that there should be a fairly even flow of women who marry within the teams, the record appears somewhat

TABLE 4.2
MIGRATION IN MARRIAGE TO AND FROM CHANG YING BRIGADE,
1974–1984, BY DESTINATION OR PROVENANCE

Destination or Provenance	Out-Marrying (Daughters)		In-Marrying (Wives)	
	N	%	N	%
Within team	60	35.9	39	16.7
Within brigade	70	41.9	101	43.3
Neighboring brigade	15	8.9	26	11.1
Neighboring commune	3	1.7	3	1.2
Neighboring district or county within 40 kilometers	4	2.3	19	8.1
Distant county beyond 40 kilometers	0	0.0	32	13.7
City	15	8.9	13	5.5
Total:	167	100.0	233	100.0

Source. Family survey.

imbalanced. Hence, a breakdown of marriages within the most recent 10 years is presented in Table 4.2.

The data from the most recent 10 years, which we would expect to be more accurate, indicate an even higher incidence of marriage within the team and brigade. The in- and out-marriage numbers are more balanced at the brigade level in the 1974–1984 period, with a total of 140 wives and 130 daughters marrying within Chang Ying. Most of the increase in intra-team marriage is at the expense of marriages into the city. Table 4.2 reveals a 5% reduction in out-marriages to the city over Table 4.1, and a 3% reduction in in-marriages.

In their study of marriage within Chen Village, a southern Han village, Chan et al. (1984, pp. 186–191) found that endogamous marriage within the lineage was so taboo that its recent initiation by poorer villagers who could not find outside spouses constituted a veritable "marriage revolution." Lineage endogamy was encouraged by local government policies in order to break down local lineage power. This was gradually adopted by the poorer villagers as a preferred marriage strategy, accounting for 70% to 80% of the total marriages.

The convenience of keeping Hui daughters nearby has been known to Chang Ying villagers for a long time. While this may be a recent trend among the Han in Chen Village, the Hui in Chang Ying have preferred not to marry their daughters out since before 1949, as Table 4.1 indicates. For Chen villagers, poverty kept them from being able to bring in wives. For Chang Ying villagers, ethnicity keeps them from wanting to bring in outside Han women, or marry their daughters out to non-Hui villages. Economic considerations are also an important factor in Chang Ying,

TABLE 4.3
CHANG YING HUI SURNAMES AND SURNAME ENDOGAMY

Surname	N	%	Surname Endogamous Marriages		Within Last 10 Years	
			N	%	N	%*
Zhang	234	20.7	20	57.1	10	29.4
Ma	114	10.0	6	20.0	2	5.8
An	99	8.7	1	2.8	1	2.9
Yang	78	6.9	2	5.7	1	2.9
Wang	59	5.2	3	8.5	2	5.8
Bai	48	4.2	—	—	—	—
Hai	43	3.8	—	—	—	—
Guan	38	3.3	—	—	—	—
Li	36	3.1	—	—	—	—
Hou	29	2.5	1	2.8	1	2.9
Wu	27	2.4	—	—	—	—
Jin	22	1.9	1	2.8	—	—
Qin	22	1.9	—	—	—	—
He	22	1.9	—	—	—	—
Du	18	1.6	—	—	—	—
Liu	18	1.6	—	—	—	—
Xue	18	1.6	—	—	—	—
Kang	16	1.4	—	—	—	—
Mu	14	1.2	—	—	—	—
Xia	14	1.2	—	—	—	—
Yi	13	1.2	—	—	—	—
Ding	12	1.1	—	—	—	—
Gao	11	1.0	—	—	—	—
Chen	10	0.88	—	—	—	—
Wan	10	0.88	—	—	—	—

(Continued)

TABLE 4.3 (CONTINUED)
CHANG YING HUI SURNAMES AND SURNAME ENDOGAMY

| Surname | N | % | Surname Endogamous Marriages | | Within Last 10 Years | |
			N	%	N	%*
Xiao	10	0.88	—	—	—	—
Hu	9	0.79	—	—	—	—
Hao	8	0.70	—	—	—	—
Mao	7	0.62	—	—	—	—
Han	6	0.53	—	—	—	—
Liang	4	0.35	—	—	—	—
Hui	3	0.26	—	—	—	—
Cao	2	0.12	—	—	—	—
Dai	2	0.12	—	—	—	—
Feng	2	0.12	—	—	—	—
Lu	2	0.12	—	—	—	—
Lou	2	0.12	—	—	—	—
Xu	2	0.12	—	—	—	—
Zhong	2	0.12	—	—	—	—
Zhao	2	0.12	—	—	—	—
Bi	1	0.08	—	—	—	—
Fan	1	0.08	—	—	—	—
Hong	1	0.08	—	—	—	—
Ping	1	0.08	—	—	—	—
Su	1	0.08	—	—	—	—
Wei	1	0.08	—	—	—	—
Total:	1,095		34	100.0	17	50.0

Note. *Percent in last two columns is of total surname endogamous marriages.

which contributes to their preference for endogamy. Government policies have restricted marriage of Chang Ying women into the city and have led to their own rapid economic development as an autonomous village. Chang Ying daughters may well have few preferable hypergamous destinations outside the village.

Endogamy is one of the most important ways Hui in this community express their descent from foreign Muslim ancestry. They keep their community pure by not marrying their daughters to non-Hui or bringing in Han women. Tables 4.1 and 4.2 also reveal that, for the Hui, there are important levels of endogamy. Since we know that virtually all out-marrying daughters are going to Hui homes, and in-marrying wives are coming from Hui families, it becomes important to ask how far out these networks extend, and how ingrown they have become. Ethnic identity for the Hui leads them to bring in wives from much farther away than the Han. It also leads them to consider marrying women from an even closer radius. In order to preserve the purity of their descent, Hui in Chang Ying do something that Han would never do: They engage in surname endogamy. By this practice, thought immoral and even unhealthful by most Han, Hui seek to perpetuate their community. It is the closest level in a hierarchy of intimate endogamous relations.

Marriage Bonds in a Close-Knit Community

For the Hui in Chang Ying, the obvious preference is to find a mate within one's team. Barring that, one should try to at least find someone from the other neighboring seven teams within the village. Of course, most younger Hui say they would much prefer to marry into the city, but strict control over migration to the capital from the countryside makes that almost impossible. With the improvement in the living conditions and education in the suburban villages, there has been a trickle of urban women out to Chang Ying. But for most Chang Ying Hui women, their world is fairly bounded by the village and team.

Each of the eight Hui teams is primarily comprised of families with one surname. From Team One to Eight, they are: Zhang, Hai, Yin, An, Ma, Zhang, Xia, and Bai and Wang (both in Team Eight). These surname groups may be better understood as clans instead of lineages, since the Hui do not recognize that all of those with the same surname are descended from the same ancestor. The Hui maintain the belief that their surnames were translated into Chinese from the names of their foreign Muslim ancestors during the Yuan and Ming dynasties. This, they explain, is the reason they feel free to engage in endogamous marriages with other Hui of the same surname—a practice eschewed by the Han as unfilial (Chan et al., 1984, p. 186).[3]

Out of the 200 families analyzed from my survey, there are 34 families with surname endogamous marriages (see Table 4.3). Seventeen of those marriages took place in the last 10 years. One family, surnamed Zhang, has had two surname endogamous marriages in two generations. The surname Zhang is the most numerous in Chang Ying, representing the majority in both Teams One and Six. These are frequently encountered surnames among Hui villagers in Northern China. This survey of Chang Ying Hui surnames presented in Table 4.3 is the first systematic analysis of Hui surnames based on one extended community. Comparisons of other communities in other regions of China are needed before we can draw any generalizations as to the frequency and distribution of these Muslim surnames.[4]

This high rate of same surname endogamy is extraordinary in the Chinese context where it is regarded as immoral at best and scientifically unhealthful at worst. The principal of the Hui elementary school suggested that one of the reasons Hui do not do well in school is that they have a high rate of mental birth defects. Hui preference for close marriage with their relatives, he argued, has led to a high incidence of mental ill-ness among their offspring (*jinhunbing*). More than 20 out of every class of 600 Hui students have severe learning disabilities to the extent that they cannot continue school beyond the first grade—a condition he attributes to close intermarriage. This reflects a common view among nationality cadres working among the Hui: Much of their economic and educational problems stem from their close intermarriage. As a re-sult, the five-generations law is strongly promoted among the Hui: No intermarriage with anyone that is a close relative within five generations. This criticism of Hui en-dogamy practice was also found as one of the main points on a "Large Character Poster" targeting the Hui during the Cultural Revolution:

> Posters were seen in Peking in autumn 1966 calling for the abolition of Muslim cus-toms. One poster proposed that the authorities should:
> Close all mosques;
> Disperse [religious] associations;
> Abolish Koran study;
> *Abolish marriage within the faith;*
> Abolish circumcision.
> (MacInnis, 1972, p. 292, emphasis added).

This represents a traditional Han criticism of the Hui, reflecting Han values of filial piety and scientism, which repeats itself in various "scientific" policies aimed at reforming them. Interestingly, the effort to prevent close in-marriage and en-dogamy within the Hui ethnic group goes against the 1957 marriage law, which dis-couraged intermarriage between ethnic groups. In most Hui villages I visited, if a Hui couple or their parents really wanted them to get married, and they were too closely related according to the five-generations law, they generally found a way to get around it.

Far-Away Hui: Remote Origins and Destinations of Chang Ying Women

Most Chang Ying women stay within their team or the brigade when they get mar-ried. But when they do move outside the village in marriage, they tend to go to or come from Hui villages quite distant from Chang Ying. There is a rather large gap between the number of women marrying within the brigade and team and those mar-rying outside the district (refer to Table 4.1). Very few marriages occur outside Shuangqiao Commune but within Chaoyang District. Even though there are many Hui satellite villages within the suburban Chaoyang District, few Hui wives come from them or marry their daughters out to these Hui villages. Between 1922 and 1984, only 2% of wives married into Chang Ying from within the district, while 27% of wives married in from neighboring or distant rural areas within or beyond 40 kilometers. Most of these distant places were areas with concentrated Hui villages.

According to Table 4.1, 47.4% of the wives marrying into Chang Ying came from outside the brigade. The majority of these women came from known Hui areas. It would be interesting to know the ethnic compositions of the communities these women married in from. Unfortunately, 1982 census data at the county level for minority population have not yet been made public. In order to find out if the women came from Hui areas, I interviewed Hui leaders and scholars familiar with the distribution of Hui villages in the North China plain. I found that Hui tended to marry their daughters out to distant areas that were not major Hui centers. Hui daughters-in-law who married in, however, tended to come from villages nearby that were almost all-Hui. A higher proportion of those Hui daughters marrying out of Chang Ying end up in areas with few Hui, than wives who come into Chang Ying. Chang Ying Hui apparently prefer to bring in wives and daughters-in-law from concentrated Hui areas. Fifteen percent of the wives who married in came from villages that were more than 70% Hui. Once they have decided to marry a daughter out, however, it seems that there is less concern that they are destined for a Hui area. Only 6% of the daughters who married out went to villages with more than 70% Hui. More than two-thirds (67.5%) of the out-marrying daughters went to villages where there were less than 30% Hui. It was noted previously that the vast majority of Hui women will be marrying Hui no matter where they go, even to a village that is mostly Han. So far, I have only found two cases of marriage with Han women, and informants could never remember any cases of Chang Ying Hui women marrying Han outside the eight Hui teams in the village. These Han living among the Hui in Chang Ying village, as I have described, had already accepted the Hui way of life.

It is noteworthy that often the women move in only one direction. The largest group of wives marrying into Chang Ying from Hui areas (32.6%) come from Dachang Hui Autonomous County, less than 40 kilometers away. However, there are as yet no cases of Chang Ying daughters marrying out to Dachang. The imbalance of women exchanged between villages in Dachang and Chang Ying may be explained by the continuing practice of marriage hypergamy in contemporary China in which women marry "up" for social, political, and economic advantages (see Lavely, 1991). Madsen (1984, p. 36) and Chan et al. (1984, p. 187) have discussed how men from poorer Han villages often have difficulty finding wives. The local girls marry up and out. Dachang Hui women may wish to marry into Chang Ying because it is a suburban village near Beijing. In China, prosperity and opportunities to work in suburban factories often come with proximity to urban centers. When local Chang Ying daughters marry outside of Chang Ying—and they seldom do—they prefer to go to Beijing. With the recent enforcement of restrictions on migration to the city, however, out-marrying Chang Ying daughters must find other destinations. Of the few that do marry-out of Chang Ying, the majority of them, the survey reveals, choose to marry far beyond the district to distant Hui areas that are economically much better off than Chang Ying. If they marry within the area at all, they are likely to stay within the bounds of the commune and marry into all-Hui villages, like Yangzha. In this case, ethnic choice is intimately tied to state policy.

PRESERVING PURITY THROUGH ETHNIC ENDOGAMY: ETHNORELIGIOUS STRATEGIES AND GOVERNMENT POLICY IN CHANG YING

This chapter has focused on one rural Hui community, Chang Ying, located on the outskirts of Beijing and its efforts to preserve the purity of its ethnoreligious identity through mate selection. For these Hui, *qing zhen* is expressed in maintaining the purity and cohesiveness of their community through marriage endogamy. Ethnic endogamy expresses their belief in uninterrupted descent from Muslim ancestors. Its maintenance insures the continuance of that heritage for future Hui generations.

Hui women of Bai culture and language, training to become mosque leaders, Eryuan County, Yunnan. Note the standard head covering despite Bai nationality clothing. The woman with the veil in the center is their teacher, having trained for 5 years in a Kunming mosque. February 1985.

In order to preserve *qing zhen*, these Hui people who are spread throughout isolated Han majority areas have developed extensive marriage networks that connect them with Hui communities throughout northern, if not all, China. While there are many other concerns confronting these Hui, the issue of community maintenance through the exchange of Hui women reveals much about their ethnic identity and the social context of Hui life in Chang Ying.

Marriage will become even more of an issue as the community is faced with increasing industrialization and urbanization. Beijing is gradually expanding to the east and south, since it is bordered by mountains to the west and north. Chang Ying is also within 30 kilometers of the airport where development has been rapid in the last few years. The Lido Holiday Inn, Jianguo, and Great Wall Sheraton hotels are all within 20 kilometers of Chang Ying, but as yet culturally remote from the villagers, who have never visited these Western hotels and know little about them.

This chapter has also told us something about the social world of Hui villagers. In some ways it is much smaller than that of their Han neighbors, in that Hui rarely marry beyond the confines of their village, and even prefer to stay within their production teams. Unlike the Han, Hui do not hesitate to engage in same surname endogamy. Only enforced government policy stands in the way of even more frequent endogamous marriage within Chang Ying. In Han villages, government policies have sought to encourage same surname endogamy to help break down the power of the lineage (Chan et al., 1984, p.186). In Chang Ying, the local government has tried to encourage exogamy. Local cadres believe that Hui preference for endogamy

Hui nationality woman of Bai culture and dress, Eryuan County, Yunnan. Note that although these people speak Bai and follow Bai culture, they are Muslims and registered members of the Hui nationality. February 1985.

has led to birth defects among the children of these close marriages, reflecting Han ideas of propriety.

At the same time, this study has revealed something about the networks connecting Hui communities. The Hui in Chang Ying exchange women in marriage with other Hui villages hundreds of kilometers away. This marriage network is maintained by contacts through the Ahong and business associates. It needs to be further studied. The networks that connect disparate Hui communities are tenuous but important. They have assisted the Hui in preserving and expressing an ethnic identity that extends well beyond their local identity.

The Hui in Chang Ying have said that better times are a result of Allah's blessing for maintaining a *qing zhen* village. They are proud of their ethnoreligious heritage and determined to maintain the purity of their identity. The exchange of Hui women in marriage is one of the main strategies for preserving that identity in isolated Hui villages. The phrase, "Out of ten Hui families, nine are related" is often used by Han to express their disapproval of Hui close intermarriage and the "unfilial" practice of surname endogamy. Yet, for the Hui, this phrase expresses the unity of their identity. Hui are not only one family because of descent from a common ancestry, they are also related affinally through extensive networks. Ethnic endogamy embodies their ideas of uninterrupted descent from a Muslim ancestry and the preservation of the purity of that ancestry through establishing affinal relations with all other Hui throughout China, as "one family under Heaven."

Notes

[1]More extensive quantitative data and analysis are presented in Gladney (1987b).

[2]Lavely (1991) reports less than 26% of marriages within the commune. Parish and Whyte (1978, p. 169) found as many as 45% of their informants married within the village.

[3]Hugh Baker (1968, pp. 174–175) also found strict observance of surname exogamy required the building of extensive intervillage marriage networks in Sheung Shui.

[4]In the Northwest, Ma is the most prominent surname, with other Hui surnames not found on this list, including: Fen, Ga, Gai, Ha, Hei, Huang, Jing, Na, Nie, Niu, La, Peng, Sa, Sai, She, Shen, Shi, Sun, Ye, Yü, Zheng, and Zhou. Leslie (1981, pp. 64–65,189–192) gives the most comprehensive list of Hui Muslim surnames based on the occurrence of the names of Hui authors in the Ming and Qing dynasties. The frequency of certain Hui surnames in some areas, like Ma and Hui, have led to many puns and sayings, the most often heard of which is, "out of ten Hui there are nine named Ma, if they're not named Ma, then Ha, if not Ha, then La" (see also Andrew, 1921, p. 25).

5 / Oxen Street: The Urban Hui Experience in Beijing

The Hui are China's most urbanized minority nationality. They constitute the vast majority of official ethnic groups in every Chinese city, with the exception of cities in the border regions of Tibet, Xinjiang, and Inner Mongolia. The ethnic identity of these Hui and the expression of that identity, however, is quite different than the Northwestern Hui Muslim communities and the rural Hui villagers that previously were discussed.

Maintaining the *qing zhen* lifestyle, getting an education, arranging a job, finding a mate, and achieving upward mobility are issues continually faced by the urban Hui, who are spread thinly throughout China in every city. With the liberalization of nationality and economic policies, many traditional Hui strategies have emerged to deal with these issues. Many of their concerns revolve around the problems facing other urbanites: arranging a job, finding a mate, getting an education, maintaining adequate housing, health, and social security. Because the Hui are members of a state-recognized nationality, however, these issues and the strategies for resolving them take on a different meaning for life in the city (see also Gladney, 1993c).

Although the Hui inhabit every major metropolitan center and are considered China's main urban ethnic group, they have received little attention in the growing anthropological literature on China's cities. The comprehensive Whyte and Parish (1984) study of urban life in contemporary China makes only passing mention of Muslims. Unfortunately, the study also drastically underestimates the population of the Hui in Beijing, stating there are only 16,000 Hui Muslims in the city (Whyte & Parish, 1984, pp. 296, 306), whereas the 1982 census revealed there are 184,693 Hui, with 46 mosques and hundreds of *qing zhen* restaurants. Morton Fried's (1969/1953) ethnography of a Chinese city in Anhui neglected the important Hui community and mosque complex in the city, their role in the local market, and the government's treatment of them (partly because he was not allowed in the mosque). While many Hui live in a city where they are concentrated in one area, the issues of Hui identity are even more pronounced in cities where the Hui are widely dispersed. This chapter will explore these different conditions of Hui urban life and introduce the cultural, social, and political aspects of Hui urban identity with particular reference to the Niujie (Oxen Street) community in Beijing.

Ramadan prayer, Niujie (Oxen Street) Mosque, Beijing City. Note that the pavilion in the background houses a Qing Dynasty stele recognizing the legality and morality of Islam. June 1984.

OXEN STREET: AN URBAN HUI ENCLAVE

Based on the 1982 census, the Hui people represent almost two-thirds (57%) of the minority residents of Beijing. While all 55 of China's minority nationalities can be found in Beijing, occupying 3.5% of the 9,230,687 population, the Hui minority are 2% of the total population. In other Chinese cities, the Hui occupy an even higher percentage of the ethnic minorities: In Tianjin the Hui constitute 87% of the minority residents, 142,847 out of a total of 163,637; and in Shanghai, the Hui represent 89% of the minority residents, 44,123 out of 49,552. The Hui are spread throughout Beijing and especially concentrated in several neighborhoods, including Oxen Street, Ma Dian, Haidian, Chongwai, Chaowai, Chaonei, and Sanlihe. While there has not

The late Imam Shi Kunbing and the late Ma Songting, celebrating Ramadan prayer, Niujie Mosque, Beijing. June 1984.

been any published data on the exact distribution of the Hui in Beijing based on the 1982 census, a good indication of Hui concentration is the location of mosques and

TABLE 5.1
BEIJING MOSQUES: NAME, LOCATION, AND FOUNDING

Name	Location	Founding
Libai Si	Niujie (Oxen Street)[†]	916–1125
Qingzhen Nusi	Niujie Shouliu Hutong[*]	1926
Qing Zhen Si	Dongsi (East Mosque)	1271–1368
Pushou Si	Funei Jinshi Fangjie	1271–1368
Faming Si	Andingmennei Ertiao Hutong	1271–1368
Qing Zhen Si	Andingmen Guan	—
Yongshou Si	Jiaozi Hutong	1662–1722
Qing Zhen Si	Qianmenwai Guanzhou Hutong	1368–1644
Qing Zhen Si	Tianqiao Fuchangjie	1926
Qing Zhen Si	Huashi (Flower Street)	1368–
Qing Zhen Si	Chongwenmenwai Tangzi Hutong	1821–1850
Qingzhen Nusi	Chongwenmenwai Liujia Hutong[*]	—
Qing Zhen Si	Tangdao Hutong	1883
Qing Zhen Si	Suzhou Hutong	1796–1820
Qing Zhen Si	Lumicang	1644–
Qing Zhen Si	Douyacai Hutong	1796–1820
Qing Zhen Si	Wangfujing	1875–1908
Qing Zhen Si	Chaoyangmenwai Nanzhongjie	1662–1722
Qing Zhen Si	Chaoyangmenwai Xiapo	1662–1722
Qingzhen Nusi	Chaoyangmenwai Xianpu si[*]	—
Qing Zhen Si	Chaoyangmenwai Balizhuang	1736–1795
Qing Zhen Si	Zhongjian Zixiang	1862–1874
Qing Zhen Si	Dongzhimennei Nanxiaojie	1821–1850
Qing Zhen Si	Gulou hou	1911
Qing Zhen Si	Shishahai	1644–
Qing Zhen Si	Nanfan Xihongmen	1368–

(Continued)

TABLE 5.1 (CONTINUED)
BEIJING MOSQUES: NAME, LOCATION, AND FOUNDING

Name	Location	Founding
Qing Zhen Si	Dongzhimenwai Erlizhuang	1271–1368
Qing Zhen Si	Anyongwai Daguan	1796–1820
Qing Zhen Si	Deshengmenwai Daguan	1662–1722
Qing Zhen Si	Deshengmenwai Ma Dian	1662–1722
Qingzhen Nusi	Deshengmenwai Xicun[*]	—
Qing Zhen Si	Xizhimenwai Nanguan	1736–1795
Qing Zhen Si	Xizhimennei Gouyan	1821–1850
Qing Zhen Si	Xisi Fenzi Hutong	1821–1850
Qing Zhen Si	Xi Dan	1875–1908
Qing Zhen Si	Xuanwumennei Shoupa Hutong	1821–1850
Qing Zhen Si	Xuanwumennei Niurouwan	1875–1908
Puning Si	Hepingmennei Huihuiying	1765
Qing Zhen Si	Fuwai Sanlihe[†]	1794
Qing Zhen Si	Haidian	1662–1722
Qing Zhen Si	Xijiao Siwangfu	1662–1722
Qing Zhen Si	Xijiao Landingchang	1662–1722
Qing Zhen Si	Xijiao Anheqiao	1662–1722
Qing Zhen Si	Xijiao Shucun	1662–1722
Qing Zhen Si	Beijiao Qing He	1662–1722

Note. [†]Indicates attached woman's mosque; [*]Indicates woman's mosque.
Sources. Wang, 1937; Gamble, 1921, p. 511; Yang Yongchang, 1981; Personal interviews.

qing zhen restaurants (see Figure 5.1). While there were relatively few privately run restaurants in Beijing, the state restaurants were established in areas of higher Hui concentration. The restaurants indicated on the map do not include smaller qing zhen cafes or getihu-run food stands. They represent only those published on city maps. Most of the more than 40 mosques existing in Beijing before 1949 (S. Wang, 1937) have been reopened or rebuilt (see Table 5.1). The presence of a mosque generally indicates at least 100 Hui families (500 individuals), with more famous mosques, like the Niujie Mosque, serving hundreds of households.

The Oxen Street area of the Xuanwu City District in the southeast corner of the city has the highest concentration of Hui. Oxen Street is known for the largest and

Figure 5.1   Hui Mosques and Restaurants in Beijing

oldest mosque in Beijing, the Niujie Libaisi, founded in the Liao Dynasty (tenth century). The street derives its name from the concentration of beef butchers in that district during the Qing dynasty (S. Wang, 1930). Stories dating from that time tell of the strong Hui community concentrated along Oxen Street where Han rarely dared to walk alone. The street now has two small *qing zhen* restaurants, eight *qing zhen* noodle and pastry shops, and several Hui *getihu* selling pastries and fruit. There are 51 *qing zhen* restaurants in the Xuanwu district, with 51 *qing zhen* meat shops and many *qing zhen* food stores selling pastries, noodles, and sundries.

The 1982 population of the Oxen Street district was 55,722, with minorities occupying 24.7% (13,755), of which 96.6% are Hui (13,307). The Hui are even more concentrated along Oxen Street itself. Out of a population of 2,446, 1,763 (70.2%) are Hui. Of the 649 households along the street, 475 (69.3%) are Hui. There are also two Manchu households and one Mongolian household on Oxen Street. In neighborhoods on either side of the street, the ratio of Han to Hui drops to about 50% and continues to decline as one moves further away.

THE RECURRING TEXTS OF OXEN STREET HUI IDENTITY

What does it mean to be a Hui in the city, and what influence does that have on one's life, social interaction, and the effect of local government policies? While it is difficult to generalize regarding the various important rituals and culturally shared ideas of identity in the city, there are certain recurring texts that are of interest to urban Hui, including legends of origin, aspects of *qing zhen* lifestyle, religious holidays, traditional specializations and handicrafts, martial arts practices, and the organization of social space. These concerns represent shared aspects of Hui identity that continually distinguish them from other ethnic groups in the multiethnic urban setting, and regularly reaffirm to themselves their unique ancestry. These cultural symbols serve as important markers of Hui identity and influence interethnic relations. Their recent resurgence under liberalized policies reveals much about changing Hui identity, its continued meaningfulness, and varied interpretations of *qing zhen*.

The Legends of Foreign Origin in Oxen Street

There are various legends of Hui origin and the arrival of Islam in China told by Hui from Beijing to Guangzhou. The most popular account is that the Tang emperor, Taizong, was disturbed by the appearance of a turbaned man chasing a phantom in a dream. His interpreter told him, "The turbaned man is a Hui-hui of the West. In Arabia is a Muslim king of great virtue. A great sage is born, with favorable omens" (Leslie, 1986, p. 74). The emperor was so astounded by his dream and its import that he dispatched an ambassador to the Arab lands who returned with three Muslim teachers. Impressed with the scientific knowledge and civility of these teachers, the emperor invited other Muslims to settle, build mosques, and propagate their faith. This legend is still repeated among the Hui who share the common belief that Islam entered China during the Tang dynasty at the emperor's invitation.[1]

The veracity of this legend and other Chinese Muslim accounts of the early origin of Islam in China are discounted by Leslie (1986, pp. 60–78) and other historians. They reason that the majority of the tales result from eighteenth- and nineteenth-century Hui attempts at legitimation through reference to imperial approval and ancient origin. "Nevertheless," Drake (1943, p. 23) concludes, "the insistence upon the arrival of Mohammedanism as early as the T'ang dynasty; the suggestion of Mohammedan troops settling in north west China; and the account of the early beginnings of Mohammedanism in Canton, all reflect, however dimly, the actual facts." For this study of ethnoreligious identity, the legends are important in that they continue to represent agreed-upon notions of Hui heritage.

There are also local stories told about the origin of the Hui in Beijing. The following account describes the origin of the Beijing Oxen Street Muslims and is engraved on a tablet in the Niujie mosque.

> In 996 A.D. a *Shai Hai* ("shaykh," elder) named Ge Wa Mo Ding came from the Western Regions (*xiyu*). This man often had strange dreams and gave birth to three sons. The eldest, Sai De Lu Ding, could tell the good or evil surrounding different graves. He left home with no reason for some unknown place and never returned. The second, Na Su Lu Ding, could read other people's minds. The youngest, Che Ah Dou Ding, could speak the language of birds. The two younger sons lived in seclusion and refused several

official posts offered to them. They became the Imam of the mosque and settled perma-nently in the East. They prophesied that Beijing would become a center of prosperity where emperors would reign over great causes. As a reward for their loyalty to the em-peror, they were allowed to build mosques in the east of the city [the Dongsi mosque] and in the south [the Niujie Mosque] and were given tombs inside the compound of the Niujie Mosque.[2]

In the southeastern corner of the Niujie Mosque are two small tombs belonging to two Shaykhs who came from the West and were buried in the mosque. Inscriptions over the grave record that the first belongs to Ah Ha Mai De (Ahmed), a Persian who died in 1280 A.D., and the second belongs to Ah Li (Ali), a Bukaran, buried in 1283 A.D. (Y. Yang, 1981, p. 60). While these graves are not patronized like those of Mus-lim saints in the Northwest (see Gladney, 1987a), they do represent the foreign origins of Chinese Islam to the Oxen Street Hui. I never saw anyone praying in front of the graves, nor was there incense lit for them, but on several occasions after prayer an el-derly Hui would take me back to the graves and repeat the legend about these two saints and the arrival of Islam in Beijing.[3]

On Eating Right: Pork Abstention and Urban Hui Identity

Among the vast majority of urban Hui and Han I surveyed, the primary distinction noted between the two peoples was pork avoidance. This issue, while of real con-cern to Hui in the Northwest, is not as paramount as it is in the city. In the North-west, Muslims are numerous. The Han are familiar with Hui customs and generally are sensitive to actions that might provoke the Hui. In most villages that are either Han or Hui, the issue is almost nonexistent. In Ningxia's Luo Village, where there is almost an even mixture of Hui and Han, the Hui households tend to be adjacent to other Hui homes. Han are careful to keep their pigs in the yards, and while mistakes do happen, people are aware of the issue and try to be sensitive.

In the Northwest, more conservative Hui do not even mention the word for "pig" and have created various euphemisms like "black bug" to avoid mentioning it. Some Hui with the surname "*Zhu*," homophonous with the word for pig, have changed their surnames, generally to "*Hei*." The current chairman of the Ningxia Regional Government, Hei Boli, told me that his Hui ancestors changed their sur-name from *Zhu* to *Hei*. The pork taboo is accepted in the Northwest where Hui are numerous. It is generally observed and rarely needs mentioning.

At the other end of the spectrum, southeastern Hui lineages who raise pigs and do not observe Islamic dietary restrictions are also not very concerned about the pork issue (see chapter 6). It only becomes an issue for them when outside conserv-ative Hui or foreign Muslims visit their village. Suggestions have been made that they cease raising pigs, but they have been doing so for centuries and there is no easy substitute. In the southern cities where Hui are few, there is generally less con-cern over *qing zhen* violations. Hui identity depends on lineage and ancestry, not on cultural maintenance.

This is not the case in northern cities and other urban centers with larger Hui communities. Pork is neither so scrupulously avoided that it is rarely mentioned, nor so prevalent that people inevitably accept it. Incidents involving pork are com-mon in urban neighborhoods where the Hui live packed closely together. In one dis-trict of Beijing, where the Hui are thinly dispersed, Ma Jianwei (pseudonym) complained that there was no way to avoid pork. His family of three generations lived in two-and-a-half small rooms that were part of a three-story complex built around a narrow courtyard. "The Han have nowhere to wash and cook their meat but in the courtyard or on the balconies. We put up with it but we really wish we could move to where there were more Hui."

Han often cannot understand why the Hui are so overly concerned about pork. For them, it is meat, the basic protein everyone craves. One Han said to me, "The Hui avoidance of pork doesn't make sense. They are like vegetarian Buddhist monks, but do not obtain any merit for giving up the meat." This misunderstanding is the subject of many ethnic tales and jibes told about why the Hui do not eat pork. I never heard these stories in the Northwest, but encountered them frequently in cities when I mentioned I was studying the Hui.

While the PRC government has gone to great lengths to correct these traditional ethnic biases, long-held ethnic stereotypes still find their way into print. In a brief *Youth News* article on December 31, 1982, the Shanghai editor responded to a question regarding the difference between Hinduism and Islam. Hinduism, he wrote, is more glorious (*guangrong*) than Islam. "In Islam, one hand holds the sword while the other holds the Qur'an." He later noted that the Muslims revere the pig, and that is why they do not eat pork. That afternoon several calls were made to the mosque and the City Commission for Nationality Affairs (CNA). Many Hui went to the office of the publisher to complain and letters poured in. In the next issue, the weekly *Youth News* published a formal apology, and on January 13 went to press a day early to reveal on the front page that the 29-year-old editor had been fired (a rarity in China) and the 17-year-old writer severely reprimanded. The article, it stated, "hurt Muslim religious feelings, was not beneficial to nationality unity (*minzu tuanjie*) and had a very bad influence." A cadre from the City CNA explained to me that while the writers were too young to understand (*qingnian bu dong shi*), this is still unacceptable in China today. In recent years the State Commission for Nationality Affairs has attempted to incorporate more ethnic awareness into its elementary curriculum and in 1985 published "nationality general knowledge" (*minzu changshi*) materials for middle-school students that stressed mutual respect and understanding for cultural differences. Nevertheless, a well-publicized case of national Muslim protest over a Chinese book that portrayed Muslims in an offensive light in May 1989 indicated continuing public misperceptions and prejudices toward Islam in China.[4]

The Restaurant as a Hui Cultural Center

The salience of the pork taboo for Hui in large and small cities throughout China has contributed to the importance of the restaurant as a center for cultural dissemination. While the mosque is central in the Northwest, and perhaps the ancestral hall in the Southeast, the importance of the pork taboo, the dispersion of the Hui in most cities, and the generally low attendance at mosque prayers contribute to making the Hui restaurant serve as a cultural center. The Niujie Mosque has from 50 to 100 Muslims at prayer there five times a day, with up to 600 in attendance on Friday, the main day of prayer (*zhu mari*). On holidays, more than a thousand cram into the main hall and fill the outlying courtyards. While on these days all generations are well-represented, most of the 10 to 15 young people that attend prayer during the midweek are Islamic students from the Chinese Islamic Society around the corner from the mosque. There is simply no time during the week for Hui workers in the city to leave their factories or institutes to go to the mosque. In retirement years, Hui men and women find more time to go to the mosque and they make up the majority of worshipers (the women pray behind a curtain in the back of the Niujie mosque). This is acknowledged by all and no one is troubled by it. Most Hui are satisfied to have one-and-a-half to two days off every year to attend Corban and Ramadan festivities at the mosque. As a result, when Hui need a public place to discuss issues and meet associates, they usually end up at the restaurant.

Young people like to go to the large state-run restaurants in the evenings because they can have a *qing zhen* meal and also buy wine, beer, and cigarettes. Bai Ling (assumed), a young Hui woman smartly dressed in jeans and a red T-shirt, told me that her parents would never let her meet boys at home. "Here my parents are glad to know that I am not in a Han restaurant, and boys like to eat here because they can't smoke and drink at home." One of the youths sitting with her admitted that he occasionally ate pork outside, but he never did at home. He liked to come here to eat because they had excellent lamb dumplings (*yangrou shuijiao*).

The Donglaishun ("Flows to the East") restaurant formerly located on Wangfujing Street, but torn down and relocated in 1994, was the largest and most famous Hui restaurant in Beijing. Established in 1903 by three brothers (Ding Deshan, Defu, and Degui) as a porridge stall at the northern entrance to the Dong An bazaar, it began selling its famous lamb hot pot (*shuan yangrou*, literally "instant-boiled mutton") and obtained its current name in 1906. The three-story building, dated from the 1930s, and the restaurant was collectivized in the 1950s. The bottom floor was always packed with people eating lamb *jiaoze*, the majority of whom had to stand up to eat during meal hours in the crowded space. The second floor served the famous hot pot and on the third floor people ordered their well-known Beijing Duck along with other stir-fried specialties. One of the cooks explained that many Han liked to come here and eat Peking Duck because they only used vegetable oil, not lard like some restaurants, and the duck tastes lighter and crispier. He also emphasized that even the most conservative Hui who will not eat in some of the other state-run Hui restaurants in town came there because they know all of the cooks are Hui. They have several smaller banquet rooms that have become popular with foreign tourist groups. Thus, they were always busy.

Ethnic Festivals and Recurring Rituals

Two days a year, in most large cities throughout China, Hui do not have to go to work or school, or sometimes are allowed to go home at noon. The government permits celebration of their "traditional nationality holidays" (*chuantong minzu jiere*). In the city, most youth know of Ramadan not as a month-long fast, but as a Hui holiday that takes place 1 day a year. While for many the Qurban (*Guerbang jie*) and Ramadan (*kaizhai jie*) holidays represent time to go to the park or take in a movie, the Hui in Oxen Street go to the mosque, make *youxiang* (a flat, fried traditional Hui pastry) and, especially on the Ramadan holiday, visit the graves of their ancestors. While most conservative Hui in the Northwest do not celebrate the Han holidays of *zhongqiu*, *qingming*, or even *chun jie* among the most conservative, the Hui in most of China's cities gladly participate. The Hui *qing zhen* mooncakes (*yuebing*), eaten during the Mooncake Festival (*zhongqiu*), are famous in Beijing. They are made with sesame and vegetable oil, not lard, so they are popularly regarded as light and savory.

From early in the morning on the Ramadan holiday, Oxen Street is jammed with people. The Chinese Islamic Society announces the time for breaking the fast and all mosques in the city generally follow. On the Ramadan holiday, the gates of the mosque are opened and people are allowed to crowd into the courtyard. Normally children do not play in the mosque and one can only enter through a side entrance. But on this day the children crowd around the sides of the courtyards and climb up on the surrounding shoe racks to watch their brothers, fathers, and grandfathers pray. The women use the reception room behind the minaret, east of the courtyard, in which to pray, as the mosque is too crowded to use the usual curtained-off area. On the 1984 holiday, I estimated the Niujie mosque had more than 2,000 worshipers. At the 1983 Corban Festival that I attended in the Dongsi mosque, there were close to a thousand attending. There were many foreign Muslims from the diplomatic community, as well as a large section of Uygurs.

The Niujie mosque generally is attended by local Hui, with many prominent Imams, such as Imam Hajji Abd Rahim Ma Songting, the eminent Hui scholar, reformer, and honorary president of the Chinese Islamic Association, who was seated in the front of the mosque in 1984. Imam Al-Hajji Shi Kunbing gave a lengthy sermon on the Ramadan holiday, exhorting the worshipers to follow the example of the Prophet, who was loyal to his people and his faith. As Muslims in China, he admonished them to work for their country's modernization and to remember they were Chinese citizens first. After the prayer, the Hui return to their homes for a feast or go to the Hui graveyard (*shangfen*) outside the city where they recite the Qur'an (*nianjing*) and clean the graves, in a manner similar to Han grave-sweeping in Qingming.

With the exception of the Ahong, their students, and a few elderly Hui who often fast for all or part of the month, the majority of the younger Hui in Oxen Street do not fast during Ramadan. However, there are exceptions. Among some more conservative Hui urban communities there are often many activities assisting those who fast, lasting the whole month. While many urban Hui do not know the Islamic history surrounding the festivals—one Beijing Hui told me that Qurban was to honor Allah's sparing the life of Ishmael—their regular observance reinforces the Islamic aspect of their ethnic heritage. Urban Hui have also maintained traditional Hui earthen funerals in which the body is buried in a white cloth without the use of a coffin or the elaborate ceremonies of the Han. I was told that only one unlucky Oxen Street man was cremated during the Cultural Revolution when Hui were encouraged to reject their "feudal" funeral customs. Until the white cloth ration coupons were abolished recently, the Hui received special increased allocations for funerals. Like their modern Han friends, many Hui youth are opting for simple wedding ceremonies through state registration without any ritual or going on "traveling weddings" (*luxing hunyin*), where the money normally spent on the ceremony is used for a honeymoon. Yet, Hui wedding celebrations, when they do take place in the city, are often more conservative than Han weddings without wine or cigarettes (discussed later). These recurring rituals, while not as elaborate as those among conservative Hui in the Northwest, continue to serve as salient texts giving meaning to Hui ethnoreligious identity.

Hui Specializations and Handicrafts

Hui are known in every small town in China for certain ethnic specializations: butchering beef and lamb, tanning leather, cobbling shoes, running small restaurants, processing wool, and carving stones and jewelry. In Oxen Street, there are several households that are famous for their long tradition of jade work. "Knowing jade Hui" (*shiyu Huihui*) were skilled at carving jade and especially "antiquing" jade (*zuo jiu*), a labor-intensive process of creating the right color and texture on the stone so that it appeared ancient. Hui were also known for their ivory carving and gold and silver work. The process was so involved and reaped such high rewards that they had the saying, "Do not sell for 3 years, sell and eat for 3 years" (*san nian bu kai zhang, kai zhang chi san nian*). The sale of one piece of jade or carved ivory could earn so much that there was also the popular saying, "in the morning have nothing to eat, in the evening put your money in a car" (*zao chen mei fan chi, wan shang you che zhuang*). Before 1949, outside Beijing's Front Gate (*qianmen*), almost all of the shops on Jadeware Street (*Yuqi jie*) were run by Hui. In addition to their skills with jewelry and jadeware (*zhubao yuqi*), Hui were known as excellent middlemen, particularly between foreigners and Han. With their exposure to Arabic and Persian in the mosque, they were reported to be adept at learning foreign languages.

The Jade Carver

Bai Shouyong is an elderly Hui jade craftsman. He is the third generation of jade carvers and his son is attempting to learn his special skills. Since the 1979 Third Central Committee Plenum, the revival of traditional nationality handicafts has been encouraged. Bai and several of the old jade workers in Oxen Street set up a small cooperative to train young people to work jade in the traditional Hui style. They hoped to train mainly Hui, but several Han have also studied. In 1980 they would take a 100-yuan piece of jade, rework it, and sell it for 130 yuan. While few local Chinese could purchase the expensive stones, foreign tourists have shown considerable interest. One Burmese businessman has made several large orders and it is thought that he resells the jade outside the country. While the artisans clearly sell their pieces in China as "antiqued" jade, the work is of such high quality that they are afraid they might be easily sold as real antiques elsewhere. In 1986, I spoke with one of the young workers at the tourist shop in the Summer Palace where they sell their wares. While there are plenty of foreign buyers, he lamented, even the master's son cannot exactly reproduce his special technique. He is afraid this skill might soon be lost.

"Now to return to the topic of the jewel and jadeware trade," one author complained before 1949, "it was once regarded as the most profitable business and the smartest children left school after two or three years to learn the trade" (S. Wang, 1930, p. 10). Like many Republican-period Hui reformers, he blamed the low education of the Hui for many of their economic and political woes. The jade trade declined in the Republican period with the shift of the capital to Nanjing (Nanking) and, especially in the North, was disrupted by the socioeconomic turmoil of the warlord years and Sino-Japanese War. Before it could be substantially revived, the 1950s collectivization campaigns transformed the enterprise into a state-run operation, where antiquing was discouraged. Only recently has there been an attempt to recover this and other local handicraft traditions.

The Lantern Maker

He Keming is a 93-year-old Hui artisan in Shanghai. Since he was 12 years old he has been making paper and silk lanterns that are displayed during the Lantern Festival. His work is so well-known that the *China Daily* referred to him as the "Lantern King" of Shanghai. He has developed a special technique of making small "gold-like coins" (*jinyin xiangqian*) to look like scales or feathers that make lantern figures, animals and birds, appear lifelike. He is joined by his son, grandson, and 12 other members of the family in making lanterns. In 1984, from Lantern Festival Day, February 16, through March 1, more than 180 of their works were on display at the Shanghai Youth Palace. He Keming displayed a golden dragon more than 2 meters high with more than 2,000 golden scales.

His bright eyes glistening behind a shock of white bushy eyebrows and a full beard, Master He explained to me that his religion has helped him dedicate himself to his craft. Every morning at 3:00 A.M. he rises from his bed to recite the Fatier prayer, a text dedicated to one's ancestors. "My religion is for the service of people and to respect my ancestors, it is not for myself." During the Cultural Revolution, he was severely criticized for his feudalistic art and at one point was encouraged to jump from an eight-story building. He turned to his accusers and claimed he wanted to live and "make revolution" (*gao geming*). "If they made me jump they would be opposing the revolution (*fan geming*)," he said with a wink, "so they let me live." During times when his art could not support him, he sold pastries on the street and ran a tea house. In 1956, he was invited to join the Shanghai Arts and Crafts Institute. "Allah protected me" (*zhenzhu baoyou*), he said. The main distinction of his work is a result of the influence of his faith. He says Islam prevents him from making the popular lantern figures of human personages, which would be idolatry. "But," he admits, "I have no problem making dragons!"

The Martial Arts Specialists

"I travel all over the country because of *wushu* (Chinese traditional martial arts) competitions," Bai Minxiong (pseudonym) complained, "and it's very difficult for me to maintain my *qing zhen* lifestyle." The Hui *wushu* boxing style is well-known among martial artists, and few practice as hard as young Bai. Unlike many of his secularized Hui friends, Bai struggles over the problems of maintaining his faith and *qing zhen* lifestyle while on the national sports-competition circuit. He is often encouraged by his teammates to give up his "backward" ethnic customs. In some ways, his early training reflects the traditional way Hui learned martial arts. His father was a well-known Ahong and martial arts expert who taught his students *wushu* in the mosque compound. "You never know when you might be called on to defend your religion" Bai remembers his father telling him.

The Hui look up to famous *wushu* artists that took part in "righteous uprisings" (*qiyi*) against oppressive regimes. Under the banner of Zhu Yuanzhang, who established the Ming dynasty in a peasant revolt, were well-known Hui Generals including Chang Yuchun, Hu Dahai, Mu Ying, Lan Yu, Feng Sheng, and Deng Dexing.[5]

Chang Yuchun is said to be the father of the famous "Kaiping spear method" (*kaiping qiangfa*). In the Ming dynasty, three schools of spear-play developed, the Yang, Ma, and Sha methods. These are typical Hui surnames, and Ma Fengtu, a famous Hui martial artist, argues that these were Muslim methods. The "18 fist-fighting exercise of the Hui" is a popular boxing method developed in the Ming. Wu Zhong, a Qing dynasty Hui, developed the famous "eight-diagram boxing" (*bajiquan*). When I visited the Hebei Hui Autonomous County of Mengcun in 1985, known as the home of Hui *wushu*, I was given a demonstration of his method, together with the "six-combination" (*liu he*) spear play carried on by Wu Zhong's descendants, two of whom participated in the national *wushu* competition that year.

Much of Hui martial arts technique revolves around spear play. Wang Xinwu (1983, p. 38), president of the Ningxia *Wushu* Committee and vice-president of the China *Wushu* Committee, argues that this may derive from the influence of Persian sword play. Born in a Hui *wushu* center in Shandong, Master Wang won the 1975 National Tai Ji Quan championship and is one of three masters responsible for formulating the "combined 48 Peking style" of Tai Ji Quan (also known as Tai Ch'i).[6]

Famous twentieth-century Hui *wushu* artists include Ma Fengtu, Ma Qunxi, Ma Xianda, Ma Zhengbang, Zhang Wenguang, and Wang Ziping. Wang Ziping was born in 1881 in Mengcun, Cangxian County, Hebei Province. At 80 years old, he accompanied Premier Zhou Enlai on his visit to Burma and demonstrated Chinese martial arts. During the Republican period, he became known for challenging several foreign boxers that claimed they could easily beat Chinese martial artists. *Wulin zhi,* a recent Chinese movie, portrayed his patriotic exploits in defeating a muscular Russian boxer employed by the Japanese to demonstrate the inferiority of the Chinese "sick man of East Asia" (*dongfang bingfu*). I saw the movie with a Hui friend in Yinchuan. He became quite upset when the movie did not reveal Wang Ziping's Hui identity and at one point the movie even portrayed his wife, in real life a devout Muslim, asking the Buddha to protect his life.

Wang Ziping's daughter, Wang Jurong, an accomplished martial artist in Shanghai, told me that her father's dedicated *qing zhen* life as a Muslim and his rigorous *wushu* exercise led to his long and healthy life. He developed a special set of exercises in 20 forms that would lead to health and longevity. "Wang Ziping himself also did [the exercise] regularly in his old age. The fact that he lived to 93 shows that this set of exercises is well worth the name of 'longevity'" (China Sports, 1984, p. 115).

Zhao Changjun is the 27-year-old student of Ma Zhengbang, the famous Hui *wushu* master from Xi'an. He began studying *wushu* when he was six years old. During the Cultural Revolution he continued his studies at home. He has won the National Wushu Championship five times (1980, 1981, 1982, 1983, and 1985), and has performed in more than 20 countries. "I am a Hui and I'm glad to be competing in Yinchuan, the capital of the Hui Autonomous Region," he told me at the 1985 National Competition, which he won. When I asked him why he worked so hard, he quietly told me, "As a Hui I not only have to compete on behalf of my country, but I also fight for my people. I am Chinese first, but I am also Hui."

The Social Organization of Tight Urban Space

In most respects, urban Hui homes are similar to those of their Han neighbors. There is not much noticeable difference between Hui and Han homes compared with the Northwest. Islamic paraphernalia in most urban Hui homes is generally limited to posting an Islamic calendar that gives the Muslim and Roman dates in Arabic and Chinese, published by the Chinese Islamic Society. Occasionally one comes across an Arabic sign with the *Shahadah* or a Chinese sign indicating that this is a Muslim household (*Musilin zhi jia*) mounted over the door or on the wall. I rarely saw them anywhere else, but in Tianjin's Hongqiao District, along Ma (Horse) Road, where the Hui are most concentrated, many Hui homes mount a small green sign over the outside entrance with the Arabic *Shahadah*. A local told me that they want Han to be able to see clearly which homes are Hui to prevent them from mistakenly bringing pork in through the gateway.

Before the Cultural Revolution, many Hui homes in Oxen Street were distinguished by three incense pots with Qur'anic inscriptions (*luping sanshe*) placed on a low table next to a family Qur'an.[7] This stood in the usual place of ancestral tablets in traditional Han homes. Hajji Muhammad Ali Ma Yue, the former principal of the Niujie Hui Middle School and present Niujie Mosque administrator, explained that Hui use incense in a much different way than the Han. Its purpose is to provide a fragrance that cleans the body and lungs (*muyu xunxiang*). "Besides, incense is not Buddhist in origin—it originally came from the West (*an xi xiang*)," Hajji Ma noted. "Hui incense is longer and thinner than the kind Buddhists use and is produced in Dachang Hui Autonomous County." That is why Hui like to make the distinction that they "stick incense" (*dian xiang*), not "burn incense" (*shao xiang*) as the Han do.

He went on to describe how the incense was used to indicate purity. On the Ramadan holiday, Muslims bring incense into the mosque to indicate their lives have been purified through fasting. Young Hui brides burn incense at weddings to symbolize a pure and chaste life. As the incense fills one's lungs, Imam Ma maintains, it reminds us that Islamic purity is internal. "Hui Muslims are just like our Niujie mosque. On the outside it looks altogether Chinese in style. But on the inside it is Muslim, pure and true (*qing zhen*)."

THE SOCIOECONOMIC CONTEXT OF OXEN STREET HUI IDENTITY

Radical and rapid socioeconomic change has taken place among the Hui in Oxen Street in the almost 40 years since the founding of the People's Republic. Except for the many *qing zhen* restaurants and the imposing mosque, one would not know that it is an urban minority neighborhood that once resembled many ethnic ghettos found in most large cities. One 1930s observer wrote:

> Some may ask whether in the world of business one might have a peaceful and prosperous life without education. Never! In Oxen Street there are countless beggars, peddlers, and men drawing a two wheeled cart, and many unemployed walking in the street with nothing to do—all of these prove my point to be true (S. Wang, 1930, p. 23).

This might well have described many Beijing neighborhoods in the 1930s. Yet, it is interesting that the writer singles out Oxen Street as the worst example of what happens when one refuses to get an education. The author argues that everyone knows the Hui are less-educated than the Han, and look what that did for Oxen Street.

Since 1949, the significant changes in Hui occupation can be broken down into four periods, all related to shifts in government policies: from 1949 to the Great Leap Forward (1949–1958), from the Great Leap Forward to the Cultural Revolution (1958–1966), from the Cultural Revolution to the Third Central Committee Plenum (1966–1979), and from 1979 until now. From 1949 to 1958 the city government assisted the local Hui in its drive for rapid economic development and recovery from the civil war. They recognized the relative poverty and lower education of the Hui compared to the Han and attempted to solve the unemployment problem in Oxen Street through collectivization and retraining of those young enough to study. In 1953, 54% of the Hui in Oxen Street were illiterate, 40% could recognize basic characters, like "10 jin of lamb," and 5.6% were middle-school level. Through establishing evening literacy courses, forming Hui schools that gave preference to local Hui in admittance, and training minority cadres, the state attempted to alleviate this situation. State-run *qing zhen* food stores and restaurants were established during this period to help rationalize the local economy. Hui holidays were permitted and the mosque was restored. Through the active lobbying of the local *jiedao* committee, the government agreed not to allow any buildings to be constructed higher than the mosque within 250 meters. "Not like the Dongsi mosque," one cadre complained, "where people look down on you from the apartment next door while you are praying." One Chinese Islamic Society representative said, "The older people in Oxen Street thank Allah and the party for these changes in their lives."

The period from 1958 to 1966 saw several reforms that had restricting effects on Hui ethnoreligious expression. The Religious System Reform campaigns closed many of the mosques in the city. The Socialist Reconstruction of Industry collectivized Hui private businesses and restaurants into larger state-run units. Interestingly enough, at the very time the state was establishing Nationalities Institutes and Minority Autonomous Regions and Counties, it also promoted policies that were later seen as detrimental to the Hui. This may be related to the strong emphasis on separating religious from ethnic expressions of identity. The state was also concerned during the Great Leap Forward period and the subsequent famine with strengthening its control over minorities, particularly in the border areas, and encouraging national loyalties over local ethnic loyalties.

The Cultural Revolution period saw the continuance and radicalization of many of these assimilative policies. All mosques were closed and former Hui businessmen were criticized as capitalists. Chairman Mao's wife, Jiang Qing, is often quoted as saying: "If you follow socialism, why worry about ethnicity (*minzu*)?" All of the signs for *qing zhen* food stores and restaurants were taken down. The "Hui Elementary School," originally Beijing's famous Northwest Middle School located across from the Oxen Street mosque, changed its name in 1966 to "Oxen Street Number Two Elementary School." While the Dongsi mosque stayed open on Fridays, mainly for foreigners, the Oxen Street mosque was closed and did not reopen until 1980. People were afraid to come to the mosque and risk being branded with the "four hats and eight characters" indicating feudalist superstition and antirevolutionary reactionism. "The Red Guards loved to criticize me," Imam Shi Kunbing, the head Imam of the Niujie mosque, recalled, "and they liked to use the mosque as a place to make big character posters (*dazi bao*)." Hui carried out their traditional

TABLE 5.2
HUI OCCUPATIONAL CHANGE IN A NIUJIE NEIGHBORHOOD,
BY PERCENTAGE OF THOSE EMPLOYED, 1953–1983

Year	*Total Employed	Factory Workers	Service Workers	Profes- sionals	Cadres	Skilled Workers	Farmers	Clergy	Busi- ness
1953	33.1	19.5	0	1.1	0	5.3	2.9	11.7	39.6
1964	35.4	54.9	13.1	5.7	3.3	9.5	5.8	7.1	0
1983	49.4	55.2	15.9	5.1	5.1	1.7	0	0	0

Note. *Total of Hui surveyed varied by year: 1,580 in 1953; 2,306 in 1964; 1,305 in 1983.
Source. Beijing Oxen Street Administrative Committee interview.

funerals quietly, ate at home or at restaurants they knew were still *qing zhen* without the sign, and when asked where they lived often gave only their local street or a false address so people would not know they were from the Oxen Street district.

The years from 1979 to the present may be seen as the fourth period, created by shifts in government policy. After the fall of the Gang of Four in 1976 and the Third Central Committee Plenum in 1979, recognition was given to the importance of nationality identity. The director of the Oxen Street *jiedao* committee, Imam Al-Hajji Salah An Shiwei, recommended the new agenda include the following: correcting the errors of the Cultural Revolution, restoring work units with nationality characteristics (nursery, elementary, middle, and religious schools, hospitals, restaurants, and stores), carrying out the new policy of strengthening minority education, training minority cadres, solving the "living problems" (*shenghuo wenti*) the Hui experience in maintaining the *qing zhen* lifestyle, allowing traditional Hui handicrafts and private businesses to reemerge, and repairing mosques and religious structures. Initially the Oxen Street mosque was given 400,000 yuan for reopening and reconstruction, with further major repairs planned.

The Business Hui: Urban Entrepreneurial Traditions

The Hui have long been known for their penchant for small enterprise. "Eight legs on the ground, two occupations" (*ba gen shang, liang ba dao*) was the characterization of the Oxen Street Hui: They operated food stands on small tables that sold either meat (beef and lamb) or pastries. The Hui in Niujie, however, are no longer engaged in small private enterprises. As in most cities, the majority of the Hui are factory workers. This has been the norm since the instigation of the 1950s Socialist Transformation of Industry campaigns, when small businesses were combined into larger collectives. The radical shifts in Niujie occupation over the last 30 years are reflected in Table 5.2.

These changes in occupation have led to major alterations in income and lifestyle. While Hui have traditionally been known as small merchants and tradesmen, their largest population is involved in agriculture. In chapter 2, Table 2.4 indicated that while the largest number of Hui are engaged in agriculture and husbandry (60.75%) they are more engaged in production and transport (22.25%) than any other nationality. This supports the traditional proclivity of Hui for trade, transport, and small enterprise.

TABLE 5.3
INCOME AND HOUSEHOLD COMMODITIES CHANGE IN NIUJIE, BEIJING, 1953–1983

Year	Household Monthly Income[*]	Individual Monthly Income	Bicycles	Radios	Sewing Machines	Watches	Television Sets
1953	36.12 (yuan)	6.12	5	2	1	0	0
1964	94.30	16.71	19	81	32	217	0
1983	125.30	34.08	519	256	187	831	349

Note. [*]Total of Hui households surveyed varied by year: 410 households in 1953; 410 in 1964; 355 in 1983. In 1983, new commodities reported included: 76 washing machines, 243 electric fans, 9 refrigerators, 9 recorders.

Source. Beijing Oxen Street Administrative Committee interview.

While change in income and ownership of household luxury items is difficult to measure, because of inflationary fluctuations and the cheaper availability of some new technologies, Table 5.3 helps in gaining some insight into recent changes in Hui households.

In 1953, it was found that there were 3,000 unemployed Hui in Oxen Street, representing about 70% of the population (see S. Wang, 1930, p. 9). Of 1,305 Hui surveyed in 1983, 49.4% were employed and 10.9% were retired. There are just over 100 *qing zhen* restaurants in the city and about 250 small food stands (*xiao chidian*; refer to Figure 5.1). The study noted that only about three to five workers out of ten in *qing zhen* restaurants are Hui, with about half the workers in *qing zhen* food stores (*fanshipin*) as Hui. This breakdown matches with my own informal survey. The vast majority of Hui in Oxen Street are engaged in factory work or in service professions (*fuwuyuan*), such as clerks in department stores or waiters in restaurants.

The Girl Next Door: Finding a Mate in a Han City

"I just don't know what to do," Yang Dexin (assumed), my older Hui friend told me. "Both of my daughters should be married, but my wife and parents just won't allow them to marry a Han. Many of our friends' children have intermarried and we have seen how inconvenient it is. They never meet any Hui boys at work, and our neighborhood does not have any likely prospects. And young people today refuse to let us make the arrangements. They turn down everyone we suggest. I guess I'll go talk to the Ahong and see if he knows of anyone." Yang Dexin had not been to a mosque in years. He was a member of the Communist Party and a cadre in a prominent institute. Yet, he was still adamantly opposed to allowing his daughter to intermarry. Nevertheless, intermarriages often take place in urban areas, and studies indicate there has been some increase. Most recent intermarriages revealed in the 1982 census, however, suggest that the Hui in Beijing are continuing to follow the traditional pattern of bringing in Han brides rather than marrying their women out. This tradition continues despite official policy that encourages intermarriage.[8]

This is a sensitive issue among the Hui in Oxen Street. While local cadres did not discourage me from asking any economic or political questions in the course of

TABLE 5.4
ETHNIC COMPOSITION AND INTERMARRIAGES OF HOUSEHOLDS IN MA DIAN

Household Type	Households With Han (Households)	(Individuals)	Households With Hui (Households)	(Individuals)	Households With Manchu (Households)	(Individuals)
All Han	608	2,196	—	—	—	—
All Hui	—	—	250	845	—	—
All Manchu	—	—	—	—	6	21
Hui–Han marriages	30	30	30	72	—	—
Manchu–Han marriages	22	40	—	—	22	42
Hui–Manchu marriages	—	—	2	5	2	2
Totals:	664	2,270	286	939	30	65

Source. 1982 Census. Adapted from Chen, 1983, pp. 48, 51.

my research, they warned that the Hui on Oxen Street would be upset if I asked about intermarriage. Conservative Hui are embarrassed if anyone in their family has intermarried, and they often will deny it. As a result I rarely asked this question in my Oxen Street interviews and had to rely on outside studies for data. The *jiedao* committee reports that in the Oxen Street district there were 37 mixed Hui–Han households, only two of which were Han men with Hui wives. There were no households on Oxen Street with two generations of intermarriages.

Studies based on the 1982 census reports have revealed much regarding increasing intermarriage trends in two Beijing Hui neighborhoods. The demographer Zhang Tianlu (1986, p. 30) reports that whereas a survey of 350 households in the Niujie area found only two Hui–Han intermarriages in 1953, and another survey in 1964 turned up none, the 1982 census revealed 38 Hui–Han intermarriages out of 491 households. In the multiethnic northern Beijing neighborhood of Ma Dian, 11.2% of the 939 Hui have intermarried with either Han or Manchu, 7.8% of the 2,270 Han have intermarried with Hui or Manchu, and 80% of the 65 Manchu nationality members have intermarried with Han or Hui. Table 5.4 gives the multiethnic structure of the intermarriages.

It is noteworthy that as the concentration of Hui goes up, there is a decrease in intermarriage. In the Tang Fang neighborhood of Oxen Street, there are a third more intermarriages among the Han than among the Hui. Of the 1,814 Hui, 10.2% have intermarried; among the 1,272 Han, 15.3% have intermarried; and among the 21 Manchu, 83.3% have intermarried. In addition to the increased possibility of finding a Hui spouse in the Oxen Street area where Hui are more concentrated, this lower percentage might also have something to do with a more conservative Hui population. Clearly, when possible, the Hui tend to marry their own.

TABLE 5.5
COMPOSITION OF ETHNIC INTERMARRIAGES
IN TANG FANG NEIGHBORHOOD, NIUJIE DISTRICT

Household Type	Households	Individuals	Hui	Han	Manchu
Hui–Han Marriages					
Male Han—Female Hui	35	132	94	38	—
Male Hui—Female Han	17	76	52	24	—
Manchu–Han Marriages					
Male Manchu—Female Han	7	27	—	11	16
Male Han—Female Manchu	3	7	—	4	3
Totals:	62	242	146	77	19

Source. 1982 Census. Adapted from Chen, 1983, pp. 72–74.

But when they do intermarry, it is important to know who it is that marries out. Traditionally the Hui have taken in Han girls and rarely married their women out. The continuation of this practice in the city is substantiated by the 1982 data in Table 5.5.

There is a similar structure of intermarriage in Ma Dian, where slightly more of the intermarriages had Hui women marrying out (7 out of 34, or 20%), as opposed to Tang Fang where 11% of the intermarriages involve Hui women marrying out (24 out of 208). The interesting feature in comparing Manchu–Han and Hui–Han marriages in Ma Dian is that among both groups, 13.6% and 20% of the women marrying out were Hui and Manchu, respectively, whereas 86% and 80% of the women marrying in were Han. In Tang Fang, 67.3% of the Hui men and 70% of the Manchu men intermarried with Han women. Both Hui and Manchu seem to be reluctant to give their women away.

The question of intermarriage is a personal one that involves much decision making and debate. A Hui–Han intermarriage ceremony that I attended in 1984 in the Tianqiao district, a concentrated Hui area in south Beijing with 80 to 90 Hui households, was one of the few cases where a Hui woman married a Han man. However, in this case she did not marry out. After much discussion, the groom decided to move in, a traditional uxorilocal practice in Chinese society known as "seeking a son-in-law" (*zhao nuxu*). It is unfortunate that the census data discussed earlier does not reveal if any of the intermarriages were uxorilocal. We might find that it is quite common when the bride is a Hui. In this case, the couple had known each other since high school, 6 years earlier, but did not become interested in each other until recently. They became reacquainted through a mutual friend and decided to get married 1 year ago. At first the parents on both sides disagreed. Neither family had experienced any intermarriages, and the Hui were especially antagonistic to the idea. The Han side happened to live in the Oxen Street district, and since they were familiar with many Hui, they were the first to agree. After the groom promised his family would clean all the pots when the bride ate with them and respect the Hui customs wherever possible, the bride's side reluctantly agreed. "Besides," her mother said, "the two are in their mid-twenties, both high-school graduates, and there are no other prospects in sight."

It was only later, when they began to discuss the lifestyle problems, that the groom accepted the father-in-law's invitation to move in. They would build them a separate room in the small family courtyard. While the groom agreed to move in, it was atypical in that they are not planning on giving their future child the bride's surname, the usual Chinese uxorilocal custom. "It was merely more convenient to live here than with my family," the groom cheerfully admitted.[9]

Most urban Hui intermarriages are simple and do not involve the mosque. This one was unique in that the girl came from a fairly religious family and she "believed in Islam in her heart" and encouraged her spouse to do the same. They went to the mosque together and spoke with the Ahong. "Before I had no religion," the groom said, "I didn't believe in anything. But, after talking with the Ahong, I became interested in the Hui religion and decided to believe." Imam Shi Kunbing, of the Niujie Mosque, relates the four conditions of his marrying a Han and Hui: They must (1) believe in only one God, Allah; (2) follow Muhammad's teachings; (3) agree to the rules of Islam regarding marriage, i.e., no divorce or adultery; and (4) learn that the basis of this is all in the Qur'an.

On the day of the wedding, five Ahong, two from the Niujie Mosque and three from the local Tianqiao Mosque, gathered in the home of the bride. After going to the groom's house for a short *qing zhen* meal and an exchange of gifts, the new couple returned to the bride's home accompanied by his family, their gifts, and the popping of firecrackers as they entered the alleyway. While the groom wore a Western-style suit, the bride was dressed in a traditional red velvet *qipao*. On the gateway to their yard they posted a large red sign with gold Arabic lettering of the *Qing Zhen Yan* instead of the traditional Chinese ideographs for "double happiness" (*shuangxi*). Over the door to the couple's new room they posted a new green placard with the Arabic *Shahadah* lettered in white. It was the first time the two families had met each other. After exchanging greetings in the courtyard, the couple went inside to meet with the Ahong who were drinking tea and eating snacks.

When they entered the room, the five Ahong were led in prayer individually by the senior Oxen Street Mosque Ahong. The father and mother's brother (*jiujiu*) of the bride joined them in the room and donned white Hui hats. Portions of the Qur'an were recited by all the Ahong simultaneously, and when they finished, the senior Ahong addressed the couple (*yizabu*). He asked if the woman was willing (*yuanyi*) to marry and if the man would accept (*jieshou*) her, and whether both parents agreed (*tongyi*). When they assented, he lectured them on the importance of Islam in their lives, belief in God, and preserving the Hui *qing zhen* lifestyle. "If your job makes it difficult for you to live the Hui life, then change your work. It's easy to change your job, but not your life." They then signed their names on a special registration card that the Ahong also signed, and the bride gave her husband some candy, her first act in her new but traditional role as wife and hostess. The two Yihewani Ahong departed and the Gedimu Ahong remained for the subsequent feast (*ninzhi ganjing*). No wine or cigarettes were served at the wedding. Later that evening the groom had a party with his friends where both items were in abundance.

TABLE 5.6
ETHNIC COMPOSITION OF ENTERING HIGH SCHOOL STUDENTS
FROM NIUJIE, 1979–1981

	1979		1980		1981		Total	
	Han	Hui	Han	Hui	Han	Hui	Han	Hui
Students	54	3	37	2	35	2	123	10
Percentage of ethnic group	0.13	0.03	0.09	0.2	0.8	0.04	0.29	0.07
Percentage of class	94.7	5.3	95.0	5.0	86.0	14.0	92.0	8.0

Source. Adapted from *Beijing City,* 1984, p. 21.

The relatively low percentage of intermarriages that I found in Niujie and Ma Dian is far surpassed by the many Hui–Han intermarriages occurring in southern urban areas. Among 20 Hui households I interviewed in Shanghai, there was not one without a member of the extended family married to a Han. There were Hui–Han intermarriages among all of the married children in seven of the households. One Hui student from a southern city told me that though his parents were both traditional Hui, his wife was Han, his three sisters were married to Han, and all of his cousins on both sides were married to Han. He began to eat pork at the age of 17 during a long hospital stay while away at school.[10] Now he eats pork all the time. His son, of course, is also registered as a Hui. He told me that his son was "100% Hui." When I asked him what he meant, he said: "My son's blood is Hui." While Pillsbury (1976) has noted that this is a common response among Hui in Taiwan, I rarely encountered it in the PRC, and then only in southern areas. Hui indicated that the children of Han–Hui marriages were "just as Hui" as other Hui children.

EDUCATING FATIMA: RELIGIOUS ISSUES AND URBAN MOBILITY

Despite a great deal of emphasis on minority education since the "golden period" of the 1950s, the Hui still lag behind the Han, especially in post-primary education. Out of 364 Han who graduated from Beijing's Number One Middle School in 1982, there were 47 (12%) who went on to either college or higher technical schools. Out of the seven Hui who graduated, not one went on to higher schooling (Beijing City, 1984, p. 20). Table 5.6 gives differences in Hui and Han high school entrance from 1979 to 1981 in the Oxen Street District.

From 1979 to 1981 there was a slight decline among both Han and Hui entering high school. Although the Hui occupy about one-fourth of the Oxen Street population, they represent only 5% to 14% of those entering high school. Less than 6% of the Oxen Street area Hui had attended middle school prior to 1955. A 1983 education survey of the Xuanwu district (where Oxen Street is located) revealed that out of every 1,000 Hui, 5.1% are college graduates, 22.7% are high school graduates, 30.7% are middle school graduates, and 41.8% are primary school graduates. The same survey among Han in the Xuanwu District revealed that 23.34% are college

TABLE 5.7
EDUCATIONAL LEVEL OF MUSLIM MINORITIES IN CHINA IN PERCENT, 1982

Educational Level	Hui	Uygur	Kazakh	Dong-xiang	Kyrgyz	Salar	Tadjik	Uzbek	Bao'an	Tatar	All Ethnic Groups	All China
University graduate	0.5	0.2	0.4	0	0.3	0.2	0.2	0.2	0.2	39.0	0.2	0.5
Undergraduate	2.5	0.1	0.1	0	0.1	0.2	0.1	0.9	0.1	11.0	0.1	0.2
Senior middle school	7.0	5.0	5.0	1.0	5.0	1.0	4.0	11.0	2.0	15.0	5.0	8.0
Junior middle school	19.0	12.0	17.0	3.0	11.0	5.0	11.0	22.0	6.0	25.0	15.0	20.0
Primary school	30.0	37.0	49.0	8.0	40.0	18.0	38.0	40.0	12.0	40.0	37.0	40.0
Illiterate*	41.0	45.0	29.0	87.0	41.0	74.0	49.0	20.0	78.0	9.0	45.0	32.0

Note. *Population age 6 and above who cannot read or can read very little.
Source. Adopted from Population Census Office, 1987, pp. xvi, 29; Gladney, 1996, p. 20.

graduates, 21.54% are high school graduates, 25% are middle school graduates, and 17.58% received an elementary education. More than four times as many Han graduate from college as Hui in this area, and there are almost two and a half as many Hui with only an elementary school education as there are Han. In 1982, 1.2% of the Han students who took the high school exam were admitted, whereas only 0.67% of the minority examinees were admitted (Beijing City, 1984, p. 21).

While it is generally true that Hui educational level is lower than that of the Han majority among whom they live, at the national level, Hui educational level has apparently fared well. Table 5.7 reveals that the Hui have kept pace with the national average and are substantially better educated than the other Muslim minorities.[11] The main advantage the Hui have is language: Other Muslim minorities have to contend with learning the Han language as a second language to enter middle school and university.[12] The Hui speak the Han dialects wherever they live.

While educational levels had not changed dramatically for Muslims in China by 1990 (see Table 5.8), in the 8 years since the 1982 census, there were some gains. The gains do not appear to have been as dramatic as for all of China, however, and this may indicate that resistance to sending Muslim children to coeducational schools is still strong. In addition, the state continues to unilaterally administer a centrally controlled curriculum, with the result that minority students receive little information about their history, least of all such religious subjects as Islam. This may propel more devout families to seek other educational alternatives in the mosque or to keep their children, especially their daughters, at home, in the fields, or in the marketplace, rather than sending them to school.

Some Hui parents in the Oxen Street district have told me that, while they are glad for the Hui schools and the priority Hui are now receiving in education, they feel their children would be more motivated to study if there was more ethnic content. Many of them remember that Hui schools in the early 1950s often invited famous Hui scholars, such as Bai Shouyi and Ma Songting to give lectures on Hui

TABLE 5.8
EDUCATIONAL LEVEL OF MUSLIM MINORITIES IN CHINA IN PERCENT, 1990

Educational Level	Hui	Uygur	Kazakh	Dong-xiang	Kyrgyz	Salar	Tadjik	Uzbek	Bao'an	Tatar	All China
University graduate	0.6	0.5	0.5	0.05	0.3	0.3	0.2	2.6	0.2	3.6	0.5
Undergraduate	0.9	0.4	0.7	0.08	0.5	0.3	0.3	1.9	0.1	2.5	2.4
Technical school†	1.6	1.6	2.6	0.3	2.4	0.9	2.1	4.7	1.0	5.8	17.6
Senior middle school	6.2	3.5	5.5	0.6	3.4	1.6	2.5	10.8	2.9	11.0	6.4
Junior middle school	19.9	11.9	16.4	2.8	10.2	6.3	9.3	20.3	7.2	22.0	23.3
Primary school	29.1	43.3	43.9	12.0	43.4	18.8	40.4	33.7	16.2	32.7	37.2
Semiliterate or illiterate	33.1	26.6	12.3	82.6	24.9	68.7	33.5	8.3	68.8	4.9	22.2

Note. †Data for "Technical school" was not provided for 1982 figures.
Source. Adopted from Department of Population Statistics, 1994, pp. 70–73, 76.

history and on historic Muslim Chinese personages. The Hui middle school also offered Arabic as a second language, so they did not have to go to the mosque to learn it. Beijing Hui parents are not tempted to withdraw their children from school and send them to the mosque for religious education like many Northwestern Hui. Instead, they argue that there is more of a need to integrate secular and religious education in order to motivate their children. They also point out that the Islamic schools, even with the course for training Imams at the Chinese Islamic Association in the Oxen Street district, cannot supply enough Imams for as many mosques as need them. One of the reasons is that many young men, upon graduation, use their Arabic or Persian to become interpreters or translators overseas, where they can travel and earn more money, instead of becoming Imams. The distinction between ethnicity and Islam in the city is still too strong for most Hui parents and they think it might help the country if the two were brought closer together.

GOVERNMENT POLICY AND URBAN STRATEGIES

The state's favorable policy toward its urban minorities is having a significant impact on their ethnoreligious identity. The Hui receive many small "special considerations" as a minority nationality that may be insignificant when taken alone, but together are beginning to have an influence in their status and living conditions.

Lifestyle Benefits

Most work units with many Hui workers give a lifestyle bonus (*shenghuo butie*) of four to six yuan to help offset the cost of buying more expensive beef, lamb, or chicken. While this is not a lot of money for the individual, a frugal family with several working members might save a fair amount over time. Urban Hui receive special oil and meat coupons that allow them to purchase beef, lamb, and vegetable oil in larger quantities at a reduced price. In Niujie, Hui could buy twice as much vegetable oil as Han and with their coupons they can buy twice as much beef or lamb from the state stores. Beef and lamb are becoming more popular among the Han with the result that the free market price is considerably higher than pork. The state ration system allows Hui to have better access to the limited supplies of beef and lamb at an affordable price.

Han coworkers of one young Hui factory worker I knew were constantly joking that even though he ate pork, he continued to receive his five yuan a month and extra ration coupons. They thought he had the best of both worlds: He could buy oil and beef at a cheaper rate and was not afraid to eat pork. No one was angry with him because, they said, "it was the government's money" (*guojia de qian*) and everyone should seek to receive all to which they are entitled.

Privileges in Education and Birth Planning

Like other minorities, the Hui in Niujie receive special consideration on their exams for entrance to middle school, high school, and college. In general, they receive two "levels" of 10 points each for college entrance preference. For example, if the threshold for college entrance on the state exams is 300 points, a Hui who scores 280 points will be accepted. This may make a difference. I knew a Hui who scored 281 on the exam and was admitted to Beijing Normal University (*Beijing Shifan Daxue*). His Han neighbor complained bitterly of this to me, as he scored 295 and was not admitted to the college of his choice, but had to go to a "television university" (*dianshi daxue*) where most courses are taught on videocassette. Athletes who place among the top six (*qian liu ming*) in provincial competitions are also given two stage preferences. Hence, it is conceivable that a Hui athlete could score 260 on the exam and still be admitted to college with a total score of 300 since he receives four stage preferences. Preference for high school and college minority education is just beginning to show long-term effects, and 1990 records should reveal a significant improvement over the 1979 to 1981 figures cited earlier.

Urban Hui are allowed to marry 2 years earlier than Han, but they are not allowed to have two children with urban residency. Only Hui with rural residency or those who recently moved to the city are allowed to have two children. This is leading to a growing number of hypergamous marriages between Hui women from the countryside and urban Hui who are interested in having at least two children (see chapter 6). Most urban Hui, like the Han (Whyte & Parish, 1984, pp. 161–162), do not want more than two children, especially if at least one is male. Minority members also tend to receive other special considerations when there are opportunities for promotion, wage increase, or assignment for housing. It is a slight edge, but an edge nevertheless.

Local Response to Favorable Policies

This edge, of the minority population receiving special considerations, is having an influence. In the Oxen Street district, out of 34 district representatives to the city government, 12 are Hui (35.3%), more than their one-fourth population ratio. Two

TABLE 5.9
ETHNICITY SELECTION AMONG OFFSPRING
FROM INTERMARRIED HOUSEHOLDS IN MA DIAN

Household Type	Total Households	Total Children	Select Hui	Select Han	Select Manchu
Hui–Han marriage	30	33	33	0	—
Manchu–Hui marriage	2	3	3	—	0
Manchu–Han marriage	22	35	—	16	19

Source. Adapted from 1982 Census, unpublished report.

Hui from this district are national Chinese People's Political Consultative Conference (CPPCC) representatives, 5 are city representatives, and 16 represent the district. For the first time, many young urban Hui are seeing participation in the local political organizations as real upward mobility strategies.

The rise in the status of local Hui, and possibilities for income and lifestyle improvements through favorable policies, has also led to a significant shift in Han–Hui relations. Once reluctant to marry Hui as culturally different, and sometimes thought inferior to Han, many local Han are now more open to interethnic marriage. The children of these intermarriages are now invariably given minority status. Table 5.9 reveals that in 1982 all of the offspring of Hui intermarriages, whether with Han or Manchu, were registered as Hui, whereas only 19 of the 35 children of Manchu–Han intermarriages chose Manchu status.

The fact that offspring of Manchu–Han marriages are less inclined to be registered as minorities than the offspring of Hui intermarriages reveals the importance of preserving and passing on ethnic identity among the Hui. This may be related to the special privileges accorded to the Hui due to their dietary restrictions that are not applicable to Manchu (detailed later). Out of 48 Hui–Han intermarriages in Tang Fang, Oxen Street district, only eight offspring chose to be Han. The government requires parents to decide the registration of their children until the age of 18 when they are allowed to choose for themselves. I have not yet met anyone who chose Han registration in recent years.

In his fascinating comparison between three multiethnic communities based on the 1982 census, Zhang Tianlu (1986, p. 32) found some interesting data regarding interethnic marriage. In the Niujie district, out of 38 Hui–Han intermarried households with 45 offspring, 33 children, or 75%, were registered as Hui. By contrast, out of six Han–Manchu intermarriages, only four of the eight children chose Manchu ethnicity (50%). In Beimujialing Hui Autonomous Village on the outskirts of Beijing, there were 16 Hui–Han intermarriages. Of 19 children, 17 chose to be registered as Hui (89.47%). In the one Han–Manchu household, the two children were registered as Han. Most striking, however, was his discovery that in the Tanying Manchu and Mongol joint autonomous village, also in the rural suburbs of Beijing, there was a high number of intermarriages between Manchu and Han (146 out of 175 intermarriages in the village), 20 Mongol–Han intermarriages, seven Mongol–Manchu intermarriages, one Hui–Han intermarriage, and one Hui–Mongol

This billboard indicates Islamic tourist sites in Oxen Street, including the Niujie Mosque, Hui Hospital, China Islamic Association Headquarters, Hui Elementary School, and Hui High School. October 1995.

intermarriage. More than three-fourths (76.8%) of all children born to mixed couples registered as minorities. A similar percentage (73%) of the Manchu–Han offspring chose Manchu nationality; 94% of the Mongol–Han offspring chose Mongol nationality; and 100% of the Hui–Han and Hui–Mongol offspring chose to be registered as Hui. Interestingly, children born to the Mongol–Manchu households registered only slightly more often as Mongol (60%) than as Manchu (40%). This indicates that there is not much of a difference in preference for nationality selection between urban and rural areas. When they have a choice, most people want to be a minority nationality in the People's Republic.

THE CULTURE OF PURITY: HUI IDENTITY IN THE CITY

This chapter has examined some of the interests and issues confronting the Hui in Oxen Street, an urban Hui community in Beijing. For them, ethnoreligious identity does not lie in the correct interpretations and applications of Islamic doctrines. Nor does it mean a strict accounting of genealogical descent from foreign Muslim ancestors. It lies somewhere in between. Constantly negotiated, variously expressed, Hui identity in the city is often difficult to describe. It has much to do with practical concerns, such as maintaining the *qing zhen* lifestyle, finding a spouse, testing into the right school, and obtaining advantageous employment. Yet, all of these decisions are made from the perspective of a tradition that is unavoidable. It must be reckoned with, even among those urban Hui who attempt to discount, hide, or reject it. For those who accept, reinterpret, and sometimes manipulate it, ethnoreligious identity is often authenticated and judged by one's *qing zhen* lifestyle. Cultural traditions that are maintained or rejected represent one's ancestral heritage. The truth and relevance of urban Hui ancestry is expressed in terms of a pure (*qing zhen*) life.

It is a popular belief, particularly among those influenced by assimilationist ideas, that Hui in the urban areas of China have been thoroughly sinicized. Measured against Middle Eastern Muslims, or even Northwestern conservative Muslim communities, the Hui hardly appear different from the Han. Pointing to the fact that the Hui in urban areas are more secularized, rarely wear Muslim dress, and sometimes even (among the young) eat pork, they have generally been ignored and absented from the social landscape. Indeed, many accounts of China's cities have almost thoroughly ignored ethnicity, as if China's urban context, like China itself, was monocultural. This study has shown otherwise. Not only do Hui maintain a vibrant sense of their identity and community, but they play an important role, and have for centuries, in China's urban affairs. Hui traditions have influenced much of China's urban life, as anyone who stops for a skewer of roast mutton on almost any street corner or a "Mongolian hot pot" in many Hui restaurants will discover. These ethnic foods have become so popular that even Han restaurants have tried to imitate them; but locals know the Hui cooks still do it better.

Hui are no longer reluctant to admit their ethnic heritage. The promulgation of recent policies and socioeconomic change has radically altered the ethnoreligious setting for Hui. Not only are the Hui prospering economically, but they are growing in population. As a direct result of this policy, Han are becoming more interested in marrying minorities, and the offspring of mixed marriages are increasingly choosing minority ethnicity. That one has the legal right to formally choose one's nationality at the age of 18 demonstrates the state's strong hand in shaping ethnic identity in China. The resurgence of Hui identity and its relevance in the social setting demonstrates that ethnic identity is quickly being disassociated with feudalism and backwardness in China. Attention to which aspects of that identity are being revived reveals much about the nature of Hui identity and its relation with government policy in the urban social context.

Notes

[1]This legend is found in the seventeenth or eighteenth century anonymous *Huihui yuanlai* (*The Origin of the Hui*) and reproduced in several Western accounts (Broomhall, 1910, pp. 61–83; Leslie, 1986, p. 74; Mason, 1929, pp. 46–53; Parker, 1910, pp. 245–251; Li & Luckert, 1994, pp. 237–240). A Soviet Dungan version is also discussed in Dyer, 1981-1983, pp. 545–570.

[2]A version of this story is given in Wang Shoujie, 1930, p. 2; and the historical background is in Yang Yongchang, 1981, pp. 60–62.

[3]Note that the second son, Na Su La Ding, bears resemblance to the famous Yuan Dynasty official, Nasredin (also, Na Su Lu Ding), the supposed ancestor of the Hui in Na village, Ningxia (see chapter 3) and of the Ding in Chendai, Fujian (see chapter 6).

[4]For an extended analysis of this incident, known as China's Salman Rushdie case, see Gladney, 1994d.

[5]Not only do the Hui believe that there were many Hui generals who helped overthrow the Yuan, but in a fascinating example of ethnohistory, one Hui historian has argued that he is a direct descendant of the Ming Taizu Emperor, Zhu Yuanzhang, who was married to a Muslim and he himself may have been a Muslim (Chang, 1988, pp. 1–4).

[6]Wang Xinwu is pictured demonstrating his Tai Ji Quan style in *Inside Kungfu,* September 1985, p. 11, and discussed in the report on an Australian teams' participation in the 1985 China National *Wushu* Championship that took place in Yinchuan, Ningxia which I attended.

[7]Several exquisite, antique porcelain vases and incense holders with Islamic insignia are on display in the reception room of the Oxen Street Mosque.

[8]The following is drawn from a 1978 policy statement that was based on an historical survey of ethnic intermarriage over the centuries in China:

"This serves as historical evidence of the fact that 'interracial marriage' adds to unity among nationalities.... The 'gang of four' totally negated 'interracial marriage.'...In fact, 'interracial marriage' expands and strengthens economic and cultural exchanges among fraternal nationalities in our country. It is conducive to social development and pushes history forward" (in Banister, 1987, p. 319).

[9]While Gamble (1933, pp. 198–242) gives extensive descriptions of several traditional weddings in Beijing, he does not give any cases of uxorilocal or minor marriage. More study needs to be done on this before we can tell if this case of uxorilocal marriage is typical in northern cities. Whyte and Parish (1984, pp. 144–145) find that though urbanites expressed an openness to living "wherever there is room," and even some new preferences for uxorilocal marriage, their data revealed that only 3% of couples lived with the wife's parents, with the vast majority establishing their own separate neo-local residence according to work and school assignments, generally related to the husband's work-unit. Male-oriented arrangements, they conclude, continue to be the norm.

[10]In order to insure that Hui in Beijing can stay in the hospital without fear of violating *qing zhen,* the city built a Hui hospital in the Niujie district. While this hospital practices only Western and Chinese traditional medicines, Hui doctors interviewed in Beijing, Xi'an, and Shanghai have said that there are certain Hui treatments for illnesses that differ from the Han and they claim that early Islamic practices had an early influence on Chinese traditional medicine. These have never been catalogued systematically.

[11]The Uzbek and Tatar minorities have fared very well in education since they are almost exclusively living in urban areas in Xinjiang.

[12]Note that the Dongxiang have the highest illiteracy rate in China, at 87%.

6 / Chendai: Ethnic Revitalization in Quanzhou, Fujian

At the end of 5 day's journey, you arrive at the noble and handsome city of Zaitun [Quanzhou], which has a port on the sea-coast celebrated for the resort of shipping, loaded with merchandise, that is afterwards distributed through every part of the province. . . . It is indeed impossible to convey an idea of the concourse of merchants and the accumulation of goods, in this which is held to be one of the largest and most commodious ports in the world.

—Marco Polo

Ding Yongwei beeped me. On a February 1994 visit to Quanzhou city in southern Fujian province, Ding called me from his private car on his cellular phone.[1] I received the call on the beeper (in Chinese, known as a "*bi pi ji*") that he had lent me (and had to show me how to use, since I had never used one before).[2] When I first met Ding in 1984, I had just begun to study the collection of villages where the people surnamed Ding resided, officially recognized as members of the Hui minority nationality in 1979 (see Gladney, 1996a, pp. 290–295). The villagers at that time still depended primarily on agriculture and aquaculture for their living and had only just begun to experience the rapid rise in income that would lead to Ding lending me his beeper just 10 years later. In a formal interview, Liu Zhengqing, the Vice-Mayor of Chendai Township, told me that the Ding villagers were so wealthy that in one village of 600 households, there were 700 telephones, most of them cellular.

When I asked my old friend Ding Yongwei if he was doing well, he held out his cellular phone and declared: "If I wasn't wealthy, could I be holding this?" (*Bu fu de hua, zheige nade qi ma?*). He later explained that the government's decision to recognize the Ding community as members of the Hui minority in 1979 was primarily responsible not only for their newfound economic prosperity, but also for a tremendous subsequent fascination for their ethnic and religious roots. In this case, the Ding claim to be descended from foreign Muslim traders who settled in Quanzhou in the ninth century. When I first began learning about this area in the early 1980s, these Hui were known not only to be among the least developed in southern Fujian, but also the most assimilated into the local Han Chinese culture (Zhuang, 1993). Now just 10 years later, the members of the Hui nationality in this township have prospered far more quickly than the Han Fujianese, accounting for one-third of the township's income, even though their population amounts to only one-seventh of the total.

Ding Hui lineage hall, Chendai Township, Fuijan Province. June 1986.

In February 1940, representatives from the China Muslim National Salvation Society in Beijing also arrived in Quanzhou in search of its ancient Muslim community, just as I did in May 1984. They also interviewed Ding lineage members who resided at that time in Chendai Town, Jinjiang County. In response to a question on his ethnic background, Ding Deqian answered: "We are Muslims [*Huijiao ren*], our ancestors were Muslims" (Zhang, 1940, p. 1). It was not until 1979, however, that these Muslims became *minzu*, an ethnic nationality. After attempting to convince the state for years that they belonged to the Hui nationality, they were eventually accepted. The story of the late recognition of the members of the Ding lineage in Chendai Town by the State Commission for Nationality Affairs as members of the Hui nationality and their more recent ethnic revitalization reveals much about ethnogenesis and state policy in China.

Outside of Quanzhou, there are 13 villages with the single surname of Ding, with a population numbering more than 16,000 and known as "*wan ren Ding*" (the 10,000-person Ding). When I spoke with members of the Ding lineage in 1984, they also strongly affirmed their ethnic identity as Hui people (*Huimin*), twentieth-generation descendants of Arab and Persian ancestors. They pointed to an abundance of preserved family genealogies, grave stones, stele inscriptions, and dynastic records as undeniable proof of their claim. For these Hui, their claim to ethnic status is based on the veracity (*zhen*) of their ancestral heritage, rather than the purity (*qing*) of their Islamic belief.

If the evidence is so overwhelming that the Ding lineage are descendants of Arab and Persian ancestors, why did it take so long for them to be recognized officially as members of the Hui minority? The answer lies in the nature of their lifestyle and the current policy of ethnic identification in the People's Republic of

China. Ding identity is radically different than the Hui identity of Na villagers described in chapter 3, representing the other extreme of ethnoreligious expression among the Hui in China.

Along China's southern coast are several lineages of Hui for whom Islamic purity is not nearly as critical as the truth of foreign ancestry to their ethnic identity and understanding of *qing zhen*. Most of the lineages that were not recognized, and several that have yet to be officially accepted as Hui, are located along the Southeast Coast and include Hui surnamed Ding, Guo, Jin, Bai, Ma, Huang, and Pu (see Figure 6.1). In Quanzhou, Fujian, a typical response to a question about Hui ancestry was:

> Of course I know my family are descended from foreign Muslims. My ancestor was an Arab, and our name was changed to Jin in the Ming dynasty. We have our family genealogy to prove it. . . .We are Hui because we are descended from these foreign ancestors.[3]

This interview was conducted in a Hui household that openly includes pork in its diet and practices Chinese folk-religious traditions in ancestral worship. While cognizant of their Islamic heritage, these Hui have not practiced Islam nor attended the mosque for generations. Because they do not follow Islamic practices, until recently, the Chinese State Commission for Nationality Affairs did not recognize many of these individuals in Quanzhou as members of the Hui nationality.

It is not surprising that under a Chinese policy resembling the culture unit model, the Chendai Hui, who lack most of the outward cultural traits that should distinguish them as Hui, would have difficulty in being officially recognized. Chendai Hui, in almost every respect, are culturally similar to their Han nationality neighbors: They speak the Southern Min (Hokkien) dialect, light incense to ancestors in their lineage temple, do not believe in Islam, and, remarkably, publicly eat pork. The last item is most critical for understanding why it has taken so long for the Ding in Chendai to attain recognition as being Hui. Yet, there are Hui who do not follow Islamic dietary restrictions, as the instance of the Fujian Hui demonstrates. Many urban Hui youths in Shanghai and Beijing say they respect their family's traditions while at home, but are more casual (*suibian*) when outside, often eating in Han restaurants. There are also many instances in China of Hui who do not believe in Islam, but continue to emphasize their Hui ethnicity. However, since the Chendai Hui do not fit many of the cultural criteria of what Hui are like, their official recognition has been late in coming. Under the current ethnic identification policy in China, which, as I have argued, relies on a Stalinist cultural trait approach, these Hui did not fit the cultural criteria. Hence, they were not recognized by the state until 1979, when changes took place not in cultural criteria, but in sociopolitical conditions.

The purpose of this chapter is not only to introduce the ethnographic data on a controversial southeastern Hui lineage, but also to analyze why existing ethnic identification policy in China has difficulty justifying their inclusion as part of the Hui nationality. Since they have been recognized as members of the Hui minority, the influence of local government policies has led to further changes in their ethnic identity. An example is provided of how modern Western ethnicity theory has difficulty identifying similar "Taiwanese Hui" in Taiwan, who have almost lost their ethnic identity under unfavorable government policies and state that they are "not Hui"

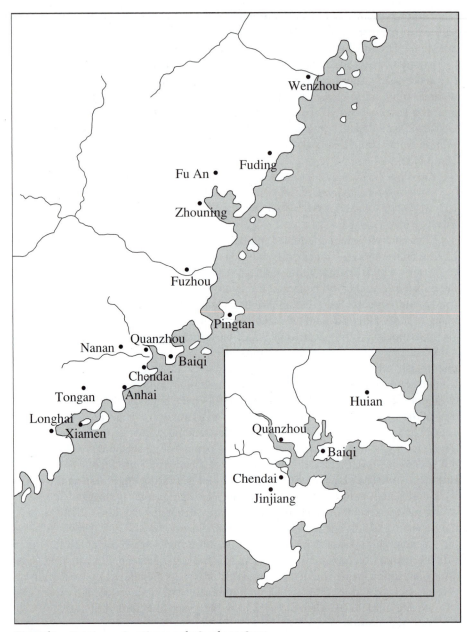

Figure 6.1   Hui Lineage Locations on the Southeast Coast

(Pillsbury, 1973, p. 145). By contrasting these divergent approaches to the ethnic identification of the Hui minority in Fujian and Taiwan, a relational approach more fully accounts for the nature of their ethnic identity due to the interaction of government policy and their specific social context.

THE CULTURAL BASIS FOR CHENDAI HUI IDENTITY

The logic of ethnic identity is based on the idea of descent—the idea, factual or fictive, of belonging to a group of people descended from ancestors different from the others with whom a group interacts. Discovering how these ancestral connections are transmitted and then appropriated in a socially relevant way is thus one of the characteristic tasks in the study of ethnic identity. Records, legends, stories, symbols, and rituals become the most critical texts by which people transmit their sense of "otherness." In the case of the Hui in Chendai, they are in the unique position of possessing numerous historical artifacts that authenticate their descent from "foreign" ancestors. For the Hui in Chendai, their *otherness* has been etched in stone.

Investigations in Quanzhou over the last few decades have unearthed "more than 200 pieces of structural stone components of Islamic gravestones, grave cover stones, mosques, and Muslim residences" (Huang & Liao, 1983, p. 201).[4] While many of these stone inscriptions are unintelligible to present Hui descendants of the Ding lineage in Chendai, the symbolic fact that their ancestors' graves bear Arabic inscriptions hold great import for their identification with these "*fan ke*" (barbarian guests) or "*semu ren*"—the official Chinese terms for foreign Muslim residents of Quanzhou before the Ming dynasty, when the term "Huihui" became widely used. Present Ding residents can point to the graveyards of their ancestors as important texts of their present Hui identity.

Historical Monuments to Hui Islamic Heritage

In a highly symbolic move, the Ding lineage relocated its earliest ancestors' graves to the historic Lingshan Holy Islamic Tombs outside Quanzhou in August 1980. These historic tombs are among those monuments preserved by the Chinese government's Historic Artifacts Bureau and generally belong to foreign Muslim or famous Hui personages buried in Chinese soil. These include the various tombs and monuments erected to the supposed Muslims who served as officials, militia, and merchants from the Southern Song through Qing dynasties (eleventh through nineteenth centuries) and are buried in special graveyards in southern China, especially Quanzhou, Guangzhou, and Yangzhou. Historic tombs also contain the graves of Hui who played a major role in China's development and interaction with the West. These individuals included Zheng He, Hai Rui, Sai Dianchi (Sayid Edjell), Li Zhi and, more recently, the Panthay rebellion leader, Du Wenxiu.

The historic tombs of Arab and Persian ancestors of the Hui in Quanzhou are also important in the interaction between Islamic identity and government policy. In 1961, the Fujian provincial government declared the Lingshan Muslim tombs and the Ashab Mosque in Quanzhou (founded in 1009–1010 A.D.) to be historic monuments.[5] Since 1979, the state, provincial, and city governments have provided substantial funds to restore these structures, to the extent that now the tombs have been refurbished and rededicated with a large tract of land and a sign at the entrance proclaiming: "Lingshan Holy Islamic Tombs." All tourist maps for Quanzhou city highlight these two Islamic sites as important attractions.

The Lingshan tombs are primarily those of two Muslim saints who, according to legend, were said to be sent to China by the Prophet Muhammad and were buried

Ashab mosque, founded 1006 A.D. Note the Arab architectural style. Quanzhou City, Fujian Province. May 1984.

Holy Islamic Cemetery, thought to contain the tombs of two cousins of the Prophet Muhammad. Lingshan Cemetery, Quanzhou City, Fujian Province. February 1991.

in their present location during the Tang dynasty (seventh to tenth centuries). According to He Qiaoyuan's 1629 *Minshu*, the two Muslim saints buried in Quanzhou are Imam Sayid and Imam Waggas from Medina. These were two of four foreign Muslims said to have visited southern China during the Wu De period of the Tang Emperor Gao Zu (618–626 A.D.).[6] Substantial research has been carried out on the more than 300 Islamic carvings and artifacts left by the Muslim communities concentrated in Quanzhou when it was a key international harbor on the Southeast Coast from the Tang to the Yuan dynasties (seventh to fourteenth centuries; see Clark, 1981).

The Ding graveyard is presently located on the southeast side of Lingshan Hill outside the Renfengmen Gate of Quanzhou. It was moved to this location and refurbished by provincial authorities and members of the Ding lineage in August 1980. The style of the two tombs is similar to those found in other Muslim graves in Quanzhou, with what has been called a pagoda-shaped tomb cover (Chen, 1984, p. 56) resting on a rectangular stone base of five tiers. Each tier is intricately carved with Islamic designs of clouds, lotus flower petals, a full moon, and Qur'anic inscriptions (for translation and description see Chen, 1984, pp. 107–108). Behind the tombs is a tablet in Chinese and Arabic indicating that this is the first ancestor of the Ding lineage in Chenjiang (now Chendai) and the ancestor of the fourth generation of the Ding lineage from Jinjiang County. On the back of the tablet is the following Chinese inscription:

> I bought this famous hill Luyuan and it was my intention to have my parents buried here, my brothers all agreed with me without objection. Litchis are planted to give shade just as our ancestors shall protect us forever. Mind you, my descendants, safeguard this important place. Written by Uncle Chengzhai in the eighth month of the second year of Xuantong (1910 A.D.) (Chen, 1984, p. 108).

This verse is significant for it clearly sets forth the "rights and obligations" of Ding descendants to maintain the traditions of their ancestors. In return for preserving their identity, they will be "protected forever." The survival of the Ding lineage as a people supports the veracity of this promise. "Ethnicity in its deepest psychological level is a sense of survival. If one's group survives, one is assured of survival, even if not in a personal sense" (De Vos, 1975, p. 17). If nothing else, the Ding are tenacious survivors.

In addition to stone inscriptions on tombstones attesting the Ding lineage's descent from foreign Muslim ancestry, there are numerous imperial edicts originally inscribed in public places depicting the important historical position of their Muslim forbears. While these do not specifically name Ding members as descendants, and are written in a classical style (*wenyan*) unintelligible to modern Chinese speakers, they do serve as important symbols signifying the glory of Hui past. Ding residents of Chendai Town pointed out several of these important edicts inscribed in the ancient Quanzhou Qingjing mosque. One such inscription is on a pedestal built against the east wall under the second arch in the passage from the entrance. It dates from 1407 A.D. and reads:

> The Emperor of the Great Ming instructs Miri Haji: I think he who is sincere and honest will revere God and serve the Emperor; he will also guide the good people, thus giving invisible support to the royal system. Therefore God will bless him, and he shall enjoy infinite bliss. You, Miri Haji, have long since followed the teachings of Muhammad; you are pious and honest, and are guiding the good people; you also revere God and

Ding ancestral tombs, Lingshan Cemetery, Quanzhou. These tombs were relocated to the cemetery in 1980 after the Ding lineage became recognized as members of the Hui nationality. February 1991.

serve the Emperor with loyalty. Such good deeds deserve praise and approval. Thereby I am giving you this imperial edict to protect your abode. No official, military or civilian personnel should despise, insult or bully them; whoever disobeys my order by doing so should bear the blame. This edict is hereby issued on the eleventh of the fifth month of the fifth year of Yongle (Chen, 1984, p. 11).

The original scroll from which this edict was copied was discovered in the home of Lan Xiaoyang, the hereditary Imam of the Puhading Mausoleum in Yangzhou, and is now kept in the Beijing Minorities Cultural Palace (Chen, 1984, pp. 11–12). This edict, originally composed in Chinese, Persian, and Mongolian, was posted in mosques throughout China by Hui in order to protect themselves against discrimination at that time and to document imperial endorsement for future generations. It is an important legitimation text for the Ding lineage and other Hui attesting that theirs is a religious and cultural heritage that was valued by the Chinese host rulers since imperial times. This text legitimates the dignity of their ancestry in the face of ethnic discrimination. It also documents the Ding lineage's early incorporation into the Chinese state system. The text thus becomes meaningful to Hui both then and at any time when their cultural traditions are brought into question.

Ritual Remembrance of Ding Identity

Probably more significant for the Hui descendants of the Ding lineage than stone inscriptions, which rarely impinge on their daily lives, are the prescriptions for properly remembering their ancestors recorded in their genealogy.[7] These prescriptions are adhered to four times a year when the Ding lineage celebrates the traditional Chinese agricultural holidays and remembers its ancestors. Like their Han Chinese neighbors, Ding members go to their ancestral lineage temple, burn incense, perform "*baizu*" rituals, and make offerings. Unlike their Han neighbors, however, they strictly prohibit the use of pork or pork byproducts in the offerings. When asked why, they say: "It is because we are descended from Hui ancestors, and they have instructed us in our genealogy not to offer them pork."[8] In addition to beef, several vegetables and seafood, including razor clams, are prescribed. Tea is also placed on the ancestral altar to assist the departed in "cleaning his mouth" of any pork residue before encountering his ancestors. Most significantly, instead of the traditional paper money that is burned by Han villagers as an offering to the ancestors to be used in the afterlife, these Hui have burned red paper with Islamic inscriptions. I could not discover where this tradition originated, but local Hui said that when there was an Ahong available in the mosque they would ask him to write Qur'anic scriptures on the paper. They said that it would help "purify" the deceased upon his meeting with Allah in the afterworld.[9] With the Han, the burning of the object is for the use of the ancestor in the afterworld. Yet, this also parallels the placing of Qur'anic text-inscribed bricks and other objects with the deceased in the graves that I have witnessed in the Northwest. For most Hui, and Muslims throughout Central Asia who do not have access to the Qur'anic text in Arabic, the text itself takes on talismantic quality and is used in burial, healing, and adornment to gain protection and power.

Other distinctives that the Ding members maintain include the making of a certain Hui food, a large deep-fried pastry, known as "*youxiang*," on holidays. On the first day of the sixth month, according to the agricultural calendar, this *youxiang* cake is prepared and the day is referred to as *baibing jie* "cake offering day." Eating this food on holidays is distinctive of Hui throughout China. That these rituals have been continued through the centuries attests to the Ding lineage's strong desire to "not disobey" the demands of its ancestors.

The regularity of these rituals at the lineage temple also helps to reinforce the ethnic identity, the "otherness" (De Vos, 1975, p. 26), of the Ding lineage. While modern Ding members might not be able to read their genealogies in classical Chinese, or explain why they cannot eat or use pork on ritual holidays, nevertheless they are regularly reminded that their ancestors are different and so are they by maintaining ritual remembrance of them. Pu Zhenzong in 1940 told his interviewers that even though he is no longer Muslim, he is descended from Muslims, and that "the Pu family has had a secret custom—never offer pork in ancestor worship" (Zhang, 1940, p. 2).

Ding members have maintained this taboo against pork during ancestral rituals for centuries, but they do not proscribe pork for their own consumption. They have an explanation for this in the form of an often-told legend, which was related to me as follows:

> Our ancestors were very sincere Muslims. At the time of our eleventh-generation ancestor, Ding Qirui, who served during the Ming dynasty as a government secretary in the Ministry of Justice, he was accused with a trumped-up charge of attempting to usurp the throne of the emperor. Because of this the emperor attempted to exterminate the Ding

A public welcoming ceremony at the Ding Hui lineage hall for the UNESCO-sponsored conference on Islam in China, Quanzhou, Fujian. February 1991.

Nationality Middle School (Minzu Zhongxue), *Chendai Township, Quanzhou. Note the sign is in Chinese and Arabic; also note the pig foraging in the foreground. February 1991.*

family. The main mark of the Ding family was their being Muslims. In order to save their lives, the Ding family could not "practice Islam (religion) for a hundred generations" (*Baidai Zhanyang*). Thus, at that time we began to eat pork and became assimilated to the Han (*tonghua*).

This is the same story, almost word for word, told to the investigation team that interviewed the Chendai Hui, Ding Deqian, in February 1940 (Zhang, 1940, p. 2). It has become an accepted text that explains the reason for the Ding Hui leaving Islam and eating pork. In the 1940 interview, as well as in mine, the Ding members explained that the phrase "practice Islam for a hundred generations" is taken from an inscription on a wooden tablet on the front of their lineage temple, parallel to another inscription on the temple itself: "pacify ourselves for future success" (*suiwo sicheng*).[10] In both interviews, the Ding speakers pointed out that the structure of their ancestral temple was built in the shape of the Chinese character for "*Hui*," one small square within a larger one, signifying they are of the Hui people. Most Han ancestral halls have covered corridors connecting the hallways on the perimeter with the main hall in the center of the courtyard. The absence of these connecting corridors is the one feature that differentiates their hall from most other Han lineage halls.

The forced-assimilation legend is extremely important for providing textual support through which modern Ding members interpret their behavior. More than the genealogy and stone inscriptions, the legend not only ties them to their ancestors but explains the difference between them and their Han neighbors, as well as why they differ from other Hui who maintain Islamic customs. The legend summarizes a common experience of suffering and persecution that Hui throughout China say took place during the Ming dynasty when, by imperial decree, they were no longer allowed to speak Arabic or Persian, wear foreign dress, and live in completely separate Muslim communities. It was at that time, they say, that Hui lost their former high status under the fallen "foreign" Mongolian dynasty and were forced to be "Sinicized" in a Chinese dynasty that prohibited foreign names, clothes, and languages (see Chan, 1953, p. 209).

SOCIOECONOMIC FACTORS IN CHENDAI HUI IDENTITY

The Ding have lived in Chendai since the Wanli period of the Ming dynasty (1573–1620) when they supposedly fled from Quanzhou to avoid persecution. Since that time, they have been known for their specialized aquacultural economy. The town of Chendai is on the Fujian coast and well-suited for cultivating the razor clams for which the Ding lineage are famous. Before 1949 they were not only engaged in this industry, but also produced opium and had many small factories that made woven bags and sundry goods. These goods were exported extensively and led to the migration of many Ding Hui to Southeast Asia and Hong Kong in their business endeavors. After 1955, when private industries were collectivized in China, these small factories were either curtailed or transferred to the larger commune of which the Ding lineage occupied seven brigades.

Since their recognition as a nationality in 1979 and the implementation of the economic reform policies in the countryside, the Ding members have once again

TABLE 6.1
INCOME FROM FACTORY AND INDUSTRIAL ENTERPRISES,
CHENDAI TOWNSHIP, 1979–1993

Year	Income (Yuan)
1979	1,440,000
1980	3,220,000
1981	5,630,000
1982	6,150,000
1983	8,780,000
1984	29,040,000
1985	36,240,000
1986	41,450,000
1987	46,880,000
1988	56,720,000
1989	68,410,000
1990	92,200,000
1991	156,140,000
1992	334,540,000
1993	620,170,000

Source. 1994 Township Records; 1989 figures from Ding, 1991, p. 3).

become engaged in private small factories, producing athletic shoes and plastic goods, like the brightly colored plastic sandals, rugs, and other sundries found in most Chinese department stores. Of the 3,350 households in the seven villages (former brigades) in Chendai (in which 92% are Hui) more than 60% ran small factories in 1991. By 1994, the majority of all households derived their primary incomes from these "sideline" enterprises. In the larger factories there are more than a hundred workers, and in smaller factories only 10 or more. Workers can work as long as they wish, usually 8 to 10 hours a day, 7 days a week.

As a result of these many factories and their output, the Ding have begun to do extremely well. Several Ding families have registered as "wanyuanhu" (10,000-yuan families), with one family who banked at least 100,000 yuan ($33,000 U.S.) in 1986. That was an extraordinary amount then, but in 1994 it became commonplace. Average annual income in the predominately Hui Chendai township in 1983 was 611 yuan per person, whereas in the larger Han-dominated Jinjiang county it was only 402 yuan in 1982 (Population Census Office, 1987, p. 175). By 1984, Chendai

TABLE 6.2
INCOME FROM AGRICULTURAL AND INDUSTRIAL SIDELINE ENTERPRISES,
CHENDAI TOWNSHIP, 1979–1993

Year	Income (Yuan)
1979	4,490,000
1980	4,920,000
1981	7,460,000
1982	11,770,000
1983	13,880,000
1984	17,770,000
1988	60,940,000
1989	74,010,000
1990	92,200,000
1991	173,820,000
1992	353,490,000
1993	639,690,000

Source. 1994 Township Records; 1989 figures from Ding, 1991, p. 3.

income reached 837 yuan per person for the town, while the Hui within Chendai averaged 1,100 yuan. Their income increased 33% in 1985. By 1989, the entire township's income had jumped to an average annual income of 1,000 yuan per person. This indicates a substantial increase of local Hui income over Han income, in the county as well as the township. It is clear that their economic success was not limited to the Hui, as Han in Fujian also prospered during this period. Income from factory and industrial enterprises increased in the entire township from 1.4 million yuan in 1979 to 620 million yuan in 1993 (see Table 6.1).[11]

The increase of Hui over Han income was due mainly to the encouragement of Hui-owned businesses, the permitted political mobilization of the Hui community, and the reestablishment of overseas Hui family connections, all of which was still being discouraged among the Han in the late 1970s and early 1980s. While these activities became commonplace along the Southeast Coast in the late 1980s, my informants said that Han cadres in Jinjiang County were reluctant to encourage such practices among the Han until the Hui proved successful with them without political repercussions.

Finally, income from sideline enterprises in agriculture and small industry has also grown at an incredibly rapid rate (see Table 6.2). Although the Hui only occupy one-seventh of the town's population, they account for more than one-third of the income (Township Records). In 1984, Chendai was the first town in Fujian

TABLE 6.3

COMPOSITION OF THE LABOR FORCE, CHENDAI TOWNSHIP, 1978–1992

Year	Agriculture	Industry
1978	69.9%	30.1%
1984	19.9%	80.1%
1985	14.0%	86.0%
1989	13.0%	87.0%
1992	7.0%	93.0%

Source. 1994 Township Records; 1989 figures from Ding, 1991, p. 3.

province to become a *yiyuan zhen* (100-million-yuan town). Color television sets were owned by almost every household and there were more than 550 motorcycles in the seven all-Hui villages in 1991. More than half of the Hui in the town have their own two- to four-level homes paid for with cash from their savings. Many of the multilevel homes that I visited had small piecework factories in the first level (making a tennis shoe sole here, the lining there, laces elsewhere, etc.), while the various stem-family branches lived in the other levels.

For example, Ding Yongwei, mentioned at the beginning of this chapter, has two sons. On the first level of his four-story stone-block home, he has a small factory that produces the stretchy fabric that is used to line the inside of athletic shoes. He obtains the materials from a distant relative in the Philippines. His youngest son and that son's wife live on the second floor. His oldest son and the oldest son's wife and two children live on the third floor (as a Hui, Ding's son is allowed to have two children). Ding Yongwei and his wife occupy the top floor.

It is clear that economic reorganization occured in the 1980s as a result of the economic reforms. Prior to 1978, the majority of the labor force (69.9%) in Chendai was engaged in agriculture and only 30% involved in industry. By 1992 this had shifted dramatically, with 93% of the labor force engaged in industry (see Table 6.3). Income from sideline enterprises has increased eight times over 1979. The Ding believe that this was due to their recognition as Hui. Whatever the reason, it is clear that economic reforms and their advantageous usage of ethnicity led to dramatic changes in the political economy of the area.

Ethnic Aspects of Ding Prosperity

Ding Hui do not attribute their prosperity to industriousness alone. Since they were recognized as part of the Hui nationality in 1979, they became eligible for assistance as members of an underprivileged minority. They have received several government subsidies that have spurred their economy. From 1980 until 1984, the government has given more than 200,000 yuan to the seven Hui teams. With the funds, they built a running water system, ponds for raising fish, and the means to expand their razor clam industry. The Ministry of Education has given 40,000 yuan to build a middle

New mosque, built in 1990 adjacent to the Ding lineage hall, Chendai Township, Fujian Province. February 1991.

school and 33,000 yuan for a primary school. They also receive benefits as a minority nationality in preference for entering high school and college. Under special birth-planning policies for minorities, they are allowed to have one more child than the Han. Hui representation in the local government is also higher than their proportion in the population. Two of the ten party committee representatives (*changwei*) are surnamed Ding, as well as the town's party secretary.

More than 50% of the Ding lineage members have overseas relatives—mainly in the Philippines, Indonesia, and Singapore—a higher proportion than among their Han neighbors. They have reestablished communication with these relatives and have been assisted by frequent remittances. This outside income is an important factor in the rapid economic development of the seven Ding villages. All seven Hui villages have elementary schools, thanks to donations from overseas relatives, averaging 20,000 yuan each. Neighboring Han villages have one elementary school for every three or four villages. The Ding say that their close and frequent contact with overseas relatives is a result of their strong feelings of ethnic identity, which they say surpasses that of neighboring Han lineages with their overseas relations.

These government subsidies and special benefits are important factors in the Ding Hui claim to ethnic minority status. The manipulation of ethnic identity for special favored treatment has been well-documented by anthropologists and is an important factor in explaining why the Ding lineage's ethnic identity has become even more relevant. Changes in socioeconomic conditions and the local political economy are conducive to rapid ethnic change. Even before such policies were promulgated, however, Ding Hui occupied a distinct ecological and commercial niche that they had maintained for generations. It is significant that part of the *jipin* ("requirements of remembrance") stipulated in their genealogy was the offering of razor clams to their ancestors (Ding, 1980, p. 30). This indicates that an almost ethnic specialization of labor was maintained in southern Fujian where Hui were known to be involved in selected aquacultural industries. The Guo in Xiamen City were known to be excellent repairmen and builders of motorboats before liberation. Virtually all mechanical repair shops were staffed by these Hui.

ETHNIC IDENTITY AND ETHNIC POLICY: THE "TAIWANESE MUSLIMS"

The "Taiwanese Muslims" are those Hui descendants described by the Taiwan Chinese Muslim Association as the "20,000 Taiwan-born descendants of Chinese Muslims who came to this island 300 years ago with the hero Koxinga [Zheng Chenggong]" (Pillsbury, 1973, p. 145). They are concentrated in several coastal towns and share a limited number of surnames, including Guo, Chen, Hong, Fu, Mu, and Pu. Their most prominent lineage is the Guo lineage in Lukang, of which one section is named for and inhabited mainly by this lineage, the "*Guo Zhu Li*" (Guo Family Section; see Ts'ai, 1973). There is good evidence to suggest that these Guo are descended from the same ancestors as the Guo lineage in Fujian, Huian County, Baiqi Township. Both Guo lineages claim descent from the Tang dynasty General Guo Ziyi (Pillsbury, 1976, p. 31), although the accuracy of this claim has been questioned.

There is evidence that an ancient mosque formerly stood in Lukang and the Chinese Muslim Association once sent mainlander Hui from Taibei to Lukang to instruct the "Taiwanese Muslims" in Islam and help bring them back into the faith. In a similar move, from 1983 to 1985, the Chinese Islamic Society in the People's Republic of China brought four Ahong from the Ningxia Hui Autonomous Region to teach in the four remaining mosques in Fujian, in order to help instruct the newly recognized Hui in the Islamic faith. Both attempts in Taiwan and Fujian were ineffectual, however, and the last Ahong in Fujian returned to Ningxia over the 1986 Spring Festival. The reason why there is a need for such instruction on both sides of the Taiwan Strait is the same: Both communities practice Chinese folk religion, eat pork, and in most other respects are culturally indistinguishable from the Han communities in which they live.

The Guo lineage on the mainland, however, was recognized by the Chinese Nationalities Commission as being Hui in the early 1950s. After some political lobbying, they were able to convince the state of their claims to minority status, a process that took the Ding another 20 years. The Guo in Taiwan, however, no longer claim that they are Hui, nor do they seem to have any interest in doing so. While the Guo in Fujian recognize themselves as Hui, their relations in Taiwan "except for those about 50 or older—say they are not" (Pillsbury, 1973, p. 145). In a visit in May 1995 to Lukang, I could find no locals who identified themselves as Hui, though several people surnamed Ding and Guo knew of their historical links to foreign ancestors who were known as Hui. They knew that these people did not eat pork, and therefore in some families it was still customary to not use pork in ancestor worship.

However, no one that I talked to knew the reason for the pork taboo or the connection between Hui ancestry and Islam.

This recognition of descent from Muslim ancestors is critical for understanding why Hui on one side of the strait claim to be Hui, and why those on the other side of the strait feel they are no longer able to be considered so. Yet, it may be premature to predict that "It may well be that visitors to Lukang, Taiwan, a mere decade from now might likewise find no more Hui" (Pillsbury, 1973, p. 240). This prediction, while giving insight into the changing identity of Hui in interaction with the Han majority and Taiwan government policy, does not adequately take into account the enduring presence of what it means, or meant, for these "Taiwanese Muslims" to be different from their Han neighbors. Confusion also arises in this approach when the analytical distinction between being Hui and practicing Islam is not made. The "Taiwanese Muslims" are certainly not practicing Muslims, but that does not mean that Hui identity might no longer be relevant to them. The maintenance of the pork taboo in ancestor worship indicates that, at the ritual level, there is still some significance attached to Hui identity among the Taiwanese Muslims. In the present social context, their ethnic identity may continue to recede in significance and total assimilation may well take place. But, it is also possible that Hui identity might become more relevant to them if Taiwan's policies toward ethnic minorities ever undergo reform similar to those on the mainland. This is all the more plausible given the increasing discussions of reunification of Taiwan with the mainland. In that case, the Lukang Guo would certainly be recognized as members of the Hui nationality and eligible for the attending privileges. Hui ethnic identity, though presently almost totally lost, would once again be sociopolitically salient.

It is not surprising that the Lukang Guo have adopted many of the customs of their Taiwanese neighbors given that their social context has been unfavorable to the expression of ethnic identity for centuries. They have been dispersed among a Han majority for 300 years. In the nineteenth century, they experienced 50 years of a policy of assimilation under the Japanese administration who discouraged "foreign religions." They have been subjected to the Nationalist policy that identifies Hui primarily in terms of their religious belief (explained in the following section). And, they have been geographically and linguistically isolated from other mainland Hui who arrived with the Nationalists. What is significant is that these individuals maintain any recognition at all of their separateness from their Han neighbors and that this is still salient for their lives in terms of ritual and social interaction. What is at issue here is not whether they are descended from Muslim ancestors, which is clearly the case. Rather, we need to examine how relevant that ancestry is for their daily lives and how that idea has changed in its expression over time, as I have argued for the Chendai Hui. While Hui identity may not presently be meaningful to the youth, this does not guarantee that it will continue to remain meaningless as they grow older.

For example, a certain Guo lineage of 383 members who migrated from Baiqi, Huian County to a village outside Xiamen, have also lost all major outward cultural traces of their ethnic ancestry. Despite their practice of Chinese folk religion and eating pork, they maintain they are different than their Han neighbors, even though they feel that the label "Hui" might no longer be appropriate for them. It may be possible that while the younger Guo in Taiwan no longer feel they should be called

Hui, they may be reluctant to view themselves like their non-Hui neighbors in every respect. While it may no longer be meaningful for young Guo in Taiwan to identify with mainland Hui, they probably still retain some kind of psychological sense of belonging to their own people.

Islamic Belief and Hui Identity

At issue here is not the Lukang Guo lineage's identity as Hui, but their inability to admit Islamic belief, which disqualifies them as Hui under Nationalist policy. As discussed in chapter 2, this policy regards the Hui as a religious group, not an ethnic group. Until 1939, the Hui were regarded as *Huimin* (Hui people) under Sun Yat-sen's policy of the five peoples of China, including the Han, Mongolian, Tibetan, Manchurian, and Hui (meaning all the Muslim peoples of China). The policy changed when Chiang Kai-shek presided over the first national congress of the Chinese Hui People's National Salvation Association in Chongqing and declared that all non-Han groups within China are subvarieties of an ancient Chinese race. Under this policy, the Hui were not considered a separate *minzu* (people, nationality), but a religious group with special characteristics and were to be referred to as *Huijiaoren* or *Huijiaotu*. For Lukang Guo, who are certainly no longer Muslim in religious belief and ritual, it becomes irrelevant and perhaps impossible to call themselves "Hui" under current Nationalist policy.

A result of the Nationalist policy, which maintains all Chinese peoples are descended from one race, is that ethnic differences in Taiwan tend to split along Mainlander–Taiwanese and class lines (see Gates, 1981). Only the aborigines (*Gaoshan zu*) receive a nationality status, similar to that on the mainland. The Hui are not regarded as an ethnic group, because there is no such category under the current policy. The Hui associate with the broader Taiwanese society of which they are a part.

The Communist Party leaders of the People's Republic of China have recognized that the Hui are a distinct *minzu* (nationality, people) since before the 1949 revolution, brought home to Chairman Mao Zedong and other early party leaders on the Long March. This historical experience and rationale has influenced considerably the PRC's policies toward the Hui and other minorities. The divergence of the PRC and Taiwan policies regarding religion and nationality has also affected the relevance of Hui identity and its expression in both societies. It is particularly relevant to the understanding of the recent ethnic transformation of the Hui in Chendai, which will be explored next.

PUBLIC POLICY AND ETHNIC REVITALIZATION IN CHENDAI

PRC policy that accords special privileges to these recently recognized Hui along the Southeast Coast and encourages their interaction with foreign Muslim governments has had a significant impact on their ethnic identity. Fujian provincial and local municipal publications proudly proclaim Quanzhou as the site of the third most important Islamic holy grave and the fifth most important mosque in the world. Religious and government representatives from more than 30 Muslim nations were escorted to Muslim sites in Quanzhou as part of a state-sponsored delegation in the spring of 1986. Foreign Muslim guests are frequently hosted by the local Quanzhou City Islamic Association.

As a result of this contact, construction of the Xiamen International Airport was partially subsidized by the Kuwaiti government. The Kuwaitis are also assisting in the building of a large hydroelectric dam project along the Min River outside Fuzhou. A Jordani businessman visiting in the spring of 1986 offered to donate $1.5 million dollars (U.S.) to rebuild the Qingjing mosque.[12] The many Islamic relics in Quanzhou are evidence of a long history of friendly exchanges between China and the Muslim world. As a result of China's growing trade with Third World Muslim nations, it is only natural that these historical treasures should be displayed and made available to foreign Muslim visitors. It is also not surprising that the descendants of these early foreign Muslim residents in Quanzhou—the Ding, Guo, Huang, Jin, and other Hui lineages—are interested in further interaction with distant foreign Muslim relations.

The historic Hui tombs take on added international significance in the present government's improving relations with foreign Muslim governments, which have had a long history in China.[13] These tombs have become objects of ethnic tourism and pilgrimage by foreign Muslims, as well as urban and Northwest Hui in China who wish to explore their Islamic "roots." Hui party cadres often make a point of visiting historic Muslim tombs, such as the large monument and public park outside Kunming, Yunnan, dedicated to the father of Zheng He, the fifteenth-century Ming explorer and Muslim eunuch. Hui visitors to these historic Muslim tombs reaffirm their international Islamic heritage.[14] Historic shrines, as objects of veneration and tourism, remind local Hui of their international and religious roots (see Gladney, 1987a, pp. 497–507).

International Islamic attention cannot but influence the self-perception of the Ding lineage as Hui descendants. It has also contributed to a kind of ethnic revitalization and rediscovery of their Muslim heritage. In 1990, a new mosque was completed in Chendai attracting many villagers interested in learning more about Islam. Qur'anic study courses have been conducted and some villagers have begun to learn Arabic. In 1991, they invited an Imam from Inner Mongolia, and 18 students from the Ding lineage have gone to Huhehot to study with the Chendai Imam's teacher in order to become future Imams, including two women. There are four other mosques in Fujian that formerly had Imams from Ningxia and Gansu who came at the invitation of the provincial Islamic Association between 1982 and 1989, but they all eventually returned to their more familiar homes in the Islamic northwest, and now Chendai is the only mosque with an Imam in all of Fujian province. This is particularly ironic since the mosque in Chendai is the newest mosque in Fujian, established among villagers who have only recently begun to practice the Islamic faith.

In November 1984, a grass-roots organization of Ding Hui leaders was recognized by the government as "Jinjiang County Chendai Town Commission for Hui Affairs." This was quite significant in that formal voluntary associations outside of initial government sponsorship were considered illegal in China, and in this case the state recognized the organization well after it was established. Even the "non-governmental organizations" (NGOs) in China are generally government initiated and semi-state controlled. One of the commission's first acts was to establish a small museum in the Ding ancestral hall displaying articles substantiating their foreign Muslim ancestry. The ancestral hall possesses the usual ritual objects and ancestral tablets on the domestic altar as other Hokkien temples (Weller, 1987, pp. 26–27). Locals affirmed that daily rituals of the domestic cult, lighting incense on a daily basis, and providing special offerings on festivals and feast days was similar to other Fujianese families. The main difference here is that there was no pork admitted into the ancestral hall. Ding members told me that they often rinsed their mouth with tea before making offerings to their ancestors, as a way of cleansing pork residue that might be offensive to them. In addition, they often offered tea at funerals so that the deceased could have a clean mouth when he or she meets Muslim ancestors in the afterworld.

Perhaps more importantly, this ancestral hall received special township level support and approval. Ancestral halls are now allowed in China, but generally not patronized by the state. The township provided some funding for the ancestral hall, reasoning that it also contained a historical museum of the history of the Hui, and thus, foreign relations in China. I have never seen another ancestral hall with a museum inside, and it was the nicest hall that I visited in Fujian.

The commission has also asked to be recognized as an autonomous minority county, but this has not been worked out because of redistricting difficulties. The successful promotion of Quanzhou's place in the ancient "Silk Route" and in Islamic history led to two UNESCO-sponsored conferences in 1991 and 1994, with substantial international participation, as part of UNESCO's ongoing study of the Silk Route as a medium of intercultural exchange.

The UNESCO-sponsored Silk Road Expedition arrived in Quanzhou in February 1991, as its main port of entry on China's "Maritime Silk Route," virtually bypassing the traditional stopping-place of Canton. During the 4-day conference and Silk Road festivities in which I participated, the foreign guests and Muslim dignitaries were brought to a Chendai Ding village as part of their orientation, in order to highlight the recent economic prosperity and government support for the modern descendants of the ancient Muslim maritime traders. In the 1994 conference, not only were academic papers presented, but participants were offered the possibility of paying to go on a tour of "Islamic Maritime Sites" following the conference, including visits to mosques and Muslim cemeteries in Hangzhou, Suzhou, Shanghai, Xi'an, and Beijing. During the 1994 conference in Quanzhou, participants were taken to several Hui-run factories, as well as to the Ding lineage's cemetery on the fifteenth day of the Chinese New Year, where Ding lineage elders remembered their ancestors by performing such rites as burning incense, bowing three times, reading portions of the genealogy, and in a newly "invented" tradition, presenting flowers to the ancestor's graves. In reflection of their ancestor's Islamic heritage, the Ding invited their local Imam to read a passage of the Qur'an in front of the graves. Afterwards, he invited the few foreign and local Muslims who could join him in a Qur'anic recitation. The ceremony was followed by statements by local officials, including a strong expression of support from Hei Boli, the former Chairman of the Ningxia Hui Autonomous Region and current Vice-Chairman of the People's Political Consultative Congress. Foreign Muslims, including the Director of the UNESCO project, and officials and scholars from Iran, Kuwait, Turkey, and Malaysia also made public statements of support.

Prosperity has come to the Ding lineage as a result of government minority assistance and of increased contacts with overseas relatives. Economic prosperity has been accompanied by ethnic and even religious revival. The growing Muslim identity of the Fujian Hui, in interaction with changing sociopolitical conditions and government policy, reveals a relational process that is the basis for ethnic change. These lineages have always maintained a Hui identity that, in conjunction with recent events, only now is beginning to take on a decidedly Islamic commitment.

The benefits attached to recognition of the Ding as members of the Hui nationality has led other southeastern lineages with traditional Hui surnames to apply for minority nationality status. As a result, the population of the Hui in Fujian is growing at a rapid rate. Ding lineage members have been located on Pingtan Island (more than 5,000 Hui were recognized in 1982) and several other areas in smaller numbers (see Table 6.4).

PURITY WITHIN TRUTH: HUI IDENTITY AMONG SOUTHEASTERN LINEAGES

Examination of this case of changing ethnic identity on the Southeast Coast has demonstrated the influence of government intervention and policy in shaping the resurgence of ethnic identity and practice. An overemphasis on the cultural traits of the Hui, their religion, eating customs, business abilities, and other distinctives to the exclusion of the social manipulation of ethnicity can lead to confusion over what makes a Hui "Hui." A cultural trait approach to ethnicity would exclude the Chendai Ding from official recognition as Hui, as it effectively did until 1979 in the PRC, and still does for Hui in Taiwan. Focusing on the social adaptation of the Hui to varying ecological environments under different government policies, to the exclusion of the cultural continuities of Hui identity, can lead to an assimilationist interpretation, as in the "Taiwanese Muslims." Attention must be given to how cultural meanings are expressed differently under different social contexts and, especially in the Taiwan and Fujian cases, under different government policies.

Under China's socialist policy, which especially since 1979 has distinguished clearly between the ethnic and religious expressions of a nationality's ethnic identity, Hui, such as the Chendai Ding, are given the option to express their ethnic identity without reference to Islamic belief and practice. Under Taiwan's Nationalist policy, which stresses the Islamic nature of Hui ethnicity, Guo lineage members in Lukang who no longer practice Islam have no grounds for being considered as Hui. Discussions of who the Hui are will only be fruitful if we examine how they have adapted under different socioeconomic circumstances and how their expression of ethnic identity and its relevance differs in those situations.

In some cases, Hui expression of ethnicity will take on a decidedly religious emphasis, as with many Northwest Hui communities. For these cases, as we have seen, Islamic purity is the main emphasis in the expression of *qing zhen* and Hui identity. In the case of this Southeastern lineage, the interpretation of *qing zhen* only dictates the preservation of one's true ancestry and the ability to demonstrate the veracity of that claim. In still other cases, we will see that a closer combination

TABLE 6.4
FUJIAN DING LINEAGE DISTRIBUTION BY COUNTY, 1986

Chendai	16,000	Hui an	100
Ping yang	2,000	Ping tan	4,800
Fu an	1,000	Ningzhou	300
Fu Ding	3,500	Tong an	200
Fuzhou	300	Jinjiang An Haizhen	400
Nan an	300	Jinjiang Dongshizhen	150
Total:			29,050

Source. Chart displayed in Central Ancestral Hall.

of purity and veracity, *qing* and *zhen*, will be stressed. More of a nonreligious ethnic identity will be prominent, especially in situations where young Hui may attempt to make use of special leadership opportunities for ethnic minorities to rise in the ranks of the Communist Party and other organizations. While Islam is an important and undeniable aspect of Hui heritage, in some contexts it is not necessarily critical for modern expression of Hui identity. Only by carefully examining the cultural and social expressions of Hui identity in various contexts, and under different government policies, can we be begin to interpret Hui ethnic identity consistently in its continuity and diversity.

The Hui discussed in this chapter are not concerned with the Islamic ritual purity of a *qing zhen* lifestyle. The core of their ethnic identity is stripped bare in their emphasis on the truth (*zhen*) of their genealogy. Their purity as Hui resides in the truth of this ancestry, which is rooted in the idea of descent from foreign ancestors who came from the West. Over the entrance to the tomb of the second Islamic saint in Yangzhou was displayed a Chinese epigraph proclaiming the foreign origin of Islam: "The Dao Originates in Western Lands" (*Dao yuan xi tu*).

Notes

[1]The visit was due to participation in a UNESCO-sponsored conference, "Contributions of Islamic Culture on China's Maritime Silk Route," February 21–26, 1994, Quanzhou, Fujian. The conference was hosted by the Fujian Academy of Social Sciences and the Fujian Maritime Museum. For a more detailed analysis see Gladney (1995d).

[2]A *United Press International,* 17 April 1994, article "Chinese Mobile Phone Industry Booms" reported that cellular-phone users in China increased by 20% in the first quarter of 1994 to 784,000, while pager owners increased 13% to more than 6 million. "Rapidly growing sales have catapulted China into the third largest mobile telecommunications market in the world after the United States and Japan. The 1993 sales of mobile phones reached 461,000, 2.7 times higher than all previous years combined.... Pagers, called 'beeper machines' in vernacular Chinese, and, more recently, cellular phones, known as 'big brothers,' have become something of a status symbol to China's nouveau rich. Many businessmen adorn themselves as a way of showing off their new wealth."

[3]See Huang and Liao (1983) regarding the changing of the surnames of several Hui lineages in Quanzhou during the Ming dynasty. Bai and Ma (1958) discuss the background for this discriminatory policy.

[4]Artifacts discovered thus far have been laboriously catalogued, photographed, and translated into Chinese, Arabic, and English by the Fujian Foreign Maritime Museum (Chen, 1984).

[5]For important discussions of the dating and name of the Persian style Ashab mosque in Fuzhou, see Chen Dasheng (1984, pp. 8–10); Zhuang (1983, pp. 65–82).

[6]Wahb Abu Kabcha is said to be buried in Guangzhou's famous "Bell tomb." The fourth saint is buried in Yangzhou. The early Tang date of this visit by foreign Muslims is hotly debated by Chinese Muslims and scholars.

[7]The importance of this genealogy is not its authenticity, but its acceptance by the current members of the Ding clan as validating their descent from foreign Muslim ancestors. It is also the basis for their continuing ancestral rituals (see Ding, 1980).

[8]This is spelled out in the *siyue* ("offering arrangements") section of their genealogy in the following prescriptions:

"On the dates of the ancestor's birth and death, the offerings for the worship are the same. But on the death date, a whole ox should be added in the worship. The ox used should be of the size of the ox which was offered in the worship of the feudal princes. Since our ancestors have served as high officials of the State since long ago, the offerings have been used until now, in order to spread out the honors of our ancestors.... Our ancestors' instructions must not be disobeyed" (Ding, 1980, pp. 42–43).

[9]A recent documentary entitled *Islam in Quanzhou* (*Yisilanjiao zai Quanzhou*), produced by the Quanzhou Tourism Bureau, filmed the yearly *baizu* rituals at the Ding ancestral graves in the Lingshan Islamic graveyard, including the burning of incense and paper with Qur'anic texts, offering of fruit and food, and the prayers of an Ahong sent from Ningxia.

[10]Ding share the belief that they are descended from the Nasredin, the son of Sai Dianchi, the famous governor of Yunnan, Sichuan, and Shaanxi during the Yuan dynasty. They say that the third characters of both texts cited above, when put in alignment, are the characters "*zhan si,*" the Chinese personal name of Nasredin (Ding Zhansi), indicating a hidden reflection of their foreign ancestry in the inscriptions over the entrance to their ancestral hall. Note that both the Na (chapter 3) and Ding lineages claim descent from the same foreign Muslim ancestor.

[11]Note that 1989 figures are based on Ding (1991), whereas 1979–1993 records are derived from my fieldnotes and township records.

[12]A resolution on the use of the funding has not yet been reached however, as local authorities are afraid of causing damage to the remains of the Ashab mosque during restoration. The Jordani, however, is not willing to construct a new mosque with his funds. The influx of this large contribution has caused considerable dissension among the Hui community.

[13]Shichor's (1989) analysis of the interplay between Middle Eastern foreign relations and China's treatment of its Muslim minorities does not reflect the importance of the minorities themselves in interacting with policy. See also Voll's 1985 analysis that distinguishes important differences between Muslim identity in China and Russia resulting from divergent ethnic policies. The recent study by Harris (1993) is the most complete on the subject of Sino-Middle Eastern relations (see also Gladney, 1994b).

[14]See Jamjoom (1985) for an interesting account of a Saudi delegation's visit to Islamic sites in China.

7 / Conclusion: Ethnic National Identity in the Contemporary Chinese State

The state in China has assigned ethnic labels to the peoples identified by them—labels often arbitrary and defined primarily by the state. Nevertheless, over the last 40 years, it can be argued that these labels have taken on a life of their own. Like material commodities, which Arjun Appadurai (1986) convincingly argues gain enduring sociopolitical value beyond their original intent, these state designations have contributed to a growing awareness of nationalism. Bernard Cohn's (1987) suggestion that these legal statuses led to the objectification and, in some cases, creation, of identities—perhaps previously present but loosely defined—is certainly relevant to the nationalities in China. Perhaps related to the traditional role of the Confucian Chinese state to name the essence of things, these designations take on superordinate status in China. Lynn White (1989) has argued that in China, labels, such as "rightist," "worker," and "landlord," have controlled access to employment, education, residence, and food rations—the substance of debate in every political conflict. They have certainly meant a great deal in determining one's access to state affirmative-action programs and political representation for minorities. It is not surprising that hundreds, perhaps thousands, of groups who perceive themselves to be ethnic are seeking nationality status from the Chinese state.

The Hui are perhaps the clearest case of a people who emerged in their present "pan-Hui" identity through a long process of ethnogenesis under the Chinese state. Hui in China, no matter where one travels, now refer to themselves as Hui people (*Hui min*). Descended from Persian, Arab, Mongolian, and Turkish Muslims, the people now known as the Hui emerged in a protracted process of ethnogenesis. Now these diverse peoples, who thought of themselves primarily as Muslims until the beginning of this century, see themselves as one nationality, united by a common imagined ethnohistory. This bond includes not only the traditionally accepted Hui Muslims who speak mainly Han dialects, but also the Tibetan, Mongolian, Thai, Hmong, Mien, and Hainanese Muslims, who now all call themselves Hui and are registered by the state as Hui. The Hui may be one of the few peoples ever to become a nationality before they fully thought of themselves as an ethnic group, at least not in such inclusive terms. That the Hui see themselves and their religion as "pure and true" adds an ironic twist to the state's power to label. By accepting the term, "Pure and True Religion" for "Islam," it tacitly legitimized a people generally thought to be less civilized than the majority. This chauvinism found its most derogatory expression in the Ming dynasty by adding to the Chinese ideograph for Hui the radical for "dog" or "beast" (Lipman, 1981, p. 293). In this case the state's authority to label was certainly intended to exclude and insult rather than to enlist.

Objectified Ethnonyms in the Northwest

While the Hui may be one of the more extreme examples of this invention and evolution of ethnicity, the reach of the state in the objectification of other nationalities in the Northwest is also clearly seen. The present-day Uygur are concentrated in the oasis cities of the Xinjiang Uygur Autonomous Region and are known as the settled oasis-dwelling Muslim Turkic-speaking people of the Tarim Basin. The ethnonym "Uygur" was revived by the Soviets in the 1930s, however, as a term for those oasis peoples who had no name for themselves other than their locality, *Kashgar-lik, Turpan-lik, Aksu-lik,* as well as *Taranchi, Turki,* and *Sart.* The term was adopted by a Chinese Nationalist warlord in Xinjiang in 1934 on the suggestion of his Soviet advisor. The ethnonym itself, however, had dropped out of usage after the fifteenth century when it referred to the settled oasis peoples of the Tarim Basin, who were Buddhist and expressly non-Muslim. Once these peoples began to convert to Islam from the tenth to fifteenth centuries, they rejected the ethnonym Uygur, which to them meant heathen (see Gladney, 1990b; Oda, 1978; Rudelson, 1991; 1992). It was gladly revived by the 6 million oasis-dwelling Turkic Muslims in Xinjiang as their ethnonym, since this acceptance brought with it recognition by the state, as well as an autonomous region. This reconceptualization of their ethnohistory struck deep chords in their agreed-upon sense of commonality as an autochthonous (indigenous) Central Asian people in opposition to the Han, descended from a historic Turkish empire, in a poetic recreation of historical imagination (see Gladney, 1993b). Other terms for the Muslim peoples of Xinjiang, such as Uzbek, Kazak, Tatar, Kirghiz, and Tajdik were also taken over by the Chinese from the Soviets, and these ethnonyms are not without their problems.

In this regard, the Yugur nationality, concentrated in their own autonomous county in Gansu's Hexi corridor, are also extremely problematic. It is this modern group that most preserves the linguistic, cultural, and religious ties with the Uygur empire's past. Known as the Yellow Uygur (*Shari Yugur*) who fled to Gansu after the Kirgiz invasion of 840 A.D., which had conquered the Uygur kingdom and dispersed the tribal confederation, the Yugur are the only remnants of the original Uygur kingdom to preserve much of their former Turkish language, written with Old Uygur script until the nineteenth century. Manichaean practices in their Lamaist–Buddhist religion are also still present, and they now are divided into three groups speaking Turkish, Mongolian, and Chinese dialects—all recognized as belonging to one nationality, the Yugur. One wonders why they did not inherit the label "Uygur" from the seventh to ninth century Buddhist kingdom, from whence they fled, instead of the oasis-dwelling Muslims in Xinjiang.

Several other nationality identities in the Northwest are of significant interest. I have already discussed the problematic identifications of the Dongxiang, Salar, and Baonan Muslims, who are found only in China. Each group speaks a combination of

Turkic, Mongolian, and Han dialects, and, within each individual nationality, there are some that speak only one or the other language—they are not all tri- or bilingual. The Baonan derive from Mongolian-speaking Tibetan Lamaists, later identified as the Tu (or Monguours), who upon conversion to Islam, formed a new collectivity eventually registered by the state as the Baonan. The Dongxiang ("East Village") derived their name from a Hezhou suburb. That the state chooses to identify these Muslim peoples individually in the Northwest, to accept their own formulations of identity and ethnonym, and then legalize them (yet, at the same time the state refuses individual recognition to the Tibetan, Mongolian, Bai, and Hainan Muslims), certainly reflects pragmatic sociopolitical decisions. This process and the effect of the distinct identifications of these peoples in their separate ethnogeneses cries out for further study.

This objectification of ethnic identities based on state-assigned labels was emphasized to me recently by a Han scholar who went to Xinjiang in the early 1950s as a language student and teacher. After taking a 1-month truck ride from Xi'an to Urumqi, she was assigned to a predominantly Uygur village that also had Kazak and Hui residents. At the time, she noticed that there was little division among them as Muslims. They worshiped in the same mosque and generally made little reference to their national identities. On a 1987 return trip, however, she found that they no longer prayed together and seemed to have a much stronger sense of their ethnic differences. This, of course, was the intention of Soviet Central Asian nationality policies: the creation of a plurality of Turkic ethnicities that would help prevent pan-Turkic unification. This policy has led, however, to other results in China.

The Hardening of Ethnonyms in the Southwest

In Southwest China, a plethora of officially designated nationalities masks an even greater ethnic complexity. As anthropologists have begun to study the ethnohistories of these groups, they have found that many are umbrella associations, registered during the 1950s identification campaigns, which included many peoples who did not necessarily think of themselves in the same way the state did, but were happy to be registered as something other than Han. A striking example is provided by the Bai people of Sichuan, whom C. P. Fitzgerald (1973) identified as the *Minjia*. In the famous study by Francis L. K. Hsü (1968), *Under the Ancestor's Shadow*, these people were regarded as Han and were held up as a general example for "Chinese" ancestor worship. For years, Sino-anthropologists have assigned this book to their students as an excellent ethnography of Chinese, namely Han, traditional society. Detailed ethnographic research by a Japanese anthropologist, Hiroko Yokoyama (1988), however, has uncovered their ethnic complexity and ethnogenesis as the Bai. David Wu (1990) reports that these people have gone to great lengths to maintain their minority status and in no way wish to be mistaken as, or assimilated to, the Han.

Lin Yueh-hwa's (1984, p. 90) discussion of the Yi (formerly Lolo) people in Sichuan also typically depicts a uniform history of a people that "is an old one in China. . . .Ever since ancient time, the Yis have been a member of the family of Chinese nationalities." This "redefinition" of ethnic history by the state in power masks a wide variety of sociocultural variety among a people now labeled as the "Yi." They comprise at least five separate ethnolinguistic groups who were, for the most part of their history, independent of Chinese rule. Stevan Harrell (1995, p. 63) suggests that the rewriting of "the history of the history of the Yi" from their own accounts, as well as Chinese and Western missionary accounts, is required to find out who and why they have become what they are.

The Qiang are a people whose identity has been conceived by an even greater stretch of the historical imagination. Distributed throughout Southwest and Central China, their name has been found by Chinese ethnohistorians to date from as early as the Shang dynasty. A fantastic leap is made to the modern century, however, in arguing that the peoples identified as such in Sichuan are direct descendants of these obscure nomadic peoples (see Zhongguo, 1981, p. 289). Through a sifting of historical, archaeological, and ethnographic materials, one Chinese researcher from Taiwan has demonstrated that the peoples found all over China during several periods and identified as Qiang in the historical records cannot possibly be related (M. Wang, 1983). This represents just another instance of a Confucian preoccupation with the "rectification of names." The term *"Qiang,"* according to the linguist Robert Ramsey (1987, p. 273), probably meant "pastoralist" in the early Chinese texts, and this was used to apply to any shepherding people. Nationality identification, in some cases in China, may be engaged in the somewhat Procrustean art of fitting modern peoples into the ethnonyms found in classic texts.

Incredible linguistic diversity and multiplicity found throughout the Southwest makes it almost impossible to identify many of these groups on the basis of language alone, though this is what was mainly attempted by the 1950s ethnologists constrained to follow a Stalinist model. Dai Qingxia (in press), a Chinese linguist, has recently shown that within a single Jingbo (Kachin) family in Yunnan, there are generally two, and perhaps three, languages in use depending on the generations present. Ramsey elaborates how these umbrella nationalities were created in China through language politics:

> At least two of these groups—Tsaiwa (or Atsi) and Lashi—are known to range over the Chinese side of the border. The languages that they speak natively are believed to be closer genetically to Burmese than to Jingpo. But since these tiny ethnic groups use Jingpo in their dealings with outsiders, the Chinese government classes them together and calls their languages "dialects" of Jingpo (Ramsey, 1987, p. 271).

In each of these cases the label the state has assigned, no matter how ill-suited, has led to the crystallization and expression of identities within the designated group along pan-ethnic lines. While ethnogenesis and the rise of pan-ethnic identities has happened throughout history, particularly with the incorporation of native peoples by nation–states, China represents an incubated process: What normally takes several generations for most ethnic groups has for many of the identified nationalities in the PRC occurred in the last 30 years.

"SUB-ETHNIC" IDENTITIES AND
THE QUESTION OF HAN ETHNICITY

Ethnic identities are, of course, not absent outside of the officially recognized minority nationalities. Unrecognized peoples live very ethnic lives: Emily Honig (1989;

1991) in a series of fascinating publications has documented the plight of the Subei people in Shanghai, who though not an official nationality, occupy several lower economic niches and have been stigmatized for such a long time that they have begun to think of themselves, and act, as an ethnic group. While Western scholars have been aware of cultural diversity within the Chinese for some time, these difference have generally been explained as "regional," or "sub-ethnic." This is because the vast majority of China scholars have accepted that 91% of China belongs to one ethnicity—the Han. Ethnographies on people such as the Hakka are said to teach us generalities about the rest of Chinese society, precisely because the Hakka are thought to be Han. Minority studies, no matter how close they are to the so-called "Han" in language, social structure, and culture—such as the Hui—are rarely included in studies of "Chinese" society, simply because they are not Han. Ethnic difference within Han society, while readily accepted as cuisines, cultures, and languages outside of China, within China are regarded as local dishes, customs, and dialects. The Cantonese, Sichuanese, and Hunanese are somehow not what they eat.

These extra-nationality associations cast doubt on the concept of the Han: The assumption that 91% of China constitutes one ethnic group is accepted by Chinese and most Western scholars. This should give us pause; perhaps we also have been taken in by the same political justification for Chinese nationalism as proposed by Sun Yatsen. Fred Blake's important study, *Ethnic Groups and Social Change in a Chinese Market Town* (1981), identified a plethora of ethnic groups defined by language, place, and occupation, including Hakka, Cantonese, and Hokkien, in the New Territories outside Hong Kong. While these groups are not recognized as "minorities" in China, no one has objected to his depiction of them as vibrant ethnic groups. This is perhaps because of their living under Hong Kong's jurisdiction. What will happen to these ethnic groups now that Hong Kong has reverted to China? Will Blake be criticized for confusing sub-regional identity with ethnicity? Clearly the issue of state policy and nationality identification requires further attention.

The question then becomes: When did these peoples begin to think of themselves as ethnic? For most, the process certainly did not begin with the nationality identification campaigns in the 1950s. The spread of the Chinese state always came into conflict with other cultures, whether dominated by peoples who identified with the descendants of the Wei River Valley or one of the 11 dynasties dominated by non-Chinese peoples. As I have argued, however, these cultural and even ethnic oppositions were fundamentally different in an empire seeking to establish rule over subject peoples than for a nation–state seeking legitimacy through a rhetoric of participation in governance. This enlistment required identification for purposes of representation and census-taking. This is the juncture where ethnicity began to become crucially salient and, for some, even invented. A parallel process has been documented in India, where Richard G. Fox has noted the production of "national cultures" and the "making of the Hindian" (Fox, 1990, p. 68). While India has been portrayed as the most multicultural of nations, and often contrasted to the culturally monolithic China, we see here the same kind of ethnic nationalist argument employed by Sun Yatsen with regard to the diversity within Chinese society. One must only wait to see if the "Hindian" will emerge from India much the same way as the "Han" in Chinese society. It is clear, however, that the ethnic minorities are already active and moving into the vanguard of ethnic politics in China (see Gladney, 1990a).

In China, the process of ethnogenesis is clearly not complete, as individuals in every new generation become incorporated into the state and begin to conceive of themselves in ethnic terms. This often happens at census registration, job application, or matriculation into state-run schools. I once asked a Han colleague when it was that he first realized he was a Han. No monocultural individual, he grew up in the cosmopolitan Manchurian city of Harbin, long a center of Sino-Soviet trade and northeastern ethnic diversity, populated by Russians, Manchurians, Koreans, Mongols, Olonqen, Daur, Hezhe, and Hui. Yet this 32-year-old intellectual, who was conducting post-doctoral research at Harvard, grew up in Harbin without ever realizing that he was a distinct nationality. "The first time I knew I was a Han," he told me, "was when I was 17 years old and I registered for work. I filled out the form and the man there told me to write 'Han' in the blank category for nationality (*minzu*). I didn't know what to write." It was when he applied for a job in the state-controlled sector that this Han fully realized his official ethnic status. It had little meaning for him until that time. Another Han from Beijing told me that she first realized she was Han when she entered school at age 7. She recalled her teacher saying that she must not make fun of her playmate because he did not eat pork, since she was Han and he was Hui. "Some people like ice cream, some others don't," the girl's teacher told her, "it's because different people like different things. You should respect the Hui, just as he should respect you, a Han." Han ethnicity is the unmarked category in China, that must be learned in state schools.

No Weberian "subjective belief" in common ancestry or political action will change one's ethnicity in China. Unauthorized "associations" of unrecognized groups are still illegal—unlike Irish in Chicago or Jews in New York who have political power despite their not being officially classified as underprivileged minorities in the United States. Only the officially designated underprivileged minorities and Native Americans find parallels with the minority nationalities of China and the Soviet Union. Unrecognized groups are not *ethne* for the Chinese state—no matter how much they themselves think they are.

ETHNIC PLURALISM IN CHINESE SOCIETY

Traditional approaches to the study of ethnic minorities in China have stressed their assimilation into Chinese culture, their "Sinification."[1] Certainly, a give-and-take will occur wherever divergent cultural traditions interact. However, in the case of the Han, this has become the accepted idea that is rarely seriously challenged: Ethnic change in China is assumed to be unidirectional, the inexorable grinding down of any foreign culture that comes into contact with the monolithic Chinese (Ch'en, 1966). Even studies that admit a wide cultural diversity within Chinese society are pessimistic about the possibilities of maintaining, let alone reviving, those cultures differing from the Han, or considering whether these "foreign" cultures might have exerted tremendous influence on what we now know as "the Chinese."

The kind of ethnic category-shifting or nationality reclassification that we have witnessed in China, where formerly registered Han reveal that they were really ethnic all along, wreaks havoc on Sinicization theory and state demographers. An overemphasis on the supposed ability of the Chinese, namely Han, culture to inexorably assimilate others has diverted attention from issues of power, state domination, and the resilience of ethnic identity. It is certainly in the interests of the regime in power to promote the idea that there is something germane to Chinese society that inevitably assimilates everything in its path.

This may be one reason why the Hui have generally been overlooked in studies of Chinese society. Even though they are the largest Muslim group and the third-largest minority and have played significant roles throughout Chinese history—virtually severing the empire in half during the mid-nineteenth century Hui rebellions, and powerbrokering in the Northwest between Japanese, Nationalist, and Communist armies during the warlord era of the first half of this century—little has been written about them in the past. It was generally assumed that if the Hui were not already Hanified, completely "Chinese" Muslims, they inevitably would be (Israeli, 1978).

This conclusion must necessarily be reached if "Chinese" is equated with "Han," which I have argued does not necessarily have to be the case, especially given the dubious nature of Han-ness. The problem is that, for Westerners, "Chinese" is an ethnic designation, so that it gets glossed as Han in China. Whereas, in China, "Chinese" (*Zhongguo ren*) refers to those who live in China, minority or otherwise. Whether they like it or not, those residing in China are Chinese (citizens, at least), though certainly not of Han ethnicity.

At times in China's history, the state certainly has attempted to assimilate those it regarded as barbarians into some notion of civilized identity. In the modern era, however, the Chinese nation–state has been predicated on the idea, if not the myth, of pluralism. In the past, hegemonic empires, many established by foreigners, may have allowed pluralism, but from it they certainly did not derive their *raison d'être*. If the Chinese state pursues more multiethnic policies, as it has officially done since 1978, then there is further hope for the Hui and other ethnic minorities. Attention to the state's role in influencing Hui identity takes us beyond positions that saw the Hui as assimilated Chinese Muslims, as if there was some pure unassimilated Muslim community, defined by a reified notion of Islam in the Middle East. It also helps to understand how the Hui as a collection of Muslim peoples could manage to survive for 1,200 years and evolve into their current identity.

The Sinicization paradigm also ignores the tremendous contributions Muslims and other minorities have made to Chinese culture. In the past, many regions and cities were governed by famous Muslim officials, like Sayyid ^CAjall, state expeditions were led by Muslim explorers, like Zheng He, and contributions were made to Confucian scholarship by Muslim gentry schooled in the classics, like Liu Zhi and Ma Chu. The Muslim astronomer Jimal al-Din introduced a Western calendar to China that was used for more than 400 years. The architect Ikhtiyar designed Beihai Park and much of the capital city. The famous "Hui hui cannon" was, of course, built by Muslims (the military engineers Alaw al-Din and Ismail), and had a long-term impact on the development of Chinese weaponry (which, it must be noted, they are now exporting back to the Middle East). Famous Yuan and Song dynasty poets were Muslims, including Gao Kegong (1248–1310 A.D.) and Zhao Zhan, a tradition that continues today, with several Hui Muslim authors enjoying a widespread audience throughout the country, such as Gao Shan (Ningxia), Bai Chongyi

(Xinjiang), Ma Zhiyao (Ningxia), Ma Li (Jilin), and Zhang Chengzhi (Beijing; see Schwarz, 1984, p. 203).

THE WIDE SPECTRUM OF HUI IDENTITY EXPRESSION

The diverse expression of the Muslim communities now recognized as Hui *minzu* may be seen as attempts to preserve ethnic integrity and identity in relational inter-action with the state and other oppositional ethnicities in each local sociopolitical context. For Hui communities in Northwest China, Islam is taken by the Hui as the fundamental marker of their identity—to be Hui is to be Muslim. Islam becomes the signifying practice of identity. The meaning of *qing zhen* for these Hui is expressed in Islamic ritual purity. Islamic movements have arisen in these communities as Hui reformers sought to resolve the tensions created by adapting the ideals of *qing zhen* to the Chinese social world. Government policy that permits freer expression of Hui ethnic identity has also allowed the resurgence of Islam. In response to the rerooting of Hui identity in Islam, local government cadres have reformulated central policies in recognition of the important place of Islam in Northwestern Hui identity.

In northern rural Hui communities that are isolated among Han majority areas, ethnic identity is often expressed and perpetuated through strategies of community maintenance. One of these strategies is ethnic endogamy. To be Hui in these com-munities is to be ensconced in a community that expresses its foreign Muslim an-cestry through the maintenance of a tradition of endogamy; *qing zhen* is expressed in maintaining the purity and cohesiveness of their community through marriage with other Hui. In order to preserve *qing zhen*, Hui marriage networks extend hun-dreds of kilometers beyond their immediate village. The promotion of government policies on urban migration, nationality marriage, surname endogamy, and birth planning have led to the expansion, and in some cases contraction, of Hui endoga-mous practices over time. Depending on fluctuations in government policies, Hui have often had to go far beyond their local area to find a Hui spouse. At other times they have been less willing to marry outside the confines of their village, lest they disrupt the cohesion of their community. Hui community interests concerning mar-riage and the changes in movement of Hui women through marriage over time re-veal the important influence of government policy on Hui identity.

Hui urban communities tend to express their identity in terms of cultural tradi-tions such as the pork taboo, entrepreneurship, and craft specializations. For these Hui, *qing zhen* means the cultural maintenance of those markers salient to their identity. To be Hui in these urban communities is to express the purity of one's an-cestral heritage through living a Hui lifestyle. This leads to the growing influence of institutions, such as the restaurant, in preserving and expressing Hui identity in the city. Liberalized nationality and economic policies have contributed to the cultural and economic expansion of those specializations and small businesses that most re-flect urban Hui descent from Hui ancestors.

In Southeastern Hui lineages, genealogical descent is the most important aspect of Hui identity—to be Hui is to be a member of a lineage that traces its descent to foreign Muslim ancestors. The concept of *qing zhen* for these Hui on the Southeast Coast is embodied in the veracity of their claims to foreign ancestry. Recent state recognition of these lineages as members of the Hui nationality has led to ethnic resurgence among previously unrecognized Hui lineages throughout the nation. In turn, contact with state-sponsored Hui and foreign Muslim delegations has led to a growing interest for many of these Hui in their ethnoreligious roots and even in practicing Islam.

Each case study illustrates a spectrum of Hui identity expression, with Islamic foci stressed in the Northwest, to ethnic endogamy and specializations in the northern urban and rural communities, to ethnic lineage stripped of any religious connotation in the southeast. Yet, in each of these communities one might find representatives of the other modes of expression all claiming Hui authenticity, such as the religious Hajji Imams in Quanzhou or the secularist Hui party members in Ningxia. Much of this has to do with the nature of local, and even individual, interactions.

It has been argued in the previous chapters that the Hui people, once members primarily of religious communities, through interacting with changing social contexts and state policy, now very much see themselves as a bona fide ethnic group. Their solidarity is clearly seen when conceptions of ethnic identity do not become preoccupied with the search for a set of static or common cultural criteria. The diversity of ethnic expressions found among the four communities discussed reveals that Hui identity is dynamically involved with and adapted to distinct social contexts. Everywhere, however, such identity has been particularly influenced by state policies implemented at the local level. Hui ethnic identity is not meaningful solely in terms of Islam, as Israeli (1978) would have us believe. While Islam is intimately related to Hui ancestry, as we have seen in Na Homestead, it may not always be as salient to Hui ethnic expression in every social context, as in Quanzhou. Yet, Islam cannot be ignored or divorced from Hui identity either, as the state has attempted to do in the past. We must look at each specific Hui community, its interests, involvements, and interaction in local contexts before coming to a more consistent understanding of Hui identity. In each context, Hui will stress those markers of identity, those signifying practices that most express to themselves, and to the salient others with whom they interact, their unique ethnicity.

THE EXTENSIVE UNITY OF HUI IDENTITY

While I have found remarkable diversity among the Hui, it has also been established that they regard themselves as "one family under Heaven," and one "united nationality." The idea that all Hui are one people becomes particularly meaningful when called into question by radical shifts in socioeconomic contexts. It became especially relevant to many Hui when they migrated from different backgrounds to Taiwan with the Nationalists in the late 1940s.

Various religious and socioeconomic networks that link disparate Hui communities together have been mentioned in this study. These networks deserve further research. They support and reinforce Hui shared ideas of a common ancestry. Religious networks include links between Sufi leaders and the appointed members of their orders, extending hierarchically from the *murshid* through his personally chosen *reyisi* and Ahong to the individual follower (*mulide*). Non-Sufi religious networks are often established by influential Ahong who attract students from all over

China, as we have seen for Linxia, Gansu, and Weishan, Yunnan. Itinerant Hui book salesmen who travel throughout China peddling the Qur'an and popular religious works reveal the importance of these religious and trade networks. As purveyors of information about distant Hui communities, these peripatetic Hui are another example of the tenuous ties between Hui communities. Social networks developed through the exchange of women in marriage also link isolated Hui communities. We have seen that one village, Chang Ying, has built contacts through establishing and maintaining affinal ties with distant Hui villages located hundreds of kilometers away, contacts often initiated and maintained by the itinerant Ahong.

Socioeconomic networks linking Hui communities were strongest before 1949 in the wool and leather long-distance trade, which the Hui dominated along the Yellow River throughout the north, and along the Burma Road in the southwest. Smaller-scale trade networks have reemerged in recent years with policies allowing freer participation in the market economy. Hui tradesmen from the Northwest are found throughout China, selling carpets and sundry factory goods in Lhasa, buying tea in Yunnan, ordering textiles in Shanghai, and trading money in Beijing. In each place they travel, mosques and newly established private *qing zhen* restaurants are the nodes in the extended network that sustains them.

State incorporation has contributed much to this process of ethnogenesis. The construction of roads, improved telecommunications, and establishment of national representative organizations have brought the formerly isolated Hui communities together as never before. State-sponsored associations whose purpose was to carry out state policies and improve nationality conditions, such as the Nationality Affairs Commission, the Nationalities Institutes, and the Chinese Islamic Association, are also playing important roles in the establishment of Hui networks and the strengthening of a national pan-Hui identity. While the Nationalities Institutes were set up to educate the minorities in Han culture, incorporating the future nationality leaders into the Han vision of the state, they have often led to the building of national associations among minorities who have come from around the country to study. Rather than assimilate into the Han, the students tend to keep to their own minority groups. Throughout China, Hui can subscribe to the periodicals *China's Muslims* (*Zhongguo Musilin*) and *Muslim World* (*Musilin Shijie*), receiving them in one's town or village through an incredibly efficient postal system. These state-sponsored organizations endorse the unity of Hui identity, and facilitate the building of relationships among Hui throughout China. The China Islamic Association has reported that between 1980 and 1987 it had organized 25 delegations of 73 members to Islamic countries, hosted 36 groups from more than 20 countries and regions, sponsored more than 2,000 pilgrims on the 1986 Hajj, trained more than 129 *manla* Islamic students from 6 nationalities at the Chinese Islamic Theological College (*jingxue yuan*) in Beijing from more than 27 provinces and regions, sent 10 students to study at the Al-Azhar in Egypt in 1982, with a second group in 1986, three of whom went to Libya, and began sending students to Pakistan from Xinjiang and Gansu (MacInnis, 1989, pp. 241–242). These state-sponsored national organizations have promoted international exchange with the Muslim world, and assisted inter-referentiality among the disparate Hui communities, which is what Michael Fischer (1986, p. 223) has suggested ethnicity may entail. These state-sponsored enterprises have contributed to the objectification and crystallization of a national ethnic group from what were once isolated "patchwork" (Lipman, 1984b) communities and more fluid identities. Few villagers need be isolated any more.

International business networks with foreign Muslims are starting to reemerge with the establishment of state-sponsored "Hui Muslim Construction Collectives" that gain contracts in Third World Muslim countries. International ties are beginning to be reestablished with the Islamic world as more Hui are trading across the western borders with Central Asian states, undertaking the Hajj and taking part in state-sponsored foreign Muslim delegations. The advent of Islamic tourism in China has literally redrawn the map for foreign Muslims and exposed local Hui to international Islam as never before.

Before 1949, several of these networks were nonexistent, and many of them were disrupted in the early 1950s. Their reemergence and the effect they are having on Hui identity are a result of liberalized economic and nationality policies. The creation of a pan-ethnic identity is intimately tied to these transnational organizations and movements, as they have furthered Hui ethnogenesis, the reconceptualization of local identities in terms of a broader imagined community.

The Give-and-Take of Nationality Policy and Ethnic Identity

Contrasting Nationalist and Communist policies toward the Hui are an important illustration of a sort of Hui "give-and-take" with different social contexts created by different policies. In "push-me, pull-you" fashion, to paraphrase the two-headed llama in *My Fair Lady,* Hui are both pushed by their ethnic background and pulled by state policy, and in the process much is given and much taken away. In Taiwan, Hui identity is regarded solely in terms of religion. Thus, for the Taiwanese Muslims who no longer practice Islam, Hui identity no longer has any relevance. Hui who came from the mainland have sought to adapt themselves to this policy, express their Islamic identity, and, at the same time, continue to emphasize the ethnic and blood differences that distinguish them from the Han. In the PRC, the Hui are free to express their identity without reference to religion. At one time, ethnic expression was encouraged to the point of excluding religious expression and Hui Islamic identity was suppressed. Now that freer religious expression has been allowed, Islamic resurgence has taken place in those areas where Islam is the most salient expression of Hui ethnoreligious identity. Even where Islam is no longer of central importance to local Hui identity, however, Islam has begun to take on new meaning, as we have seen among Hui lineages on the Southeast Coast. In both Taiwan and Mainland China, the state has attempted to define Hui identity in terms of its own state ideology. In response, the Hui in both places have reformulated their own ethnic ideologies in order to preserve and express their identity.

The state reconstructs mosques and historic Islamic sites as places for tourism and religious pilgrimage for the Hui and foreign Muslims. As a result, local Hui identity often becomes expanded in its perspective. Hui villagers, many for the first time, experience participation in the national and international Islamic world. Expanded awareness of the importance of Islam to Hui identity leads local government officials to revise policies that had previously encouraged a stricter distinction between ethnicity and religion. Many of these policies were originally intended to encourage economic development and the Four Modernizations. In the process, they have allowed freer religious expression of Hui identity. With this resurgence of ethnoreligious identity, socioeconomic development has also improved.

Now that the state once again has promoted policies favorable to the Hui and other minorities, there has been a resurgence in those aspects of ethnic identity most relevant in each social context. In China, people now want to be ethnic or at least members of a minority nationality. Children of mixed marriages choose to be registered as a minority. Han young people in Beijing are willing, and perhaps even prefer, to find minority spouses. While autonomous regions, counties, and villages were thought to possess little real autonomy, this study has shown that enough benefits are attached to them for people to want them. Not only in Chendai, Fujian, where the Ding have applied for recognition as an autonomous county, but throughout China, autonomous administrative units have become important issues in contemporary ethnopolitics. In China, as well as the former USSR, autonomy may not have meant much in the past, but it did give people a voice in the political process and a legal wedge by which to push for social change.

THE POLITICS OF ETHNIC SEPARATISM

On June 17, 1993, two bombs exploded in an office building next to the Oasis Hotel in Kashgar, a large market town in southern Xinjiang, killing three people and ruining the entire front of the building. A group agitating for an independent "Eastern Turkestan" claimed responsibility for the explosion, convincing Beijing that its fears regarding Uygur separatism and the increasing influence from the new independent Turkic states on its borders were well-founded. Throughout the long hot summer, various reports surfaced that at least two bombs exploded in Xinjiang per week, with as many as 30 separate bombings over the next three months. The long-standing struggles of Tibetan independence movements have also been well-documented (Goldstein, 1990, pp. 129–167; Kelly, 1991). However, until now, most China scholars have dismissed the possibility of separatism as remote and the violent incidents as minor, on the periphery of China's great land mass and of no serious threat to the central authority. The Hui, Uygurs, Kazakhs, Tadjiks, Mongols, and even the Tibetans are still felt to be marginal minorities that were expected to go the way of the Manchu and others who have been thought to be long-assimilated into the Chinese mainstream.

China's 55 "official" minority nationality groups include 10 Muslim nationalities located primarily on China's borders with Russia and the new Central Asian states, whose majority populations are mainly Muslim. With a total Muslim population of at least 20 million, this places China among the most numerous of Muslim nations (more than Saudi Arabia, Iraq, Libya, or Syria). In 1991, Xinjiang became linked directly to Kazakhistan by rail, and overland roads to Pakistan, Kazakhistan, Tajikistan, and Kyrgyzia are becoming much more open to cross-border travel. Weekly flights leave from Urumqi, the capital of Xinjiang, to Istanbul, Saudi Arabia, and Central Asia (Gladney, 1992a, p. 3). Through cross-border trade and increased foreign trade relations with the Middle East, involving significant exchanges of cheap Chinese labor, consumer goods, and weaponry, China has become closely tied to the Muslim Middle East. In order to maintain close ties with the Muslim world, China has had to pay closer attention to the treatment of its Muslim minorities. The recognition of China by Saudi Arabia in 1990 and increasing numbers of Muslim pilgrims from China to Mecca indicates improving relations. Yet, these relations will be jeopardized if Muslim, especially Uygur, discontent continues over such issues as limitations on mosque building, restrictions on childbearing, and mineral and energy development in Muslim minority regions without attention for local concerns.

Protests by Uygurs and other Muslims in the past have covered a wide range of religious, family, and environmental issues. These issues have been exacerbated by increasing income disparities between the Southeast and Eastern coastal regions and the primarily Muslim areas of the north and northwest. As contact increases between Central Asian Muslims on both sides of China's northwest border, moves for local autonomy and even independence may need to be balanced against the desire for economic growth. Xinjiang's Muslims are well aware of the ethnic and political conflicts in Azerbaijan and Tajikistan, and the fact that many of them are better off economically than their co-religionists across the border. The challenge to the state government is to convince Northwestern Muslims that they will benefit more from cooperation than from resistance.

In the south, there are nearly 12 million Kam-Thai speaking Zhuang people on the Vietnam border, and more than 24 separate minority groups in Yunnan province alone, where cross-border relations with Myanmar (Burma), Cambodia, and Thailand have increased dramatically in the last few years. Weekly flights connect Yunnan's capital, Kunming, with Bangkok and Chiangmai, and increased overland traffic has led to a rising problem of smuggling and drug trade across the Chinese border. The settling of disputes in Cambodia, Vietnam, and highland Burma have continued to be a high priority for state planners in Beijing, perhaps because of the significant potential for ethnic wars to spill over China's southern borders.

The importance of the minorities to China's border areas and long-term development is disproportionate to their population. Although they are less than 9% of the total population, minorities are concentrated in mineral and natural resource rich areas spanning nearly 60% of the country's land mass. In many border counties of Xinjiang, Tibet, Inner Mongolia, and Yunnan, minorities exceed 90% of the population. The state has recognized the minorities' importance and distinctiveness by creating ascending levels of minority autonomous administration. In minority-populated areas, there are 5 autonomous regions, 31 autonomous prefectures, 96 autonomous counties and banners, and countless autonomous villages as well. "Autonomous" primarily means that there is more local control over the administration of resources, taxes, birth planning, education, legal jurisdiction, and religious expression. It does not mean that true political control is in minority hands. Whereas most minority regions and districts have minority government leaders, the real source of power is in the Communist Party, which in all of these areas is dominated by the Han majority, reflecting China's active watch over these autonomous areas. As a result, these "autonomous" regions actually come under closer scrutiny than other provinces with large minority populations, such as Gansu, Qinghai, and Sichuan.[2]

Nevertheless, while "autonomy" seems to be not all that the name might imply, it is still apparently a desirable attainment for minorities in the PRC. Between the 1982 and 1990 censuses, 18 new autonomous counties were established, with three new counties in Liaoning Province for the Manchu alone who previously had no autonomous administrative districts of their own. The majority of the earlier autonomous districts were set up shortly after the identification programs were completed in the late 1950s. While it is clear that the government is trying to limit the recognition of new nationalities, there seems to be an avalanche of new autonomous administrative districts. In addition to the counties and numerous autonomous villages whose total numbers have never been published, there are at least eight new counties scheduled to be set up in the future.[3] The establishment in the late 1980s and 1990s of more autonomous districts reflects a real desire for increasing independence from central jurisdiction. No matter how circumscribed that autonomy is in actuality, it is clear that many want it.

POPULATION POLITICS: "COMING OUT" IN THE 1990s

The increase in autonomous administrative districts and minority population reflects what may be described as an explosion of ethnicity in contemporary China. While Han population grew a total of 10% between 1982 and 1990, minority population grew 35% overall (Figure 7.1). Significantly, Muslim populations grew by an average of 30 to 40%. The Hui, who were the main focus of this study, grew in population from 7.2 million in 1982 to 8.6 million in 1990, an increase of 19%. The Manchu, who conquered China in 1644 and established the Qing dynasty, were a group long thought to have gradually assimilated to the Han Chinese majority during their 286-year rule (Ch'en, 1966). Yet, not only have the Manchu added three new autonomous districts in Northeast China, but they have grown a total of 128%, increasing their population from 4.3 million to 9.8 million. Indeed, it has now become popular, especially in Beijing, for people to "come out" as Manchu or other ethnics, admitting that they were not "Han" all along.

The Tujia, a group widely dispersed throughout the Southwest, more than doubled their population from 2.8 million to 5.8 million, and they will secure five of eight new autonomous counties scheduled to be set up. Even more remarkable is the case of the Gelao people in Guizhou who grew an incredible 714% in just eight short years. Clearly, these rates reflect more than mere fecundity and extensive use of minority exception to the national one child per family birth restriction. Such large population increases reflect "category-shifting" or reclassification where people redefine their nationality, either from Han to minority or from one minority to another. Children of mixed parents due to inter-ethnic marriages are allowed to choose their nationality at the age 18; before then, the parents can decide. At the same time, people who can prove minority ancestry, as is the case of the Hui in Fujian, can apply for reregistration. There must have been much of this "category-shifting" for the total minority population in China to grow from 67 million to 91 million in just eight short years.[4] One scholar predicts that if this rate continues, the population of minorities will be 100 million in the year 2000, 131 million in 2010, 221 million in 2030, and 864 million in 2080 (Tien, 1983, p. 147). China has begun to limit births among minorities, especially in urban areas in the last few years, but can it limit the avalanche of applications for redefinition? What about the hundreds of groups applying for first-time recognition?

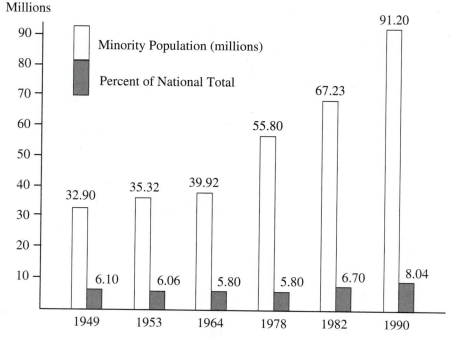

Figure 7.1   Minority/Majority Population Growth, 1949–1990

There are also new international pressures being brought to bear on China's domestic minority policies. China's efforts to promote a more open policy toward its Muslim minorities has been noted, which would be more amenable to its Mideast trading partners. By contrast, international pressure still has had little effect on China's treatment of Tibetans, perhaps due to the lack of real geopolitical support for Tibetan complaints in the United Nations and elsewhere. Of more influence will be China's growing trade with South Korea and its impact on the Korean populations in Liaoning and Manchuria. The Koreans are already the most educationally advanced of all nationalities in China, including the Han, and their local economy is booming due to South Korean investment, tourism, and abundant natural resources. International tourism and travel to China's minority areas has had a significant impact on local economies, particularly with successful "Silk Road" tourism to Xinjiang, and recent marketing of package tours to the "colorful" minority regions of Yunnan and Guizhou for Japanese, Taiwanese, and Southeast Asian Chinese tourist groups.

The most striking change in China's policy toward a single minority, as a result of changing international relations, has been recent discussions of recognizing the Chinese Jews (*youtai ren*) as an official nationality, just after the improvement in Sino-Israeli relations in 1992. The Chinese Jews, once thought extinct, are now said to number from 2,000 to 8,000 in population. It is known that China's last active synagogue was in Kaifeng, where the Jewish community mentioned by Marco Polo are thought to have eventually assimilated to the Hui Muslims in the area by the mid-nineteenth century, due to declining population, probable persecution, and lack of contact with other Jews. Gradual assimilation to the large Muslim community in the area was not surprising due to shared dietary and religious similarities, amidst a Chinese population that ate pork and practiced polytheism. The "Chinese Jews" were distinct from the European Jews who began arriving in the nineteenth century to China's northeastern and eastern coastal cities from Europe and Russia, many of whom left China when the communists took over in 1949. The reawakened interest in the Chinese Jews of Kaifeng and their reappearance has as much to do with rising ethnic consciousness (many of them claimed to have been unwillingly absorbed by the Hui and the Han), as it has to do with international, especially American Jewish, academic interest in the "lost" Jews of China.

Clearly, it has become popular to be "officially" ethnic in 1990s China. But why? One explanation may be that in 1982 there were still lingering doubts about the government's true intent at registering the nationalities during the census. The Cultural Revolution, a 10-year period when any kind of difference—whether it be ethnic, religious, cultural, or political—was ruthlessly suppressed, had officially ground to a halt only a few years previously. Mosques, Buddhist temples, churches, lineage halls, and other cultural institutions were torn down in the name of destroying the "Four Olds." By the mid-1980s it had become clear that those identified as an "official" minority were beginning to receive real benefits due to the carrying out of several "affirmative action" and other entitlement programs. The most significant privileges included permission to have more children (except in urban areas, minorities are generally not bound to the one-child policy), pay less taxes, obtain better (albeit Chinese) education for their children, have greater access to public office, speak and learn their native languages, worship and practice their religion (often religious practices such as Shamanism that were still banned among the Han), and express their cultural differences through the arts and public culture. These have become real advantages and privileges that, though rarely honored in the past, have begun to have an impact in the last 10 years. In the 1990s, people want to be "officially" ethnic. But what about the "unofficial ethnics" among the so-called Han?

ETHNICITY AND NATIONALISM IN THE PEOPLE'S REPUBLIC

Understanding of the Hui and other ethnicities in China in the past has been hampered by models and policies that could not account for the wide diversity and present unity of ethnic expression. Models that relied on a cultural-trait analysis, such as the Stalinist and cultural approaches, do not begin to account for the dynamic context and politicized nature of ethnicity in China. In the example of the Hui, these models foundered on the similarity between Hui and Han and on the diversity found within the Hui. Although the Hui did not fit the Stalinist model, the government chose to recognize them on the basis of prerevolutionary ideas for the political goals of incorporation and state-building, in a careful rewriting of history. Utilitarian situational approaches had trouble with the continued meaningfulness and power of ethnic identity in the face of hegemonic oppression. Attention to power relations in the ongoing relations between the state and local ethnic groups, both externally and internally, is critical for our understanding of the current resurgence of ethnic identities, their significance, and salience in the modern world.

At the same time, the role of the state must not be overprivileged. Even the most totalitarian of regimes has its limits. As the example from the former Soviet Union illustrates, ethnic identity has a power and resilience of its own that acts in relational fashion with the state apparatus. At the same time, ethnicity itself need not be over-essentialized. Peoples disappear or merge into other groups through processes of ethnogenesis. The emphasis here is on relations, not essences.

Hui identity is rooted in the idea, factual or fictitious, of descent from foreign Muslim ancestors. This idea links all Hui together—religious and nonreligious, Ahong and cadre, farmer and factory worker—under the shared belief that "All Hui under Heaven are one family." When this shared idea of descent interacts with changing social contexts, new expressions of identity emerge in relation to the old. This leads to the wide variety of Hui ethnoreligious expression in different social settings. As has been described in the discussion of four Hui communities, expressions of Hui identity and understandings of *qing zhen* will be altered and adapted to each specific context. Cultural symbols of Hui identity, such as the pork taboo, Islamic ritual, genealogy, occupational specialization, and endogamy become salient for each Hui community in the social situation where they express their ancestral heritage. The markers of identity that become salient in each context often has much to do with state policy and power. These policies are often influenced by international alignments and shifts in relations.

Since the founding of the PRC, international and strategic considerations—particularly the desire for Third World, often Muslim, investment—have encouraged favoritism toward minorities, so that goals of pluralism and assimilation have constantly shifted, depending on local and international politics. Chinese Marxists were surprised that these identified groups did not fade away with post-colonialism, land reforms, collectivization, and erosion of class-based loyalties. Ethnicity is a vertical phenomenon that cuts across class and socioeconomic stratification, and it has maintained its salience despite the land reform campaigns and other efforts to reduce class differences in Chinese and Soviet societies, which, it was thought, would lead to the disappearance of social and ethnic difference. Charles Keyes has suggested the metaphor of a gyroscope for understanding ethnicity: Rooted in constructed notions of descent and ancestry, it is constantly changing and propelled by its very dynamism. This has certainly been true for the Hui across China and their notions of self, history, and Islam (which they translated *qing zhen*). This notion was perfectly expressed by Ma Zhu (1681), an early Qing dynasty scholar, who in 1681 published a work on Islam, which he entitled: *Qing Zhen zhi Nan* "The Compass of *Qing Zhen*."

In recent years, the Hui have been significant players in China's efforts to maintain close political–economic ties with largely Muslim, Middle Eastern nations (which involve trade, development contracts, silkworms, and the like). As we have discovered, China's nationality policy is a "derivative discourse," combining Western, Japanese, and Soviet notions of nationalism, awkwardly constructed on top of traditional ideas of identity, ethnicity, and race. The contradictions and complementarities of these discourses, mainly inculcated in China at the beginning of this century, have combined with China's traditional notion of country and race as defining nationality to produce a multilevel debate on Chinese national identity that continues to rage across the country.

The rise of ethnic nationalism among Muslims is caught up in the national debate over national identity. The Muslims, and other minorities, have much at stake in this debate. If it should resolve itself in a traditional Chinese racist approach, as it did in the "Han chauvinist" periods of the Cultural Revolution and Anti-Rightist campaigns, they have much to fear. If, however, their call for pluralism has been heard we may see a new openness throughout Chinese society, a rediscovery and reflowering of many different ethnic roots, once subsumed for nationalistic goals as merely "regional" or "sub-ethnic." While this may be a threat to an insecure rulership, it may also be the only way to engender the support of all the people of the People's Republic without resorting to force.

As the Hui and other ethnic groups interact with local contexts, both their ethnic identity and the government policies influencing them will change. This interaction has led to the Hui emerging as a people who are an important part of the fabric of Chinese society. The Hui are no longer "strangers in a strange land" as the Protestant missionary G. Findley Andrew (1921, p. 12) suggested in the 1920s. With recent favorable nationality policies that have allowed freer expression of Hui identity, special nationality privileges, and further exposure to the Islamic world, we should expect newer Hui collectivities and interpretations of *qing zhen* to emerge. This relational process has produced a Muslim minority in China, the Hui, who have emerged in the last 40 years as an ethnoreligious group, with a vibrant national and even transnational identity.

Notes

[1] A notable exception to the assimilationist view of Chinese Islam is found in Lombard and Salomon (1994).

[2] I know of only two minority First Party Secretaries in minority Autonomous Regions: Ulanfu, the famous Mongol Communist who dominated Inner Mongolia in the 1950s and 1960s, before being transferred to Beijing and Wu Jinhua, a Yi minority from Sichuan who was Party Secretary in Tibet from 1985 to 1989.

[3] The new autonomous counties scheduled to be set up are: In Qinghai Province—the Datong Hui-Tujia Autonomous County (A.C.) and the Minhe Hui-Tujia A.C.; in Sichuan Province—the Qianjiang Tujia-Miao A.C., the Pengshui Miao-Tujia A.C., the Shizhu Tujia A.C., the Mabian Yi A.C., and the Ebian Yi A.C.; and in Guizhou Province—the Yuping Dong A.C. Cited in Ma Yin (1989, pp. 434–448).

[4] Few minorities experienced population increases between 1982 and 1990 due to migration, with notable exceptions perhaps being the Vietnamese (Jing nationality, 58% growth) and the Russians (Eluosi nationality, 360% growth). The Russian population is important to watch as events in the former Soviet Union have led to a large influx of Russians to China in the last few years, primarily for trade and employment possibilities, but some are attempting to settle due to fears about latent Central Asian and Siberian hostilities toward Russians in those regions.

References

Abu-Lughod, L. (1991). Zones of theory in the anthropology of the Arab world. *Annual Review of Anthropology, 18,* 267–306.

Alles, E. (1994). L'islam chinois: femmes ahong. *Etudes Oriental, 13/14,* 163–168.

Alonso, M. E. (Ed.) (1979). *China's inner Asian frontier.* Cambridge, MA: Peabody Museum, Harvard University.

Anderson, B. (1991). *Imagined communities: Reflections on the origin and spread of nationalism.* London: Verso Press.

Andrew, G. F. (1921). *The crescent in North-West China.* London: China Inland Mission.

Anonymous. (1944). Japanese infiltration among Muslims in China. Unpublished report, Office of Strategic Services, Research and Analysis Branch.

Appadurai, A. (1986). Introduction: Commodities and the politics of value. In A. Appadurai (Ed.), *The social life of things: Commodities in cultural perspective.* Cambridge, MA: Cambridge University Press.

Armijo-Hussein, J. (1989). The sinicization and confucianization in Chinese and western historiography of a Muslim from Bukhara serving under the Mongols in China. In D. C. Gladney (Ed.), *The legacy of Islam in China: An international symposium in memory of Joseph F. Fletcher* (Conference volume). Harvard University, Cambridge, MA.

Aubin, F. (1986). Chinese Islam: In pursuit of its sources. *Central Asian Survey, 5* (2), 73–80.

Bai, S. (1951, February 17). Huihui minzu de xingcheng [The nature of the Hui nationality]. *Guangming Rebao.*

Baker, H. D. R. (1968). *Sheung Shui: A Chinese lineage village.* Palo Alto, CA: Stanford University Press.

Banister, J. (1987). *China's changing population.* Stanford, CA: Stanford University Press.

Barnett, A. D. (1963). *China on the eve of the communist takeover.* New York: Praeger.

Barnett, A. D. (1993). *China's far west: Four decades of change.* Boulder, CO: Westview Press.

Barth, F. (1969). Introduction. In F. Barth (Ed.), *Ethnic groups and boundaries: The social organization of cultural difference* (pp. 9–38). Boston: Little, Brown.

Befu, H. (Ed.) (1993). *Cultural nationalism in East Asia: Representation and identity.* Berkeley, CA: Institute of East Asian Studies.

Beijing City Sociology Committee, et al. (Eds.) (1984). Beijing shi canzaju xiaoshu minzu jiaoyu wenti diaocha baogao [Research report on the problem of education among dispersed minorities in Beijing City]. *Central Institute for Nationalities Journal, 1,* 18–26.

Blake, F. C. (1981). *Ethnic groups and social change in a Chinese market town.* Honolulu, HI: University Press of Hawaii.

Bourdieu, P. (1977). *Outline of a theory of practice.* Cambridge, MA: Cambridge University Press.

Brandt, C., Schwartz, B. & Fairbank, J. (Eds.) (1931, November 7). Constitution of the [Chinese] Soviet Republic. *A documentary history of Chinese communism.* London: Allen & Unwin.

Broomhall, M. (1910). *Islam in China: A neglected problem.* New York: Paragon Books.

Burns, J. F. (1984, June 13). Chinese city is true to Moslem self. *Los Angeles Times,* p. Y4.

Chan, A., Madsen R. & Unger, J. (1984). *Chen village: A recent history of a peasant community in the People's Republic of China.* Berkeley: University of California Press.

Chan, W. (1953). The new awakening of Islam. In W. Chan (Ed.), *Religious trends in modern China.* New York: Columbia University Press.

Chance, N. A. (1990). *China's urban villagers: Changing life in a Beijing suburb*. Fort Worth, TX: Harcourt Brace Jovanovich.

Chang, H. Y. (1987). The Hui Muslim minority in China: An historical overview. *Journal, Institute for Muslim Minority Affairs, 8* (1), 62–78.

Chang, H. Y. (1988). The Ming Empire: Patron of Islam in China and Southeast and West Asia. *Journal of the Malaysian Branch of the Royal Asiatic Society, 61* (2), 1–44.

Chen D. (Ed.) (1984). *Islamic inscriptions in Quanzhou* (E. Chen, Trans.). Yinchuan, China: Ningxia Peoples Publishing Society and Quanzhou, China: Fujian People's Publishing Society.

Ch'ên Y. (1966). *Western and Central Asians in China under the Mongols: Their transformation into Chinese* (Monumenta Serica Monograph XV). Los Angeles: Monumenta Serica at the University of California.

Cherif, L. (1994). Ningxia, l'école au fémini. *Etudes Oriental, 13/14*, 156–162.

China Sports (Eds.) (1984). *Wushu among Chinese Moslems*. China Sports Series 2. Beijing: China Sports Magazine.

Ci Yuan [Etymologies] (1982). (5th ed., Vols. 1–4). Beijing, China: Shangwu Yinshuguan.

Clark, H. R. (1981). Consolidation on the South China frontier: The development of Ch'uanchou 699–1126. Unpublished doctoral dissertation, University of Pennsylvania, Philadelphia.

Cohn, B. S. (1987). The census, social structure and objectification in South Asia. In B. S. Cohn (Ed.), *An anthropologist among the historians and other essays*. Delhi, India: Oxford University Press.

Connor, W. (1984). *The national question in Marxist-Leninist theory and strategy*. Princeton, NJ: Princeton University Press.

Constable, N. (1994). *Christian souls and Chinese spirits*. Berkeley: University of California Press.

Crook, I. & Crook, D. (1959). *Revolution in a Chinese village, Ten Mile Inn*. London: Routledge & Paul.

Dai, Q. (in press). On the languages of the Jingpo nationality. In C. Li & D. C. Gladney (Eds.), *Minority nationalities of China*. Amsterdam: Mouton Press.

DeFrancis, J. (1984). *The Chinese language: Fact and fantasy*. Honolulu, HI: University of Hawaii Press.

Denzin, N. K. (1968). On the ethics of disguised observation. *Social Problems, 15*, 502–504.

Department of Population Statistics of State Statistical Bureau and Economic Department of State Nationalities Affairs Commission, People's Republic of China. (1994). *Population of China's nationality (data of 1990 population census)* [*Zhongguo Minzu Renkou Ziliao (1990 nian Renkou Pucha Shuju)*]. Beijing: China Statistical Publishing House.

De Vos, G. & Romanucci-Ross, L. (Eds.) (1975). *Ethnic identity: Cultural continuities and change*. Palo Alto, CA: Mayfield Publishing.

Dikötter, F. (1992). *The discourse of race in modern China*. Stanford, CA: Stanford University Press.

Ding Clan Genealogy (1980). In *Quanzhou wenxian congkan di san zhong* [Quanzhou documents collection, no. 13]. Quanzhou, China: Quanzhou Historical Research Society.

Ding, X. (1990). Chendai: The past and the present. In C. Guoqiang (Ed.), *Chendai Huizushi Yanjiu* [Research on Chendai Hui nationality history] (pp. 1–6). Beijing: China Academy of Social Sciences Press.

Dittmer, L. & Kim, S. S. (Eds.) (1993). *China's quest for a national identity*. Ithaca, NY: Cornell University Press.

Drake, F. S. (1943). Mohammedanism in the T'ang Dynasty. *Monumenta Serica, 8*, 1–40.

Dreyer, J. (1976). *China's forty million: Minority nationalities and national integration in the People's Republic of China*. Cambridge, MA: Harvard University Press.

Dreyer, J. (1981). The Islamic Community of China. *Central Asian Survey, 1* (2/3), 32–49.

Duara, P. (1995). *Rescuing history from the nation: Questioning narratives of modern China*. Chicago: University of Chicago Press.

Dunlop, J. B. (1983). *The faces of contemporary Russian nationalism*. Princeton, NJ: Princeton University Press.

Durkheim, E. (1915). *The elementary forms of the religious life* (J. W. Swain, Trans.). New York: Free Press.

Dyer, S. R. (1979). *Soviet Dungan Kolkhozes in the Kirghiz SSR and the Kazakh SSR* (Oriental Monograph Series No. 25). Canberra: Australian National University Press.

Dyer, S. R. (1981–1983). T'ang T'ai-tsung's dream: A Soviet Dungan version of a legend on the origin of the Chinese Muslims. *Monumenta Serica, 35*, 545–570.

Eickelman, D. F. (1981). *The Middle East: An anthropological approach*. Upper Saddle River, NJ: Prentice-Hall.

Ekvall, R. (1939). *Cultural relations on the Kansu-Tibetan border*. Chicago: Chicago University Press.

Erikson, K. T. (1967). A comment on disguised observation in sociology. *Social Problems, 12*, 366–373.

Evans-Pritchard, E. E. (1940). *The Nuer*. London: Oxford University Press.

Fan, C. (1980). In Chinese Academy of Social Sciences (Eds.), *Zhongguo de xibei jiao* [China's northwest corner]. Tianjin, China: Public Publishing House and Beijing: New China Publishing Society.

Faure, D. (1989). The lineage as cultural invention: The case of the Pearl River Delta. *Modern China, 15*, 4–36.

Fei, X. (1981). Ethnic identification in China. In X. Fei (Ed.), *Toward a people's anthropology*. Beijing, China: New World Press.

Fei, X. (1989). *Zhonghua minzu de duoyuan jiti juge* [Plurality and unity in the configuration of the Chinese nationality]. *Beijing Daxue Xuebao, 4*, 1–19.

Feng, Z. (1985). "Gedimu" bayi ["Gedimu" eight opinions]. In Gansu Provincial Ethnology Department (Eds.), *Xibei Yisilanjiao Yanjiu* [Northwest Islam research]. Lanzhou, China: Gansu Nationality Publishing Society.

Fernea, E. W. (1965). *Guest of the sheik: An ethnography of an Iraqi village*. New York: Anchor Books.

Firth, R. (1936). *We, the Tikopia*. London: Allen & Unwin.

Fischer, M. M. J. (1986). Ethnicity and the post-modern arts of memory. In J. Clifford & G. E. Marcus (Eds.), *Writing culture: The poetics and politics of ethnography*. Berkeley: University of California Press.

Fitzgerald, C. P. (1973). *The tower of five glories: A study of the Min Chia of Ta Li, Yunnan*. Westport, CT: Hyperion Press.

Fletcher, J. (n.d.) The Naqshbandiyya in Northwest China. Unpublished manuscript, Harvard University, Cambridge, MA.

Fletcher, J. (1975). Central Asian Sufism and Ma Ming-hsin's new teaching. In C. Ch'en (Ed.), *Proceedings of the fourth East Asian altaistic conference*. Taipei: National Taiwan University.

Fletcher, J. (1979). A brief history of the Chinese northwestern frontier, China proper's northwest frontier: Meetingplace of four cultures. In M. E. Alonso (Ed.), *China's inner Asian frontier*. Cambridge, MA: Peabody Museum.

Fletcher, J., Alonso, M. E. & Chorbachi, W. K. (1989, April 14–16). Arabic calligraphy in twentieth-century China. In D. C. Gladney (Ed.), *The legacy of Islam in China: An international symposium in memory of Joseph F. Fletcher* (Conference volume). Harvard

University, Cambridge, MA.

Forbes, A. D. W. (1986). *Warlords and Muslims in Chinese Central Asia*. Cambridge, MA: Cambridge University Press.

Fowler, V. (1987). The truth about *Zhen. Asian Review, 1* (1), 26–42.

Fox, R. G. (1990). Hindu nationalism in the making, or the rise of the Hindian. In R. G. Fox (Ed.), *Nationalist ideologies and the production of national cultures*. Washington, DC: American Ethnological Society.

Fried, M. (1969). *Fabric of Chinese society*. New York: Octagon.

Friedman, E. (1994). Reconstructing China's national identity: A southern alternative to Mao-era anti-imperialist nationalism. *The Journal of Asian Studies, 53* (1), 67–91.

Gamble, S. (1921). *Peking: A social survey*. New York: George H. Doran.

Gates, H. (1981). Ethnicity and social class. In E. Ahern & H. Gates (Eds.), *The anthropology of Taiwanese society*. Stanford, CA: Stanford University Press.

Geertz, C. (1973). The integrative revolution: Primordial sentiments and civil politics in the new states. In C. Geertz (Ed.), *The interpretation of cultures* (pp. 255–310). New York: Basic Books.

Geertz, C. (1968). *Islam observed: Religious development in Morocco and Indonesia.* Chicago: University of Chicago Press.

Geertz, C. (1988). *Works and lives: The anthropologist as author*. Stanford, CA: Stanford University Press.

Gladney, D. C. (1987a). Muslim tombs and ethnic folklore: Charters for Hui identity. *The Journal of Asian Studies, 46* (3), 495–532.

Gladney, D. C. (1987b). *Qing Zhen: A study of ethnoreligious identity among Hui Muslim communities in China*. Unpublished doctoral dissertation, University of Washington, Seattle.

Gladney, D. C. (1990a). The peoples of the People's Republic: Finally in the vanguard? *The Fletcher Forum of World Affairs, 12* (1), 62–76.

Gladney, D. C. (1990b). The ethnogenesis of the Uighur. *Central Asian Survey, 9* (1), 1–28.

Gladney, D. C. (1990c, February 3). The Tasaday of China? *Anthropology Newsletter.*

Gladney, D. C. (1992a). Transnational Islam and Uighur national identity: Salman Rushdie, Sino-Muslim missile deals, and the trans-eurasian railway. *Central Asian Survey, 11* (3), 1–18.

Gladney, D. C. (1992b). The Hui, Islam and the State: A Sufi community in China's northwest corner. In J. Gross (Ed.), *Muslims in Central Asia: Expressions of identity and change* (pp. 89–111). Durham, NC: Duke University Press.

Gladney, D. C. (1993a, July 27). The study of Islam in China: Some recent research. *MESA Bulletin,* 23–30.

Gladney, D. C. (1993b). The Muslim face of China. *Current History* September (575), 275–280.

Gladney, D. C. (1993c). Urban ethnicity in China: Muslim enclaves in modern Beijing. In A. Southall & G. Guldin (Eds.), *Urban anthropology and China* (pp. 278–307). Leiden, The Netherlands: E. J. Brill.

Gladney, D. C. (1994a). Representing nationality in China: Refiguring majority/minority identities. *The Journal of Asian Studies, 53* (1), 92–123.

Gladney, D. C. (1994b). Sino-Middle Eastern perspectives since the Gulf War: Views from below. *The International Journal of Middle East Studies, 29* (4), 677–691.

Gladney, D. C. (1994c). The making of a Muslim minority in China: Dialogue and contestation. *Etudes Oriental, 13/14,* 113–142.

Gladney, D. C. (1994d). Salman Rushdie in China: Religion, ethnicity, and state definition in the People's Republic. In H. Hardacre, L. Kendall & C. Keyes (Eds.), *Asian visions of authority: Religion and the modern states of East and Southeast Asia* (pp. 255–278). Honolulu, HI: University of Hawaii Press.

Gladney, D. C. (1994e). Ethnic identity in China: The new politics of difference. In W. A. Joseph (Ed.), *China briefing, 1994* (pp. 171–192). Boulder, CO: Westview Press.

Gladney, D. C. (1995a). Tian Zhuangzhuang, the fifth generation, and minorities film in China. *Public Culture, 8* (1), 161–175.

Gladney, D. C. (1995b). China's ethnic reawakening. *AsiaPacific Issues, 18*, 1–8.

Gladney, D. C. (1995c). Islam. In D. Overmeyer (Ed.), Chinese religions: The state of the field. *The Journal of Asian Studies, 54* (2), 371–378.

Gladney, D. C. (1995d). Economy and ethnicity: The revitalization of a Muslim minority in Southeastern China. In A. Walder (Ed.), *The waning of the communist state: Economic origins of political decline in China and Hungary* (pp. 242–266). Berkeley: University of California Press.

Gladney, D. C. (1996a). *Muslim Chinese: Ethnic nationalism in the People's Republic.* Cambridge, MA: Harvard University Press, Council on East Asian Studies.

Gladney, D. C. (1996b). Relational alterity: Constructing Dungan, Uygur, and Kazakh identities across China, Central Asia, and Turkey. *History and Anthropology, 9* (2), 1–33.

Gladney, D. C. (in press). Bodily positions/social dispositions: Sexuality, nationality, and Tiananmen. In W. Dissanayake (Ed.), *Narratives of agency: Self-making in Chinese, Indian, and Japanese cultures.* Minneapolis: University of Minnesota Press.

Gladney, D. C. & Shouqian, M. (1989). Interpretations of Islam in China: A Hui scholar's perspective. *Journal, Institute for Muslim Minority Affairs, 10* (2), 475–486.

Glazer, N. & Moynihan, D. P. (1974). *Beyond the melting pot.* Cambridge, MA: MIT Press.

Goldstein, M. C. (1990). The dragon and the snow lion: The Tibet question in the 20th century. In A. J. Kane (Ed.), *China briefing, 1989* (pp. 129–167). Boulder, CO: Westview Press.

Gough, K. (1967). Anthropology: Child of Imperialism. *Monthly Review, 19* (11), 12–27.

Halfon, C. (1994). Femme et musulmane a Lanzhou, au Gansu. *Etudes Oriental, 13/14,* 151–155.

Harrell, S. (1995). The history of the history of the Yi. In S. Harrell (Ed.), *Cultural encounters on China's ethnic frontiers* (pp. 63–91). Seattle: University of Washington Press.

Harrell, S. (1974). When a ghost becomes a god. In A. P. Wolf (Ed.), *Studies in Chinese society.* Palo Alto, CA: Stanford University Press.

Harris, L. (1993). *China considers the Middle East.* London: I. B. Tauris.

Heberer, T. (1989). *China and its national minorities: Autonomy or assimilation?* New York: M. E. Sharpe.

Hobsbawm, E. (1991). *Nations and nationalism since 1780* (2nd ed.). Cambridge, MA: Cambridge University Press.

Honig, E. (1989). The politics of prejudice: Subei people in republican-era Shanghai. *Modern China, 15* (3), 243–274.

Honig, E. (1992). *Creating Chinese ethnicity.* New Haven, CT: Yale University Press.

Hsieh, S. (1986, July 7). *Ethnic contacts, stigmatized identity, and Pan-Aboriginalism: A study on ethnic change of Taiwan Aborigines.* Paper presented at the conference of Taiwan studies: An international Symposium, University of Chicago.

Hsü, F. L. K. (1968). *Under the ancestors' shadow.* Palo Alto, CA: Stanford University Press.

Huang, T. & Yuanquan, L. (1983). *Mantan Quanzhou diqu ahlabo Musilin de houyi ji qi yiji* [An informal talk on the Moslem descendants of the Quanzhou area and their heritage]. In Quanzhou Foreign Maritime Museum (Eds.), *Symposium on Quanzhou Islam.* Quanzhou, China: Fujian People's Publishing Society.

Huizu Jianshi Editorial Committee (Eds.) (1978). *Huizu Jianshi* [Brief history of the Hui]. Yinchuan, China: Ningxia People's Publishing Society.

Israeli, R. (1978). *Muslims in China*. London: Curzon & Humanities Press.

Israeli, R. (with Goodman, L.) (1994). *Islam in China: A critical bibliography*. Westport, CT: Greenwood Press.

Iwamura, S. (1948). The structure of Moslem society in inner Mongolia. *Far Eastern Quarterly, 8* (1), 34–44.

Jamjoom, A. S. (1985). Notes of a visit to mainland China. *Journal, Institute of Muslim Minority Affairs, 6* (1), 208 –218.

Jin, Y. (1984). The system of *menhuan* in China: An influence of Sufism on Chinese Muslims. *Ming Studies, 19*, 34–45.

Kelly, P. K., Bastian, G. & Aiello, P. (Eds.) (1991). *The anguish of Tibet*. Berkeley, CA: Parallax Press.

Keyes, C. F. (1979). Introduction. In C. Keyes (Ed.), *Ethnic adaptation and identity: The Karen on the Thai frontier with Burma*. Philadelphia, PA: ISHI.

Keyes, C. F. (1981). The dialectics of ethnic change. In C. Keyes (Ed.), *Ethnic change* (pp. 4–30). Seattle: University of Washington Press.

Kristeva, J. (1980). *Powers of horror: An essay on abjection* (L. S. Romleiz, Trans.). New York: Columbia University Press.

Lal, A. (1970). Sinification of ethnic minorities in China. *Current Scene, 8* (4), 1–25.

Lardy, N. R. (1986). Agricultural reforms in China. *Journal of International Affairs, 32* (2), 91–104.

Lattimore, O. (1950). *Pivot of Asia: Sinkiang and the inner Asian frontiers of China and Russia*. Boston: Little, Brown.

Lavely, W. R. (1991). Marriage and mobility under rural collectivization. In R. S. Watson & P. B. Ebrey (Eds.), *Marriage and inequality in Chinese society* (pp. 286–312). Berkeley: University of California Press.

Leslie, D. D. (1972). *The survival of the Chinese Jews: The Jewish community of Kaifeng*. Leiden, The Netherlands: E. J. Brill.

Leslie, D. D. (1981). *Islamic literature in Chinese, Late Ming and Early Ch`ing: Books, authors and associates*. Canberra, Australia: Canberra College of Advanced Education.

Leslie, D. D. (1986). *Islam in traditional China: A short history to 1800*. Canberra, Australia: Canberra College of Advanced Education.

Liao, P. (1993, September 16–18). *Commentary as literature: Reading Taiwan's newspaper literary supplements in 1993*. Paper presented at the Symposium on cultural studies in Asia, the Pacific, and the United States, Program for Cultural Studies, The East–West Center, Honolulu, HI.

Lin, Y. (1984). Yizu of Liang Shan, past and present. In D. Maybury-Lewis (Ed.), *The prospects for plural societies*. Washington, DC: The American Ethnological Society.

Lipman, J. N. (1981). *The border world of Gansu, 1895–1935*. Unpublished doctoral dissertation, Stanford University, Stanford, CA.

Lipman, J. N. (1984a). Ethnicity and politics in republican China: The Ma family warlords of Gansu. *Modern China, 10* (3), 285–316.

Lipman, J. N. (1984b). Patchwork society, network society: A study of Sino-Muslim communities. In R. Israeli & A. H. Johns (Ed.), *Islam in Asia 2*. Boulder, CO: Westview Press.

Lipman, J. N. (1987). Hui-Hui: An ethnohistory of the Chinese-speaking Muslims. *Journal of South Asian and Middle Eastern Studies, 11* (1/2), 112–130.

Lipman, J. N. (1994). The third wave: Establishment and transformation of the Muslim brotherhood in modern China. *Etude Orientales, 13/14*, 89–105.

Liu, S. (1948). *Collected works of Liu Shao-ch'i, 1945–1957.*

Lo, H. (1965). *K'e chia shi liao hui p'ien* [Historical sources for the study of the Hakkas]. Hong Kong: Institute of Chinese Culture.

Lombard, D. & Salomon, C. (1994, April 57). Islam and Chineseness. *Indonesia,* 115–131.

Ma, Q. (1983). A brief account of the early spread of Islam in China. *Social Sciences in China, 4,* 97–113.

Ma, S. (1984). *Yisilanjiao zai Zhongguo weishenmo you chengwei huijiao huo qingzhenjiao?* [Why is Islam in China called Huijiao or Qingzhenjiao?] *Guangming Rebao* 9, October 1979. Reprinted in *Huizu shilun ji 1949–1979* [Hui history collection 1949–1979]. Chinese Academy of Social Sciences Ethnology Department and Central Nationalities Institute Ethnology Department (Eds.), Hui History Team. Yinchuan, China: Ningxia People's Publishing Society.

Ma, S. (1989, April 14–16). The Hui people's new awakening at the end of the 19th century and beginning of the 20th century. In D. C. Gladney (Ed.), *The legacy of Islam in China: An international symposium in memory of Joseph F. Fletcher* (Conference volume). Harvard University, Cambridge, MA.

Ma, T. (1983). *Zhongguo Yisilan Jiaopai yu Menhuan Zhidu Shilue* [A history of Muslim factions and the Menhuan system in China]. Yinchuan, China: Ningxia People's Publishing Society.

Ma, W. (Ed.) (1986). *Yunnan Daizu, Zangzu, Baizu, he xiao liangshan Yizu diqu de Huizu* [Yunnan Dai, Tibetan, Bai, and Little Liangshan mountain Yi minority area Hui peoples]. *Ningxia Shehui Kexue, 1.*

Ma, W. (Ed.) (1992). *Yunnan Huizu Shi* [A history of the Yunnan Hui nationality]. Kunming, China: Yunnan Minzu Chubanshe.

Ma, Y. (Ed.) (1989). *China's minority nationalities.* Beijing: People's Publishing Society.

Ma, Z. *Qing Zhen zhi Nan* [The compass of Islam]. (1681). 8 juan.

MacInnis, D. E. (1972). *Religious policy and practice in communist China.* New York: Macmillan .

MacInnis, D. E. (1989). *Religion in China today: Policy and practice.* New York: Maryknoll, Orbis Books.

Mackerras, C. (1994a). *China's minorities: Integration and modernization in the twentieth century.* Oxford, England: Oxford University Press.

Mackerras, C. (1994b). Religion, politics, and the economy in inner Mongolia and Ningxia. In E. H. Kaplan & D. W. Whisenhunt (Eds.), *Opuscula Altaica: Essays presented in honor of Henry Schwarz* (pp. 437–464). Bellingham, WA: Center for East Asian Studies, Western Washington University.

Madsen, R. (1984). *Morality and power in a Chinese village.* Berkeley: University of California Press.

Mair, V. H. (1989, April 14–16). Chinese language reform and Dungan script in Soviet Central Asia. In D. C. Gladney (Ed.), *The legacy of Islam in China: An international symposium in memory of Joseph F. Fletcher* (Conference volume). Harvard University, Cambridge, MA.

Marcus, G. E. (1986). Afterword: Ethnographic writing and anthropological careers. In J. Clifford & G. E. Marcus (Eds.), *Writing culture: The poetics and politics of ethnography.* Berkeley: University of California Press.

Mason, I. (1929). The Mohammedans of China: When, and how, they first came. *Journal of the North China branch of the Royal Asiatic Society, 60,* 1–54.

Matthews, R. H. (1943). *Matthew's Chinese-English dictionary.* Cambridge, MA: Harvard University Press.

Mauss, M. (1962). *The gift: Forms and functions of exchange in archaic societies.* New

York: Norton.

Mernissi, F. (1987). *Beyond the veil: Male–female dynamics in modern Muslim society*. Bloomington: Indiana University Press.

Millward, J. A. (1989, April 14–16). The Chinese border wool trade of 1880–1937. In D. C. Gladney (Ed.), *The legacy of Islam in China: An international symposium in memory of Joseph F. Fletcher* (Conference volume). Harvard University, Cambridge, MA.

Moerman, M. (1965). Ethnic identity in a complex civilization: Who are the Lue? *American Anthropologist, 67* (5), 1215–1230.

Naroll, R. (1964). On ethnic unit classification. *Current Anthropology, 5*, 283–291, 306–312.

Nash, M. (1989). *The cauldron of ethnicity in the modern world*. Berkeley: University of California Press.

Ningxia Pictorial. (1984). Yinchuan, China: Ningxia People's Publishing Society.

Norman, J. (1988). *Chinese*. Cambridge, MA: Cambridge University Press.

Oda, J. U. (1978). *Acta Asiatica, 34*, 22–45.

Pang, K. (1992). *The dynamics of gender, ethnicity, and state among the austronesian-speaking Muslims (Hui-Utsat) of Hainan Island*. Unpublished doctoral dissertation, University of California, Los Angeles.

Parish, W. L. & Whyte, M. K. (1978). *Village and family in contemporary China*. Chicago: University of Chicago Press.

Pickens, C. L. (1942). The four men Huans. *Friends of Moslems, 16* (1).

Pillsbury, B. (1973). *Cohesion and cleavage in a Chinese Muslim minority*. Unpublished doctoral dissertation, Columbia University, New York.

Pillsbury, B. (1976, August 19–24). *Blood ethnicity: Maintenance of Muslim identity in Taiwan*. Paper read at the conference on Anthropology in Taiwan, Portsmouth, NH.

Pillsbury, B. (1978). Being female in a Muslim minority in China. In L. Beck & N. Keddie (Eds.), *Women in the Muslim world*. Cambridge, MA: Harvard University Press.

Pillsbury, B. (1981). The Muslim population of China: Clarifying the question of size and ethnicity. *Journal, Institute for Muslim Minority Affairs, 3* (2), 35–58.

Polo, M. (1987). In W. Marsden (Ed.), *The travels of Marco Polo*. New York: Dorset Press.

Population Census Office of the State Council of the People's Republic of China and the Institute of Geography of the Chinese Academy of Sciences. (1987). *The Population Atlas of China*. Oxford, England: Oxford University Press.

Pratt, M. L. (1986). Fieldwork in common places. In J. Clifford & G. E. Marcus (Eds.), *Writing culture: The poetics and politics of ethnography*. Berkeley: University of California Press.

Pye, L. W. (1975). China: Ethnic minorities and national security. In N. Glazer & D. P. Moynihan (Eds.), *Ethnicity*. Cambridge, MA: Harvard University Press.

Rahman, F. (1968). *Islam*. New York: Doubleday Anchor Books.

Ramsey, S. R. (1987). *The languages of China*. Princeton, NJ: Princeton University Press.

Renmin, R. (1991, November 14). *Guanyu 1990 nian renkou pucha zhuyao shuju de gongbao* [Report regarding the 1990 population census main statistics] (p. 3).

Riftin, B. (1989, April 14–16). Muslim elements in the folklore of the Chinese Huizu and the Soviet Dungans. In D. C. Gladney (Ed.), *The legacy of Islam in China: An international symposium in memory of Joseph F. Fletcher* (Conference volume). Harvard University, Cambridge, MA.

Roff, W. R. (1985). Islam obscured? Some reflections on studies of Islam and society in Asia. *L'Islam en Indonesie, 1* (29), 7–34.

Rosaldo, M. Z. (1984). Toward an anthropology of self and feeling. In R. A. Shweder & R. A. LeVine (Eds.), *Culture theory: Essays on mind, self, and emotion*. Cambridge, MA: Cambridge University Press.

Rossabi, M. (1979). Muslim and Central Asian revolts. In J. D. Spence & J. E. Wills, Jr. (Eds.), *From Ming to Ch'ing*. New Haven, CT: Yale University Press.

Rossabi, M. (1988). *Khubilai Khan: His life and times*. Berkeley: University of California Press.

Rudelson, J. J. (1991). Uighur historiography and Uighur ethnic identity. In I. Svanberg (Ed.), *Ethnicity, minorities, and cultural encounters*. Uppsala Multiethnic Papers 25, 63–82.

Rudelson, J. J. (1992). *Bones in the sand: The struggle to create Uighur nationalist ideologies in Xinjiang, China*. Unpublished doctoral dissertation, Harvard University, Cambridge, MA.

Said, E. (1978). *Orientalism*. New York: Random House.

Salzman, P. C. (1989, May 16). The lone stranger and the solitary quest. *Anthropology Newsletter*.

Sangren, P. S. (1987). *History and magical power in a Chinese community*. Palo Alto, CA: Stanford University Press.

Shichor, Y. (1989). *East wind over Arabia: Origins and implications of the Sino-Saudi missile deal*. Berkeley: University of California Press.

Shils, E. (1967). Primordial, personal, sacred and civil ties. *British Journal of Sociology, 8*, 130–145.

Shue, V. (1984). The fate of the commune. *Modern China, 10* (3), 250–283.

Sinor, D. (1969). *Inner Asia: A syllabus*. Bloomington: Indiana University.

Sinor, D. (1990). *The Cambridge history of inner Asia*. Cambridge, MA: Cambridge University Press.

Skinner, G. W. (1965). Marketing and social structure in rural China (Pt. II). *Journal of Asian Studies, 24* (3).

Skinner, G. W. (1971). Chinese peasants and the closed community: An open and shut case. *Comparative Studies in Society and History, 13* (3).

Snow, E. (1938). *Red star over China*. New York: Grove Press.

Stalin, J. V. (1953). *Works, 1907–1913* (Vol. 11). Moscow: Foreign Languages Publishing House.

Sun, Y. (1924). *The three principles of the people: San Min Chu I* (F. W. Price, Trans.). Taipei, Taiwan: China Publishing Company.

Thompson, S. (1988). Death, food, and fertility. In *Death ritual in late imperial and modern China*. Berkeley: University of California Press.

Tien, H. Y. (1973). *China's population struggle: Demographic decisions of the People's Republic, 1949–1969*. Columbus: Ohio State University Press.

Trimingham, J. S. (1971). *The Sufi orders in Islam*. Oxford, England: Clarendon Press.

Ts'ai M. (1973, August 10, 11/November 17). *Hui-jiao zai Lugang* [Islam in Lukang]. *China Times*.

Unger, J. (Ed.) (1996). *Chinese nationalism*. Boulder, CO: Westview Press.

Voll, J. O. (1982). *Islam: Continuity and change in the modern world*. Boulder, CO: Westview Press.

Wang, M. (1983). *Zhongguo gudai Jiang, Qiang, Diqiang zhi yanjiu* [Research on China's ancient Jiang, Qiang, and Diqiang peoples]. Unpublished master's thesis, Taiwan National Normal University, Taipei, Taiwan.

Wang, S. (1930, May 25/July 5). Niu jie Huimin Shenghuo tan [Discussion of the lifestyle of the Oxen Street Hui]. *Yue Hua*.

Wang, S. (1937, May 1). Beiping shi Huimin Gaikuang [A survey of the Hui people of Beiping]. *Li Gong*.

Wang, X. (1983). Huizu Wushu chutan [An introductory discussion of Hui Wushu]. *Wulin*,

10, 38–39.

Wang, Y. (1985). Najiahucun de zongjiao zhuangkuang [The religious situation in Najiahu village]. *Ningxia Shehui kexue, 9*, 7–9.

Wax, M. L. (1983). On fieldworkers and those exposed to fieldwork: Federal regulations and moral issues. In R. M. Emerson (Ed.), *Contemporary field research*. Boston: Little, Brown.

Weber, M. (1952). *Ancient Judaism* (H. H. Gerth & D. Martindale, Eds. and Trans.). Glencoe, NY: Free Press.

Weber, M. (1958). *The protestant ethic and the spirit of capitalism* (T. Parsons, Trans.). New York: Charles Scribner.

Weber, M. (1963). *The sociology of religion* (E. Fischoff, Trans.). Boston: Beacon Press.

Weller, R. P. (1987). *Unities and diversities in Chinese religion*. Seattle: University of Washington Press.

White, L. T. (1989). *Policies of chaos: The organizational causes of violence in China's cultural revolution*. Princeton, NJ: Princeton University Press.

Whyte, M. K. & Parish, W. L. (1984). *Urban life in contemporary China*. Chicago: University of Chicago Press.

Winters, C. (1979). *Mao or Muhammad: Islam in the People's Republic of China*. Hong Kong: Asian Research Service.

Wolf, A. & Huang, C. (1980). *Marriage and adoption in China, 1845–1945*. Stanford, CA: Stanford University Press.

Worsley, P. (1984). *The three worlds*. Chicago: University of Chicago Press.

Wu, D. (1990). Chinese minority policy and the meaning of minority culture: The example of the Bai in Yunnan, China. *Human Organization, 49* (1), 1–13.

Xue, W. (1986). *Lasa de Huizu* [The Hui of Lhasa]. In *Huihui Minzu Bian Huaxia* [The spread of the Huihui nationality in China]. Lanzhou, China: Gansu Provincial Nationalities Affairs Commission, Gansu Provincial Nationalities Research Institute.

Yang, H. (1989, April 14–16). The eighteenth century Gansu relief fraud scandal. In D. C. Gladney (Ed.), *The legacy of Islam in China: An international symposium in memory of Joseph F. Fletcher* (Conference volume). Harvard University, Cambridge, MA.

Yang, Y. (1981). *Mantan Qingzhensi* [Brief discussion of mosques]. Yinchuan, China: Ningxia People's Publishing Society.

Yanov, A. (1987). *The Russian challenge and the year 2000* (I. J. Rosenthal, Trans.). Oxford, England: Basil Blackwell.

Yegar, M. (1966). The Panthay (Chinese Muslims) of Burma and Yunnan. *Journal of South-East Asian History, 7* (1), 73–85.

Yokoyama, H. (1988, November 16–20). *Ethnic identity among the inhabitants of the Dali Basin in Southwestern China*. Paper presented at the 87th Annual Meeting of the American Anthropological Association, Phoenix, AZ.

Zhang, C. (1990). *Xinling shi* [A history of the soul]. Beijing, China: People's Press.

Zhang, T. (1983). Population growth among China's minorities. *China Reconstructs, 32* (11), 45–46.

Zhang, T. (1985). Najiahucun de Huizu zhishi qingnian sixiang zhuangkuang [Najiahu village Hui intellectual youth situation]. *Ningxia Shehui kexue, 9*, 10–12.

Zhang, T. (1986). *Beijing shaoshu minzu renkou zhuangkuang fenxi* [Analysis of the Beijing minority nationality population situation]. *Zhongguo Shaoshu Minzu Renkou, 2* (6), 22–33.

Zhang, Y. & Debao, J. (1940). *Dao Chendaixiang qu—baogao* [Trip to Chendai village—report]. Unpublished report, Quanzhou, China.

Zhongguo Shaoshu Minzu (Ed.) (1981). *Zhongguo Shaoshu Minzu* [China's minority nationalities]. Beijing, China: People's Publishing Society.

Zhu, Y. (1985). Najiahucun chanye jiegou de diaocha [Najiahu village industrial production structure research]. *Ningxia Shehui kexue, 9,* 1–6.

Zhuang, J. (1993). *Chendai Dingshi Huizu Hanhua de yanjiu* [Research on Han assimilation of the Ding lineage in Chendai]. *Haijiaoshi yanjiu, 34* (2), 93–107.

Index